"An attractively broad and accessible account of democracy from the Greeks to the present... [guides] readers through the mass of difficult material with enviable clarity... [offers] impressive new evidence and analyses... Particularly timely."

New York Review of Books

"What makes the book compelling is its focus on colourful thinkers, activists, and political leaders who lived and breathed the democratic moment throughout history... Miller shows that democracy's ascent is best seen not as a gradual unfolding of a political principle driven by reason and moral destiny but rather as a grand roller coaster ride of struggle, revolution, and backlash. Today's populist outbursts look quite ordinary alongside this history."

Foreign Affairs

"[Miller] forces the reader to sit up and realize that history isn't a definitive greyed parchment beyond reproach, but actually a living force constantly capable of new interpretation and meaning in our current world... Like the ekklesia in Athens, the constituent assembly in Versailles, and the soviet in Petrograd, *Can Democracy Work?* offers insightful context on how our own body politic will survive these turbulent times."

Christian Science Monitor

"Distinguished historian of ideas James Miller's short history of democracy and its different meanings is both compulsive and compulsory reading for our sometimes shockingly disenchanted times. Ever optimistic, Miller remains enamoured of his native United States's striking experiment in cosmopolitan self-governance, and stands proudly and persuasively tall for liberal—and democratic—ideals."

Paul Cartledge, author of *Democracy: A Life*

CAN DEMOCRACY WORK?

A SHORT HISTORY OF
A RADICAL IDEA, FROM
ANCIENT ATHENS TO OUR WORLD

JAMES MILLER

ONEWORLD

A Oneworld Book

First published in Great Britain and Australia by Oneworld Publications, 2018
This paperback edition published 2020

Copyright © James Miller 2018

ISBN 978-1-78607-627-4
eISBN 978-1-78607-403-4

Typeset design by Richard Oriolo
Printed and bound in Great Britain by Clays Ltd, Elcograf S.p.A.

Oneworld Publications
10 Bloomsbury Street
London WC1B 3SR
England

When the time comes at last
And man is a helper to man
Think of us
With forbearance.

—Bertolt Brecht,
"To Those Born Later" (1940)

CONTENTS

CODA: WHO ARE WE? 213

CAN DEMOCRACY WORK?

PRELUDE:

WHAT IS DEMOCRACY?

We have frequently printed the word Democracy. Yet I cannot
too often repeat that it is a word the real gist of which still sleeps,
quite unawaken'd, notwithstanding the resonance and the many
angry tempests out of which its syllables have come, from pen
or tongue. It is a great word, whose history, I suppose, remains
unwritten, because that history has yet to be enacted.

—Walt Whitman, *Democratic Vistas* (1870)

"A GREAT DEMOCRATIC REVOLUTION is going on amongst us,"
Alexis de Tocqueville wrote in 1835, in the aftermath of the
United States' War of Independence and the French Revolution. Like many
observers of the modern democratic ideal, the French social theorist
found many of its implications troubling, if left unchecked. Yet with
twists and turns, and despite some spectacular setbacks, the "great
democratic revolution" that Tocqueville described indeed continued,
sometimes flaring up with disturbing results, throughout the twentieth
century and into the twenty-first.

Tocqueville was one of the first in a long line of modern writers
who have believed that democracy in some sense represented a logical

culmination of human affairs: for Francis Fukuyama, writing in 1989, the year that jubilant Germans tore down the Berlin Wall, liberal democracy marked "the end of history," with an American exclamation point.

But history hasn't evolved in quite the way that these theorists anticipated. Tocqueville expected democracy to produce greater equality—yet democratic states conjoined with market societies have recurrently produced growing *in*equality. At the same time, as nations have grown larger, and as new transnational institutions have changed the everyday life of millions, those who govern have become increasingly remote, often making democracy in practice seem like a puppet show, a spectacle in which hidden elites pull all the strings—not "a great word" with a "history that has yet to be enacted."

But democracy amazingly enough survives—at least as an article of faith or a figment of modern ideology. As one recent empirical study sums up the evidence: "If we take the number of people who claim to endorse democracy at face value, no regime type in the history of mankind has held such universal and global appeal as democracy does today." In a striking contrast to the low regard in which democracy was held throughout most of the rest of recorded human history, virtually every existing political regime today claims to embody some form of democracy. Vladimir Putin and his supporters have declared Russia to be a "sovereign democracy." Even North Korea calls itself a "Democratic People's Republic."

It is often assumed that democracy emerged as a global political norm as the result of a gradual evolution, realizing the best in a great heritage of Western political thought. A suspiciously reassuring tradition is then taken for granted. First practised by the ancient Athenians, fruitfully justified in the republican theories of Aristotle and his successors, developed through the struggles between people and king in England, democracy finally bursts into full bloom, most notably in the United States.

This account is misleading. Democracy before the French Revolution was generally held to be a fool's paradise, or worse. At the zenith of direct democracy in ancient Athens, one critic called it a "patent absurdity"—and so it seemed for centuries afterward to political theorists from Plato to James Madison.

It was only in the eighteenth century that theorists and militants resurrected democracy as an articulate ideal. In France, inspired primarily by the radical ideas of Jean-Jacques Rousseau and the revolutionary journalists and political leaders who championed his ideas, the common people of Paris for a few months in 1792 and 1793 practised their own form of direct democracy in local assemblies, now and then augmented through armed insurrections. In response to the radical demands of these latter-day Parisian democrats, some political observers advocated a new, indirect form of self-government, a novel regime they called (as had a few Americans before them) a "representative democracy." Instead of exercising sovereignty directly, the people in a modern democracy should exercise it *in*directly, by transferring their power to elected representatives. Under the pressure of events, one of the most ardent of modern French democrats, Robespierre, went farther and defended the need, in the midst of a democratic revolution, for a temporary dictatorship—precisely to preserve the possibility of building a more enduring form of representative democracy once the revolution was complete and law and order were restored.

Ever since the French Revolution, modern democracy has oscillated between the gradual evolution of representative democracy and radical challenges to this evolving status quo, leading to demands for more, not less, democracy, often in conjunction with demands for a reformation of the distribution of wealth, and sometimes (as in Russia after 1917) resulting in new forms of avowedly democratic dictatorships. Notable among these revolts are the Chartist uprisings of 1839, and the Chartist general strike of 1842 in Great Britain; the European revolutions of 1848, and the Paris Commune of 1871; the soviet uprisings of 1905 and 1917, and the workers' councils they inspired in Germany, Hungary, and Italy; the anticommunist workers' councils in Hungary in 1956, Solidarity in Poland in 1980, and the Velvet Revolution in Czechoslovakia in 1989. Or consider more recent events, from the ill-fated Arab

Spring uprisings of 2011 and the Maidan revolt in Ukraine in 2013 to the so-called umbrella revolution of Hong Kong in 2014—or even the Brexit "leave" vote in the United Kingdom in 2016, mobilized under the slogan "Take back control."

Recent events in the United States have been similarly tumultuous. Recall the hopes for a wider and more direct popular participation in politics briefly raised in the presidential election of 2008, when Barack Obama rallied previously indifferent voters on a platform of social change—and then recall the rapid fading of these hopes, and the subsequent rise of grassroots movements that saw themselves as battling for more democracy, such as the Tea Party on the right and the Occupy Wall Street and the Black Lives Matter movements on the left, capped by the populist revolt in 2016 against the established political elites led, improbably enough, by the billionaire showman Donald J. Trump.

What is at stake in these contradictory and often controversial political developments? What, if anything, do modern representative democracies have in common with the dictatorial democracies of contemporary communist regimes, or with such avowedly direct democratic movements as Occupy Wall Street or Spain's Indignados?

If both North Korea and the United States consider themselves democratic—and if liberals and conservatives, and socialists and communists, and nationalists and populists, and American politicians of every stripe can all claim to embody the will of a people—then what, in practice, can the idea of democracy possibly *mean*?

III

WHAT FOLLOWS IS a history of an idea—a chronological look at several episodes in our ongoing experiment in democracy. Even in such a condensed recounting, it's a dramatic saga that raises some hard questions:

Are more direct forms of popular political participation either feasible or desirable in today's world? Can liberal representative democracies survive in the face of ongoing revolts against their various shortcomings? Or are our nominal democracies at growing risk of drifting toward illiberal and authoritarian forms of rule, duly proclaimed in the name of "the people"?

Perhaps these questions are too narrowly posed. Perhaps, as Tocqueville and others have argued, democracy isn't merely a form of government, it is also a way of life, and a shared faith, instantiated in other forms of association, in modes of thought and belief, in the attitudes and inclinations of individuals who have absorbed a kind of democratic temperament. But how can democratic habits of association, conduct, and conviction survive in a setting where democracy as a political form is honoured mainly in the breach?

III

LIKE MOST AMERICANS of my generation, I came of age in a country that treated democracy as a self-evident ideal, and a source of considerable national pride. Through my father, an English professor who had been raised in a union household in the oil fields of Oklahoma, and my mother, a college-educated housewife who had been reared by an extended family of observant Lutheran small businessmen in Illinois, I absorbed a number of political pieties that were widely shared in postwar America. I was taught that we were lucky to live in an exceptional society, devoted to life, liberty, and the pursuit of happiness. And I was taught that I had a duty (my mother believed it was God-given) to make this exceptional society an even better place, in part by exercising my political rights, not only to vote but also to think for myself and to speak out against perceived injustices.

My formative years were spent in Lincoln, Nebraska, in the heart of the Great Plains of the American Midwest, a place filled with churchgoing compatriots. Both of my parents were politically engaged when I was growing up, though the two sides of the family held divergent political views: my dad and his folks were ardent Democrats, while my mom's extended family members (apart from her) were almost all equally fervent Republicans.

In order to ensure tranquil family gatherings, I was taught to avoid talk about politics and religion in polite company—even as I was encouraged to consult my conscience and to draw my own conclusions about what a good society would look like.

As I entered adolescence, and inspired by the presidential campaign of 1960, I went door-to-door canvassing for John F. Kennedy in a city that Richard Nixon would carry by a wide margin. With my parents' encouragement, I became a Young Democrat and, when a Democrat subsequently became governor of Nebraska, I was invited to give a speech in the governor's mansion about the greatness of Franklin D. Roosevelt.

When my family moved to Chicago in the Autumn of 1962, the city came as a revelation to me. Living in Hyde Park on the South Side, I was for the first time in my life surrounded by people of all races and religious views. Attending a high school founded by the great progressive educator John Dewey, I was introduced to some of his philosophical justifications for America's democratic ideals, and also taught about the challenges these ideals faced in a country like Ghana (the topic of a class I took on postcolonial Africa).

Among my classmates, there were more avowed Socialists than Republicans. For the first time in my life, I knew people for whom "radical" was a term of approval, not opprobrium. In the spring of 1965, I joined my first political demonstration, organized by the Student Nonviolent Coordinating Committee, a protest against a subcommittee of the House Un-American Activities Committee that was holding hearings at an old federal courthouse on Chicago's North Side. (What I most vividly recall is the many officials who were taking photographs of us protesters.)

In 1965, I went to college in Southern California, and at first I remained an active Democrat, attending a California Democratic Council (CDC) statewide meeting in 1966. But by then, the war in Vietnam had become a subject of fierce controversy, and I ended up at the CDC convention booing, along with many other participants, as that organization's leadership offered only tepid opposition to what seemed to many of us the misguided war policies of Lyndon Johnson. I concluded, doubtless too hastily, that the party system was rigged (even though the California Democratic Party had in fact created, in CDC, one of the most powerful grassroots political organizations in the United States at that time).

To my father's chagrin—he considered my newfound political passions puerile—I became an antiwar activist and, in the spring of 1967, I joined Students for a Democratic Society after meeting Carl Davidson, an SDS leader who visited a political sociology class I was taking at the time. He spoke of "participatory democracy" and the power to make the decisions that affected our lives. Inspired by such talk, I helped organize a local branch of SDS—and fancied myself a more ardent proponent of democracy than ever. Democracy, I concluded, wasn't just about voting and manoeuvring for power in a hierarchically organized party—it was now about direct action and becoming part of a face-to-face community of peers.

In the summer of 1968, I was back home in Chicago, where I ended up joining a chaotic protest at the Democratic convention that year. I was angry at the growing savagery of the war in Vietnam, the assassination of Martin Luther King, Jr., and the transformation of American cities like Chicago into police states, patrolled by military personnel in armoured vehicles. I was free, white, and twenty-one; and profoundly disenchanted with what I regarded as a betrayal by establishment liberals of what I had been taught were core democratic—and American—values.

After finishing graduate work in the history of ideas, I went on to write two books about the history of democracy: one, on Jean-Jacques Rousseau and the roots of modern democracy in his conception of popular sovereignty, and in the expression of his ideals in the French Revolution; the other, on the American New Left of the 1960s and the rise and fall of "participatory democracy" in that decade.

Apart from a decade spent working as a cultural critic for *Newsweek* magazine in the 1980s, I have spent most of my life teaching politics in various universities, for the past quarter century at the New School for Social Research, where one of my early heroes, Hannah Arendt, also taught.

As time has passed, I've had second thoughts about many of my old convictions, and I've tried hard to imbue my students with a sceptical outlook on their own political assumptions, no matter how fiercely held. Year after year, new students appear in my classes eager to learn more about democratic ideals—and also eager to put these ideals into practice.

And year after year, I've had to ask myself, seriously, a handful of recurrent questions:

What is living, and what is dead, in the modern democratic project?

For that matter, what *is* the modern democratic project? Is it a single project in practice, or is it realized in divergent, even contradictory forms? Is it a universal goal of political evolution, as some have argued, or a uniquely Western creation, intertwined with Christianity and the spoils of Western imperialism, and therefore of limited relevance to the citizens of other world civilizations? Is it backward-looking, as some critics have alleged, or future-orientated, as Walt Whitman prophesied?

And can it really work—especially in complex modern societies?

III

AS HANNAH ARENDT pointed out long ago, the shared political experience of exuberant new beginnings is a recurrent feature of modern democratic revolts. It needs to be stressed here that these *revolts* are a central part of the story of modern democracy: they are not an unfortunate blemish on the peaceful forward march toward a more just society; they form the heart and soul of modern democracy as a living reality.

It is a familiar story: out of the blue, it seems, a crowd pours into a city square, or gathers at a barnstorming rally held by a spellbinding orator, to protest hated institutions, to express rage and anger at the betrayals of the current ruling class, to seize direct control of public spaces. To label these frequently disquieting moments of collective freedom "populist," in a pejorative sense, is to misunderstand a constitutive feature of the modern democratic project.

Yet as Arendt also understood, these episodes of collective self-assertion are invariably fleeting and stand in tension with the need for a more stable constitution of collective freedom, embodied in the rule of law, and representative institutions that can operate at a larger and more inclusive scale, both national and international. Even worse, these large-scale institutions are prone to frustrate anyone hoping to play a more direct and personal role in political decision making.

This means that the democratic project—both ancient and modern—is inherently unstable. Frustrated in practice, the modern promise of popular sovereignty recurrently produces new efforts to assert the collective power of a people, however narrowly or expansively defined. If observers like the apparent result, they often hail an event as a renaissance of the democratic spirit; if they dislike the demands being made, then they are liable to dismiss these episodes of collective self-assertion as mob rule, or populism run amok. No matter. Since 2011, the world has seen wave after wave of democratic revolts on the streets of various capital cities, and also at ballot boxes.

Hence our current predicament. Even though the postwar consensus over the meaning and value of *liberal* democratic institutions seems more fragile than ever—polls show that trust in elected representatives has rarely been lower—democracy as furious dissent flourishes as rarely before, in vivid and vehement outbursts of anger at remote elites and shadowy enemies. And these outbursts are essential to the continued vitality, and viability, of modern democracy—even as (and precisely because) they challenge the status quo, destructive though that challenge may be.

III

IN ORDER TO tell the story of democracy, it is necessary to describe the meaning of the term in different times and places, taking seriously the history of the word itself, and its many and sometimes surprisingly various uses. "The history of philosophy, and perhaps especially of moral, social and political philosophy, is there to prevent us from becoming too readily bewitched," the Cambridge historian Quentin Skinner has argued. "The intellectual historian can help us appreciate how far the values embodied in our present way of life, and our present ways of thinking about those values, reflect a series of choices made at different times between different possible worlds."

The account that follows is the work of someone trained, like Skinner, in the field of intellectual history. But it is also a deeply personal narrative, if only because I am inescapably the product of a typically modern democratic faith that was drummed into me from birth. This makes it hard for me to draw a sharp line between my considered political beliefs and an internalized ideology that, in fact, typifies the present age.

In any case, what this book describes is not only a highly selective sequence of historically conditioned forms of government, and the series of choices people have made among them, but also a similarly selective series of moral visions, pictures of a better world that have grown out of, but also contradict, the increasingly various institutions that have claimed to instantiate some form of "democracy."

The story I tell is Eurocentric. Recently sceptics of such an approach have raised doubts about whether democracy in fact first appeared in Greece. They have suggested instead that analogous forms of self-rule independently evolved around the world, in India, in China, and in Japan; and they have pointed to the later, equally fortuitous appearances of self-government in Africa, medieval Iceland, the Swiss cantons, and among the indigenous peoples of Australia and the Americas.

It would be foolish to deny the possibility that some important examples of popular participation in governance may predate the invention of democracy in Athens, or have arisen independently of any knowledge of the Greek experience. But as the classical historian M. I. Finley tartly quipped, whatever the facts may be about such examples, "their impact on history, on later societies, was null. The Greeks, and only the Greeks, discovered democracy in that sense, precisely as Christopher Columbus, not some Viking seaman, discovered America." Similarly, in the nineteenth and twentieth centuries, it was the imperial proponents of democratic ideas from England, France, the United States, and the Soviet Union—championing both liberal and socialist forms of self-rule—who exported democracy around the world, often at gunpoint, eventually turning it into a putatively universal human right.

I have chosen to recount this frequently fraught history by describing a series of different historical responses to the question What is democracy?

The answers range from the closed, self-governing community of ancient Athens, through the assertion of popular sovereignty in revolutionary Paris in 1792, to the rise of a commercial republic of free individuals in America; from the struggle for social and political equality waged by European socialist parties in the nineteenth century, through the consolidation in the early twentieth century of rival regimes of ostensible self-rule in the United States and the Soviet Union. After World War II, democracy, understood as the self-determination of peoples, emerges as a universal aspiration, memorialized in Article 21 of the Universal Declaration of Human Rights adopted by the General Assembly of the United Nations in 1948.

By recollecting in this way the sheer variety of different answers to the question What is democracy? I can also shed some light on a puzzling outcome I mentioned at the outset: the astonishing fact that liberals and conservatives, and socialists and communists, and nationalists and populists, and American politicians of every stripe now claim to represent the will of a sovereign people. The United Nations' avowed commitment to democratic ideals is a tremendous historical achievement. But the associated propaganda claim that these nations are all conducting a democracy is, as a friend remarked to me, very nearly laughable—even in the United States.

III

BEFORE STARTING TO tell this interlocked series of complex stories, however, it is important to sharply distinguish democracy from liberalism—two value-laden words that, in recent years, have become almost hopelessly conflated and confused, especially in the work of social scientists and Western political pundits.

Unlike democracy, "liberalism" is a relatively late addition to our political lexicon. In Europe, the word first comes into wide usage in the nineteenth century by various political theorists and statesmen in France, Germany, and Italy, united in their horror at the bloodshed of the French Revolution, but otherwise varied in their positive views. Some focused on promoting commerce and free trade, some stressed juridical limits to state power, others on building a strong state to promote the common good, and still others, some religiously motivated, on fostering citizens who were "liberal" in the classical sense of being unselfish and magnanimous.

In the United States, liberalism was introduced even later into the jargon of American politics by a group of reformers who believed that the federal government could be a tool for positive social change; Teddy Roosevelt Progressives in 1912, they became Wilsonian Democrats from 1916 to 1918, and embraced "liberalism" as a way to distinguish themselves from sectarians of any political party as well as from revolutionary advocates of socialism or communism.

Democracy, when it first appeared in Greece, had nothing to do, either in theory or in practice, with any such modern conception of liberalism.

In classical Athens, democracy presupposed shared norms, a shared religious horizon, and a shared projection of egalitarian ideals; it revolved around periodic public assemblies in which all the citizens met as one, and had, as its characteristic procedure, the random selection of citizens to fill almost all the key offices of justice, administration, and government. As Socrates discovered at his trial for impiety and corrupting the youth in 399 B.C., the ordinary citizens of ancient

Athens had little patience for nonconformists. Their collective freedom to wield their power was perfectly compatible with the complete subjection of the individual to the community.

Modern democracy, which revolves around an idea of popular sovereignty utterly alien to the thinking of the ancient Greeks and most powerfully expressed in Rousseau's concept of the general will, also has no necessary connection to liberalism. The Protestant champions of the idea of popular sovereignty in the sixteenth century summoned the power of the people for the express purpose of dethroning rulers with whose religious views they disagreed: "It was not religious liberty they sought, but the elimination of wrong religions."

Rousseau, writing two centuries later, was characteristically blunt in conceding that his views of popular sovereignty had no necessary connection with any concept of natural rights. In the *Social Contract*, his 1762 treatise on political right, he argued strenuously that slavery was unnatural and illegitimate, but he also freely speculated (with good reason, as we shall see) that slavery was perhaps a prerequisite of democracy in Athens.

"What! Freedom can only be maintained with the support of servitude? Perhaps. The two extremes meet," Rousseau wrote. "There are some unfortunate situations when one cannot preserve one's freedom except at the expense of others, and when the citizen can only be perfectly free if the slave is completely enslaved"—and so it was in the first decades of the American experiment in democracy.

The great Austrian jurist Hans Kelsen, building on the work of Rousseau, but with far greater sobriety and analytic rigour, made a similarly trenchant observation about modern conceptions of democracy in his 1920 monograph, *The Essence and Value of Democracy*: "Even with the limitless expansion of state power and, consequently, the complete loss of individual 'freedom' and the negation of the liberal ideal, democracy is still possible as long as this state power is constituted by its subjects. Indeed, history demonstrates that democratic state power tends toward expansion no less than its autocratic counterpart." In other words, a majority of voters in a modern representative democracy may very well support policies that are explicitly *illiberal*, as some Americans fear had happened after the election in 2016 of Donald J. Trump as the forty-fifth president of the United States.

In sum: democracy does *not* entail liberalism, and vice versa—even if the two ideas have sometimes become intertwined, as most notably occurred in America in the course of the twentieth century.

III

WHAT'S CLEAR TODAY is that while democracy as such may be widely admired, it is in its liberal form also an embattled ideology. In 2014, the Hungarian prime minister, Viktor Orbán, explicitly opposed liberal restraints on popular sovereignty as an impediment to making Hungary competitive in the global economy, and praised instead the strengths of an "illiberal state." In the years since, the West has been at a paradoxical crossroads. As one commentator has sharply observed, "Few leaders and movements in the West dare to challenge the idea of democracy itself. Not so for liberalism, which has come under mounting attack." One result has been the rise of popular movements in which a majority of ordinary citizens have embraced a narrow conception of solidarity and rallied around a leader who claims to embody the will of such a closed community (Orbán is only one example).

Another result has been a resurgence of traditional anxieties, notably in the United Kingdom and the United States, about the worth of democracy as a form of government. Why should we entrust the fate of the earth to large numbers of ordinary citizens foolish enough to elect a manifestly unfit American president?

Such worries are nothing new: in 1975, a group of social scientists and political leaders in Europe, Japan, and the United States published a volume analysing *The Crisis of Democracy*. In 2018, however, the worries seemed to run deeper. Some feared for the future of democracy, while others began to fear modern democracy itself, for the chaos and potentially self-destructive outcomes it could obviously, in certain circumstances, produce.

It is perhaps ironic, given events in my homeland as I was writing this book, but I probably feel more proud of the American accomplishment in this context than I did as a young man. I have lived long enough to appreciate the fragility of political institutions that are responsive to citizens, however limited that responsiveness may currently be. I have come to appreciate as well the need for some measure of political representation, legitimized through voting, and also the value of having organized political parties, inevitably hierarchical in their structure, that nevertheless continue to fight for a more informed public and a more secure right to vote, supplemented by more opportunities for ordinary people, and not just professional politicians, to participate, in a thoughtful way, in making the decisions that affect the shape of a large and diverse society. And I am struck by the progress we have made as a nation, and the polyglot expansion of our citizenry as a whole, and the generosity with which Americans, at their best, have conceived of popular sovereignty in pluralistic terms. For all its faults, and despite profound racial tensions that persist in the wake of a very bloody civil war, the United States has evolved into the world's most striking ongoing experiment in cosmopolitan self-governance.

Still, as Tocqueville appreciated long ago, and as the shocking triumph of Donald Trump in the American presidential election of 2016 only confirmed, the relative historical success of a relatively liberal form of modern democracy in America is no reason for complacency.

Whether democracy in America, or anyplace else, can flourish, either as a historically conditioned set of political institutions or as a moral vision, must remain, by the very logic of democracy, an open question. Only its citizens can resolve its manifold problems and paradoxes, and only they can decide if its vistas, despite all challenges, remain as inclusive and enchantingly "democratic" as Walt Whitman once hoped—or if democracy comes to stand instead for something much narrower, even mean.

ONE

A CLOSED COMMUNITY

OF SELF-GOVERNING

CITIZENS

WHEN AMERICAN POLITICAL SCIENTISTS speak of democracy today, they generally have in mind a political system for choosing and replacing the government through free and fair elections, a system that also protects the human rights of all citizens, and one that adheres to a rule of law, in which the laws and procedures, memorialized in a written constitution, apply equally to all citizens.

By these criteria, the world's first democracy wasn't properly a democracy at all. At the zenith of its political glory in the fifth and fourth centuries B.C., Athens did not choose its government by holding elections, nor did it protect the human rights of its citizens, as it lacked any notion of such rights, nor were the fundamental powers of the Athenian polis enshrined in a comprehensive written document.

What Athens did have is a community in which every citizen was expected to participate directly in the political life of the city—and far more actively than in any known modern democracy. At the height of democracy in Athens, in the mid-fourth century, an assembly of citizens, open to all, met at least forty times a year. All political offices were held by ordinary citizens, selected by lot, and all legal judgments in the city's courts were reached by large juries of ordinary citizens, similarly selected. And all this happened in a comparatively large commercial city that dominated the eastern Mediterranean world for nearly two centuries.

Despite this apparently impressive record of accomplishments, most ancient authorities reviled democracy in Athens. Plato, perhaps the most widely admired writer in antiquity, and someone who lived under democratic rule in the fourth century, criticized the false beliefs that prevailed in a city governed by public opinion rather than true knowledge, and he deplored the "insolence, anarchy, wastefulness, and shamelessness" that the prevalence of false beliefs facilitated. The historian Thucydides, another citizen of democratic Athens, who chronicled the Peloponnesian War with Sparta that had begun in 431 and ended with the defeat of Athens in 404, essentially blamed the power of the ordinary people of Athens, and their susceptibility to manipulation by mendacious orators, for this catastrophic outcome. As a result of critics like Plato and Thucydides—not to mention subsequent political developments, from the Macedonian empire of Alexander the Great to modern European monarchies that claimed absolute sovereignty as a divine right—nobody much cared about the Athenian political system for almost two thousand years, nor about democracy as a form of government.

In the centuries between the rise of Rome and the fall of the Bastille, the world's first democracy was left largely unexamined, and possible justifications for it were rarely considered. Even in contexts where the idea still circulated, among trained jurists and experts in political philosophy, democracy was normally disparaged as the worst of the simple forms of government, inferior to both monarchy and aristocracy. It was only in the eighteenth and nineteenth centuries in Europe and the United States that a sweeping reevaluation of ancient democracy took place—helping to transform the main currents of political thought and institutional development, first in the West, and then around the world.

The reevaluation of Greek democracy continues. As a result of recent research and ongoing discoveries of previously lost documents, most notably a detailed description of Athenian political institutions likely compiled by Aristotle and his students, and unearthed in Egypt only in 1879, scholars today know much more than Plato or Thucydides conveyed about the nature of the various democratic institutions of Athens—including how radical their implications really were.

Modern scholars have also skilfully interpreted the surviving texts of Athenian orators, which contain idealizing paeans to democracy, if not a systematic political philosophy. Thus Demosthenes, perhaps the most famous Athenian orator, praised his city's democratic way of life for its "spirit of compassion for the helpless, and of resistance to the intimidation of the strong and powerful; it does not inspire brutal treatment of the populace," nor does it encourage "subservience to the rulers of the day."

III

ATHENS WAS ONE of roughly one thousand Greek-speaking political units, towns scattered in the countryside and along the coasts of the Mediterranean, Aegean, and Black Seas, "like frogs around a pond," as Plato put it. The territory of Athens was roughly the size of the modern American state of Rhode Island. It was the most populous polis in ancient Greece. Though the exact number of total residents, including slaves, foreigners, women, and children, is impossible to determine, and fluctuated dramatically over time, experts estimate that there were perhaps as many as sixty thousand citizens in 431 B.C., and about thirty thousand a century later—and that the number of adult male citizens represented around a tenth of the entire population of Attica. The majority of these people resided in rural inland villages; the rest lived either in the port of Piraeus or in the urban centre of Athens, the two most thickly settled regions.

Democracy made its surprising appearance in Athens in an archaic context where some neighbouring civilizations (such as Persia) had a king ruling over a relatively large realm, and where most of the smaller Greek-speaking city-states were ruled either by monarchs claiming divine sanction; by secular tyrants ruling by brute force; or by a small group of nobles or rich citizens—an "aristocracy," as Greeks called it if this elite was civic-minded, or an "oligarchy," if it was merely self-interested.

Insofar as ordinary citizens (the demos) had a role to play in the archaic polis, it was by acknowledging the authority of their leaders, sometimes (as in Homer) simply by shouting their collective approval in public assemblies before a crucial battle. The earliest forms of popular participation in Greece seem to have been plebiscitary—citizens acclaimed or formally elected a leader, but the leader, having secured popular approval, was then free to exercise power as he saw fit.

According to the pioneering fifth-century Greek historian Herodotus, who is one of our main sources for what little we know about these things, Athens took its first steps toward more robust forms of self-government under the leadership of Solon, who served as an archon or city magistrate in 594/3 B.C. He was legendary for enhancing the power of the city's ordinary citizens, abolishing the practice of debt slavery—and then renouncing power, leaving the city for ten years, thus abjuring the customary spoils of high office.

Solon's reforms were not universally popular. In the decades that followed, Athens was in frequent turmoil, mainly caused by feuds between rival dynastic families with clashing political programmes. A period of relative stability began in the middle of the sixth century, when a war hero named Peisistratus seized power and established a tyranny, with the support of most poor Athenians. By levying taxes on wealthier citizens, the tyrant was able to embark on an ambitious public works programme, erecting new monuments and buildings, and also devoting public funds to supporting a variety of religious cults and civic festivals. After his death in 527, the tyranny survived for another generation until Cleisthenes, a scion of the powerful Alcmaeonid family, rose to political prominence in 510.

III

A NOBLEMAN of uncommon ability, Cleisthenes was ruthless, wily— and blessed with a bold political imagination. Banished as a child along with other members of his extended family because of their on-going resistance to the rule of Peisistratus, he came of age in Delphi, the site of the Temple of Apollo and the seat of the Pythia, the high priestess regarded as the vessel of Apollo and the oracle most widely consulted in the ancient Greek world. While residing there, the Alc-maeonids won a contract to rebuild the Delphic temple. In a shrewd act of philanthropy, Cleisthenes convinced his kinsmen to pay for ex-traordinarily fine marble columns for the new temple façade out of the family coffers. Their generous gift put Delphi in the family's debt. Shortly afterward, Cleisthenes personally intervened with the Pythia. He arranged for the oracle to advise Sparta to topple Athens's tyrant, and so free the city from the iron grip of his family's enemies. Schemes like this were typical in archaic Greece.

As a result, a large army of Spartans led by their king in 510 B.C. succeeded in toppling the Athenian tyrant Hippias, triggering several years of elite infighting in Athens. By then, the growing mobilization of popular support by Athenian political rivals had unleashed what one histo-rian speculates was a gradual "process of steady expansion of political equality," from "the narrow circle of only the noble" to the broader ranks of wealthy citizens, who in turn sought increasingly explicit sup-port from the poorer citizenry.

It was apparently in this charged context that sharp conflict erupted over whether or not to define the Athenians as a people with the collective capacity to exercise political power directly. In 508, Isagoras, an oligarch who hoped to reverse the growing power of poorer Athenians, outmanoeuvred Cleisthenes to become archon—the city's highest civilian official in those days.

Contesting that result, Cleisthenes began to mobilize popular support, in part by publicizing an elaborate programme of political reforms, meant to give *more* power to ordinary citizens. His enemies in turn asked the Spartans to return to Athens, this time to drive Cleisthenes and his allies into exile, to install their army on the Acropolis, and to ensure by force that an oligarch and his allies would be able to rule Athens at will, as an ally of Sparta. Once again, Athens seemed on the verge of spiralling into violence and civil war.

Before the arrival in Athens of King Cleomenes's troops, Cleisthenes and his family and elite followers decamped, as anticipated.

But what happened next came as a shock. Instead of acquiescing in the foreign occupation, the ordinary citizens of Athens, as if spontaneously, converged on the Acropolis and surrounded the Spartan army, laying siege to the citadel. It took only three days to drive the Spartans from the city—an outcome that suggests the popular uprising had numbers and force on its side.

Though there is no scholarly consensus on the significance of this event, one modern historian, Josiah Ober, does not shrink from comparing the Athenian uprising of 508 to the storming of the Bastille that would launch the French Revolution in 1789. The result in Athens, according to Ober, was also a "revolution," in the modern sense of a new beginning, a political upheaval that inaugurates a radically new political order.

III

"ALTHOUGH ATHENS had been a great city before," writes Herodotus, "it became even greater once rid of its tyrants." Summoned back to Athens after the people had repulsed the Spartans, Cleisthenes turned to the Assembly, or Ekklesia, derived from the Greek word meaning "to summon," because citizens were summoned to meetings by a trumpeter or herald. Under the tyrants, the Ekklesia had been an essentially passive body, but Cleisthenes sought to invigorate it in order to authorize his ambitious plans for reforming the city's institutions. Henceforth all new legislation in Athens had to be validated in the Assembly, which was now open to *all* citizens, no matter how poor. (At the time, the Athenian citizenry consisted of free-born males over the age of twenty-one with a native Athenian father.) An amphitheatre was built for the Assembly, a meeting place called the Pnyx, situated on a rocky slope in central Athens.

In the most audacious aspect of his reform programme, Cleisthenes entirely reorganized the body politic. Athens's traditional kinship groupings had long given de facto political power to a few wealthy families who worshipped a divine ancestor and controlled the relevant priestly offices. Cleisthenes set out to undermine this system by creating an entirely new set of ten civic "tribes." He assigned each a new eponymous hero to worship and stipulated that its members would be drawn from each of the three broad subregions of Attica: the shore, the plain, and the uplands. Membership in a tribe was now determined more or less arbitrarily, instead of by birth or physical proximity.

One result of this new organization was to bring much closer together hitherto quite separated areas of the polis, and also to break up the regional power bases that had driven political conflict in recent decades. Another result was the creation of a new civic religion that enabled all citizens, not just the members of dynastic families, to join in the worship of a heroic ancestor, and to share in the organization of worship.

The newly empowered Assembly would be steered by an expanded Council of 500, with each tribe providing fifty members. Any citizen over the age of thirty was eligible to serve. Councillors had to take an oath and submit to preliminary review and then a final audit, as a check against wrongdoing. Infantry troops were similarly organized into tribal regiments—and "one of the first things that most forcibly struck outside observers about post-Cleisthenic Athens was how much more militarily successful it quite suddenly became."

At the same time, Cleisthenes laid a new stress on broadly based civic festivals. These events helped to knit the new civil order together symbolically, by periodically convening a very large group of people—citizens, but also women, resident aliens, even visitors from other cities—in public rituals that dramatized the new civic virtues of *isonomia* (equality under the law), *isegoria* (equal ability to speak in public), and *isokratia* (equal power).

The most important of these festivals had become the City Dionysia, celebrated annually in Athens for five days at the end of March. The Dionysia was capped by public performances of dithyrambs (choral hymns dedicated to Dionysus), tragedies, and comedies, with the poets and their elite patrons competing for prizes.

According to the myth behind the festival, a certain Pegasos of Eleutherai in the distant past had brought to the nearby city of Athens a statue of Dionysus, the most volatile of the Greek gods, associated with the cult of the bacchae, female worshippers of the god and participants in the ritual bacchanalia. The Athenians, however, failed to honour the god's statue appropriately. Angered by their effrontery, Dionysus cursed the Athenian men with a chronic genital affliction that could be relieved, according to an oracle, only by expiating the affront through an appropriate ritual observance.

As it evolved in Athens, a central role in the festival's ritual atonement of the city's guilt came to be played by its ephebes, young men between the ages of eighteen and twenty, who were sufficiently wealthy to afford armour and who were undergoing mandatory military training to become hoplites, the armed infantrymen who had long formed the backbone of the city's military forces. Each City Dionysia opened with a reenactment by the ephebes of the advent of Dionysus. The proceeding included a sacrifice at a hearth altar and a torchlight procession bearing the statue of Dionysus to an amphitheatre on the south slope of the Acropolis. A parade the next day was even more lavish. Priests and honoured participants carried a variety of offerings to the god: carved phalluses, bowls, loaves of bread, and other objects of religious significance. Ephebes marched in military formation as acolytes of the god, blurring the lines between defending the city by armed force, attending a civic festival, and participating in a religious ritual. Upon arrival at a sacred district next to the amphitheatre, a number of animals were sacrificed, and other, bloodless offerings were made.

III

WITHIN THE THEATRE during the Dionysia, seating was set aside for the ephebes, a reminder of the critical role played by its soldiers throughout Athens's history. But the best view was reserved for the Council of 500, seated by tribes. This arrangement underlined the paramount role that ordinary citizens now played in civic affairs, as a result of perhaps the most critical of all the innovations commonly credited to Cleisthenes: namely, his introduction of an annual drawing of lots to determine who would serve that year on the Council. This was a striking departure from the previous practice of selecting political officials by letting prominent men of noble birth (like Cleisthenes) vie for popular support with help from their networks of wealthy friends and clients.

To anyone accustomed to the importance of periodic elections in most modern democracies, the use of a lottery to select a city government seems counterintuitive. But drawing lots to seek the advice of the gods was a common practice in ancient Greece, as it was in many other archaic cultures; so was the use of a lottery to assure fairness (as still happens today in the selection of juries for court trials in many places). At the same time, Cleisthenes put the lottery to a novel *political* use, and he reinforced its impact by stipulating that a citizen could serve on the Council of 500 only twice, nonconsecutively. By combining rotation in office with a random selection process, the lottery nullified the corrupting advantages otherwise conferred in elections by wealth and family prominence. That is why Aristotle regarded elections as an essentially *oligarchic* political device, whereas he thought that selection by lot was quintessentially democratic.

Holding an annual lottery to staff the Council ensured that almost every Athenian citizen, at least once in his life, would participate in governing the city—just as the seating arrangement at the City

Dionysia ensured that he would be publicly honoured for this service. Over the course of the fifth century, more and more of the city's offices would be filled in annual lotteries open to even the poorest of its citizens, turning the device into a defining feature of the first democracy.

III

THE WORD that Athenians later in the fifth century retrospectively applied to the institutional reforms inaugurated by Cleisthenes—*demokratia*—described a novel and still-evolving political form, in which ordinary citizens (demos) all had equal access to *kratos* (political power). By the end of the century, there were perhaps several hundred Greek settlements besides Athens that had adopted a form of democracy, some of them allies of Athens and some forced by Athens to adopt democratic institutions modelled on its own.

Slowly but surely, lotteries were used to fill more and more Athenian offices. In 487/6, the lottery was introduced to select the city's chief magistrates, the archons. To this trend there were two significant exceptions—the city's board of ten generals and its board of ten treasurers, officials responsible for military and financial affairs. Both groups were chosen in elections (and, in the case of the financial officials, there was a property qualification prospective officeholders had to meet as well). Election was the device used in these cases because the city wanted to have experienced merchants overseeing the city's finances, and shrewd strategists leading the city's armed forces, not just any random commoner. It therefore deployed an undemocratic political method in order to produce a meritocratic outcome.

In any case, the power of all the city's officials, whether randomly selected by lot or elected by a vote, was gradually subordinated to the power wielded by the Assembly when citizens met face-to-face in the Pnyx. The polis in Athens began to eclipse in ethical significance the *oikos*, or household—a fraught transition, represented dramatically in the *Antigone* of Sophocles.

III

IN ORDER TO preserve the perceived purity of this powerful new community, membership was restricted by a number of formal exclusions that became more rigorous as the regime became more democratic. As time passed, the criteria for citizenship were tightened to ensure that no resident aliens had any access to political power; neither, of course, did women or slaves. As a result, only a small fraction of the Athenian population participated in politics. The significance of this exclusivity was incalculable: the citizens of Athens were encouraged to think of themselves as a chosen people, an example for the rest of mankind. The myth of Athenian autochthony—a strong form of nativism, stressing that citizens must spring from the land—enabled even the poorest citizen to regard himself as well-born.

All native-born male Athenians enjoyed political equality by law. At the same time, there were other marked inequalities among them—of status, of wealth, and of education. Aristotle, a careful analyst of the structure of Greek city-states, sorted the free citizens into two categories: a large group of ordinary citizens (the demos, or common people), and a smaller group of extraordinary individuals, aristocrats distinguished by family pedigree, ownership of property, cultivation, and civic achievements.

Such individuals enjoyed no special privileges *de jure* in democratic Athens. Instead, elite citizens bore special burdens: they were expected to help finance the city's warships and to help pay for the city's dramatic festivals (a distinctively Greek form of voluntary taxation, organized around the institution of "liturgies"—the Greek word *leitourgia* literally means "public service"). These public contributions brought glory to some wealthy citizens and enabled them to stand out in the Assembly and other public settings. By the mid-fifth century, it was also common for elite citizens to learn from hired experts how to speak persuasively in public—this was a preliterate society that revolved largely around the spoken, not the written, word. Still, it is a bit misleading to call such eloquent leaders of the Assembly "politicians," as Athens, lacking any such specialized way to make a living, lacked any such word for those members of the elite who chose to devote their free time to public life; in democratic Athens, profiting from politics was in fact a criminal offence.

Despite the advantages they continued to enjoy even after the reforms of Cleisthenes, distinguished Athenians who hoped to lead the demos nevertheless had, unavoidably, to come into direct and ongoing contact with the crowd of ordinary citizens who regularly convened in the Assembly. Any aspiring leader needed to court the common people and find ways to persuade them to undertake a concerted course of action with some measure of consistency. Success in this task generally required having some kind of extraordinary talent, whether as a persuasive speaker, a political tactician, or a military strategist.

Only a few men in some measure combined all of these talents—and that is surely one reason why a handful of famous leaders loom so large in most histories of Athenian democracy.

III

MY FIRST EXPOSURE to ancient democracy came as a schoolboy, through reading the funeral oration of Pericles. In assigning the text, a passage from Thucydides' *The Peloponnesian War*, my sixth-grade teacher explained the sombre occasion—an annual oration, held at the city's military cemetery, to commemorate the soldiers killed in combat in the first months of what would become a lengthy war with Sparta.

She also stressed the larger purpose of the speech, to sum up the virtues of the city these soldiers had died for, a society, not unlike our own United States, she suggested, conceived in liberty, and dedicated to the proposition that all men are created equal, and she directed our attention to the following passage:

"Our constitution," says Pericles, "does not copy the laws of neighbouring states; we are rather a pattern to others than imitators ourselves"—a reference to the radical novelty of Athenian institutions. "Our city is called a democracy because it is governed by the many, not the few"—one of the earliest, and simplest, definitions of the new political form. "In the realm of private disputes everyone is equal before the law, but when it is a matter of public honours each man is preferred

not on the basis of his class but of his good reputation and his merit"—
an indication of the egalitarian spirit that prevailed in the city.

By the time he delivered his funeral oration, Pericles, according to
the ancient Greek biographer Plutarch, had earned the nickname
"Olympian," because of the admirable nobility of his character and the
blameless way he had exercised power, with unwavering civility and
self-restraint.

His pedigree was distinguished. His mother was a niece of Cleisthenes, while his father, Xanthippus, although briefly exiled, was renowned for leading the Athenian forces that annihilated the Persian
fleet of Xerxes at Mycale in 479, a year after the first Greek victory over
the invaders at Salamis.

As a member of the Alcmaeonid family, Pericles had access to some of
the most celebrated teachers of the day: Plutarch reports that he
learned from Zeno of Elea, a logician renowned for his paradoxes, and
Anaxagoras, a naturalist who offered novel explanations of eclipses,
rainbows, and meteors.

In 472, shortly after he had come into his patrimony after the death of
his father, Pericles was asked to serve as a *choregos*, or producer, at the
City Dionysia for Aeschylus, who had been chosen as one of the three
playwrights to produce three tragedies and a satyr play for that year's
festival. The names of *choregoi* were inscribed on the annual victory lists
alongside the names of the winning poet and actors—and in 472, Pericles
and Aeschylus were both awarded first prize for *The Persians*.

The play focuses on the Greek triumph at Salamis and its aftermath. It recounts the anger of the gods at the hubris of Xerxes, whose
attempt to conquer the Greek people ends in humiliation and defeat.
But the play also commemorates the glorious victory of the Greeks over
the barbarian foe. In the words of a Persian messenger bearing grim
tidings:

> The rest of their array moved out and on,
> And to our ears there came a burst of sound,
> A clamour manifold.—*On, sons of Greece!*

On, for your country's freedom! strike to save
Wives, children, temples of ancestral gods,
Graves of your fathers! now is all at stake.

Salamis was a naval engagement, and its outcome proved the prowess of the Athenian fleet of triremes, so-called because of the arrangement of rowers in three tiers down each side of the swift boats. As many as ninety oars on each side, each manned by one rower, enabled the warships to reach a speed of ten knots in short bursts. The poorest citizens in Athens manned the oars of these long boats—and their crucial contribution to the city's emergence as a regional and eventually an imperial power earned them ever more direct access to political power, and the gratitude of the city's leaders, as Pericles attested in his funeral oration to honour the war dead: "No one, moreover, if he has it in him to do some good for the city, is barred because of poverty or humble origins."

As soon as he was eligible, at the age of thirty, in 464, Pericles was elected to serve as one of Athens's ten generals. That year he commanded a fleet of ten triremes on an expedition into the Corinthian Gulf, where he defeated an army of Corinth's neighbour Sicyon. Some historians think that his skill as a naval officer helps to explain his first appearance the following year as a key political actor. In 463, Pericles brought charges against the most prominent of the city's elected generals, Cimon, accusing him of taking bribes from the King of Macedon (apparently to prevent an Athenian attack). At the time, Cimon and his aristocratic supporters were also facing a domestic political challenge from a political newcomer named Ephialtes, who favoured giving more power to the lower classes. (Eminent Athenians routinely used litigation as a form of political harassment.)

Cimon's trial for bribery ended in his acquittal. But a few months later, while Cimon was abroad, leading what turned out to be an unsuccessful Athenian effort to help Sparta suppress a revolt by their Helots (the city's slave-warriors), he faced a different kind of democratic ordeal. His absence cleared the way for his opponents to push political reforms through the Assembly under the leadership of Ephialtes, with the help of followers like the young Pericles.

Ephialtes represented a new kind of Athenian leader: a man without wealth who was regarded as upright and incorruptible, a man *from* the people offering himself as a leader *of* the people. His most important reform was to take away the remaining judicial powers of the Athenian Aeropagus, the city's council of elders, an aristocratic body originally consisting of former archons. The vetting of members of the Council of 500 before and after they had served their annual terms in office was now transferred to the Council itself, while jurisdiction over criminal cases was transferred to popular juries chosen by lot. Officials were now accountable to the demos, not to a dynastic power elite.

Hoping to avert an open civil war, Ephialtes persuaded the Athenians to send Cimon into exile upon his return to Attica. Once a year, the ordinary citizens of Athens were given the opportunity to cast out a compatriot, if they chose. On the appointed day, citizens would assemble in the city's agora, its central marketplace, and write a name on a potsherd; if more than six thousand potsherds named the same person, he would be required to leave Athens within ten days and remain in exile for ten years—a process known as "ostracism."

All of these reforms were contentious. Shortly afterward, in circumstances that remain obscure, someone murdered Ephialtes—and Pericles emerged as his foremost political heir. But his consolidation of power was gradual. It was only in later decades that his authority became unrivalled, due to his acknowledged gifts as an orator in the Assembly—and, equally important, his leadership of the city's armed forces as the most prominent of its *strategoi*, or elected generals.

Under Cleisthenes' reforms, the city's ten elected generals jointly exercised command of the city's military forces, deciding strategy by majority vote; each general held his presidency in turn in daily rotation. There were no property qualifications to stand for election, but because the city normally favoured men with some level of education, most generals came, like Pericles, from wealthy families. Generals could serve consecutive terms in office, if reelected: Pericles was first elected general in 464 and held the post almost continually from 443 until his death in 429.

Generals in these years played an unusually large political role, if only *ex officio*. They had the right to attend meetings of the Council of 500 and to propose that it convene the Assembly. And they were often asked to address the Assembly when it deliberated over whether or not to engage in a war—a constant concern.

By the time that Pericles emerged as the city's undisputed leader, Athens had amassed the eastern Mediterranean's most feared military machine, an armada of battleships backed up by a large infantry. Its armed forces enabled Athens to create a formidable empire in the mid-fifth century, exercising a far-flung hegemony over a variety of maritime colonies and vassal Greek city-states.

Pericles proved himself in combat and helped his troops win numerous typically sanguinary campaigns, most notably against the rebellious citizens of Euboea (446), in Samos (441–439), and in Aegina (431). Although Pericles was praised by his supporters for his judiciousness and restraint as a general, he was blunt in his defence of Athenian imperialism, telling the Assembly in one speech recorded by Thucydides, "Remember, too, that if your country has the greatest name in all the world, it is because she has never bent before disaster; because she has expended more life and effort in war than any other city, and has won for herself a power greater than any hitherto known."

Athens's growing empire in these years enabled Pericles to finance a number of domestic reforms that strengthened the democratic character of the city. One innovation was to introduce daily pay for the city's armed forces. According to Plutarch, Pericles sent out "sixty triremes annually, on which large numbers of the citizens sailed about for eight months under pay, practising and at the same time acquiring the art of seamanship." He also increased the number of military garrisons assigned to subject city-states, a system that also helped the poorest of citizens. One recent historian has estimated that almost fifteen thousand individuals were supported directly in these ways by the Athenian empire. Pericles initiated a large number of public works projects, persuading the Assembly to construct new monuments and sacred buildings, creating jobs for a large number of local craftsmen. He also introduced a fund that enabled ordinary citizens to receive a per diem payment for serving by lot as a juror in one of the city's courts, or as a magistrate on the Council. As the French historian Vincent Azoulay remarks, Pericles was in these ways able "to redistribute wealth to the people on a scale never before seen in history."

Perhaps as a result of these reforms, citizenship in Athens became an even more jealously guarded privilege. (Increasing the number of citizens of course would risk diluting, if not destroying, the newfound fiscal benefits of democratic citizenship.) In addition to excluding slaves, women, and resident aliens, the Athenians passed a law in 451/450 decreeing that it was no longer enough to have a citizen father to qualify for Athenian citizenship; one needed to have a native-born mother as well. The high point of democratic egalitarianism in Athens coincided with the imposition of new, and quite restrictive, norms of citizenship, along with a renewed stress on the mythic autochthony of the Athenian people, sprung from the soil of Attica.

Thucydides, in his *History of the Peloponnesian War*, asserts that "the growth of the power of Athens, and the alarm that this inspired in Sparta, made war inevitable." Pericles himself led the Athenians into what turned out to be a prolonged and ultimately disastrous war with Sparta—but not without sharp opposition, a reminder that his power was always circumscribed by his need to cooperate with the city's other nine generals, and by his ongoing accountability to the citizens of the Assembly.

The crowd could turn suddenly, as Pericles well knew (his father, after all, had been briefly ostracized). Ordinary citizens in the Assembly routinely resorted to vocal interruptions and heckling, trying to throw an orator off his stride. When they gathered "in assemblies, courts, theatres, army camps, or any other common meeting of a multitude," the Athenian demos, Plato reports, would "blame some of the things said or done, and praise others, both in excess, shouting and clapping; and besides, the rocks and the very place surrounding them echo and redouble the uproar of praise and blame." (The place where the Assembly convened, the Pnyx, means "squeezed tight together.")

Large crowds packed into confined public spaces may have served as a visible check on the power of any one orator—they certainly can make for impressive political theatre. But they don't necessarily promote nuanced deliberation about complex issues, as many modern popular mobilizations, and also the direct democracy of the Swiss rural communes (*Landsgemeinden*), would confirm in practice.

The power of the demos was absolute, and it often changed its mind: it was for just this reason that critics considered democracy a uniquely unstable form of government. The citizens in assembly were perfectly free to reject previously approved laws, even to establish completely new institutions (as witness their adoption of the sweeping reforms of Cleisthenes). As M. I. Finley reminded readers in his classic study *Democracy Ancient and Modern*, "There were no theoretical limits to the power of the state, no activity, no sphere of human behaviour"— public or private, sacred or secular—"in which the state could not legitimately intervene provided the decision was properly taken for any reason that was held to be valid by the Assembly. Freedom meant the rule of law and participation in the decision-making process, not the possession of inalienable rights." In 430, a few months into the war with Sparta, with the city under siege by the enemy and a plague ravaging those inside the city walls, the Assembly turned on Pericles, blaming him for their plight and eventually relieving him of his duties as *strategos*.

The citizens soon enough repented of their decree and reinstated Pericles as general. But within weeks, he was dead, a victim of the plague that eventually killed nearly one-third of the population of Athens.

III

"**THE ATHENIAN COMMUNITY** during the Periclean time must be regarded as one of the most successful examples of social organization in history." So wrote the British scholar (and avid supporter of empire as a liberating force in world history) Alfred Zimmern in 1911, in his classic account, *The Greek Commonwealth*. And so I was told by my sixth-grade teacher, who encouraged her students to admire Periclean Athens along with Republican Rome and postwar America—all political systems in which ordinary citizens wielded a just measure of political power, I was taught, whether directly, in democratic assembly, or indirectly, by popular voting for public officeholders.

Years passed before I discovered that my textbook image of Pericles was not widely shared in antiquity, nor was my teacher's admiration for Athenian democracy. On the contrary: the prevailing tradition in the West, up until the late-eighteenth century, was hostile to democracy.

It is worth recalling that most Greek cities in this period were aristocracies or oligarchies, governed by a small group of men who claimed the right to rule on the basis of noble birth or wealth, or both. The anonymous author of one of our earliest sources on Greek politics, probably written sometime in the second half of the fourth century A.D., put his views this way: "Throughout the world the aristocracy are opposed to democracy, for they are naturally least liable to loss of self control and injustice and most meticulous in their regard for what is respectable, whereas the many display extreme ignorance, indiscipline and wickedness, for poverty gives them a tendency towards the ignoble, and in some cases lack of money leads to their being uneducated and ignorant." In other words, citizens free from want, and with the leisure time to become educated, are better political decision makers than those less fortunate—this was the crux of the case for aristocracy as an ideal form of government.

Athens, in contrast, let the poorest of its citizens participate in almost every level of government. By empowering an impoverished multitude in this manner, the city, critics charged, had in fact created a new kind of tyranny, a collective tyranny of the majority, a kind of "dictatorship of the proletariat" in which the Assembly and democratic orators in concert had created a redistributive regime that doled out money and patronage to the ordinary citizens who manned the imperial fleet and staffed the city's juries and civil offices.

Thucydides, though he admired Pericles as an exemplary political leader of the aristocratic type, was no fan of Athenian democracy. He nevertheless documented some remarkable public debates among the Athenians in his history of the Peloponnesian War, offering evidence of the strengths as well as limitations of the city's democratic institutions in action.

For example, Thucydides recounts how the Assembly reacted in 427 to the news that its armed forces had suppressed a bloody revolt at Mytilene. The armed uprising, fomented by an erstwhile ally with the connivance of its enemy Sparta at a time when Athens had yet to recover fully from the plague, was not the sort of act likely to excite feelings of clemency toward the rebels. In an initial meeting of the Assembly, Thucydides reports that Cleon, the most powerful popular leader after the death of Pericles, had no trouble convincing his fellow citizens to mete out the harshest possible justice, by summarily executing all the men of Mytilene and enslaving the women and children.

A master of abusive insults—some say "he was the first to shout when addressing the people"—Cleon was ruthless in his dishonesty and preening in his self-confidence. Thucydides says he was "the most violent man at Athens, and at that time the most powerful with the people." He was, in the eyes of the chronicler, a pernicious new style of popular leader (literally, *demagogos*)—a bombastic and vindictive man whose prevailing emotions, of anger and pique, he could make contagious in public settings.

In ancient Greek, before the derogatory appropriation of the term by Plato, *demagogos* meant, literally, "leader of the people"—and in this purely descriptive neutral sense, Pericles was in fact the most acclaimed leader of the people in fifth-century Athens. As Thucydides himself emphasized, the Athenian democracy flourished when incisive leaders as self-possessed as Pericles played a central role in popular decision making—and floundered when power-hungry agitators pandered to popular passions.

In his account of the Athenian deliberations over what to do with Mytilene, Thucydides proceeds to describe in detail how the demos, as it sometimes did, underwent a dramatic change of heart. The Assembly was reconvened the next day to reconsider their original decision. Cleon was this time answered by one Diodotus, who urged mercy and a calm reconsideration of what policy best served the city's interests. (Nobody questioned its right to slaughter the men and enslave the women and children.) After hearing the arguments of Diodotus, the Assembly revoted, and chose, by a narrow margin, to spare the people of Mytilene—for reasons of geopolitical prudence, not out of any humanitarian sentiment. (Admittedly, no such happy outcome occurred in the even more hair-raising episode involving the Athenian genocide of the Melians a few years later, though that policy was executed not by the Assembly but by the city's presiding officials on-site.)

The episode gives us a vivid glimpse of the demos in action—and Thucydides, despite the not unreasonable outcome in this case, was not at all reassured by what he saw.

On the contrary, the inconstancy of the crowd confirmed his view that ordinary people, quick to anger and vulnerable to flattery, had little interest in, or ability to learn, or act upon, the truth. In his opinion, the best leader in a democracy was someone like Pericles, who "led the multitude rather than being led by it . . . Whenever he saw the people were unjustifiably confident and arrogant, he would cow them into fear with his words; on the other hand, when he saw them unreasonably afraid, he would turn them back to hopefulness once more." It is in this context that Thucydides remarks that Athens under Pericles was a "democracy" in name only; in reality, it was a city "governed by its first citizen."

III

IN 404 B.C., the Peloponnesian War ended in the defeat of Athens, the dismantling of its empire—and, briefly, the destruction of its democracy. Shortly after the city surrendered to Sparta, the so-called Thirty Tyrants came to power and quickly disbanded the Council of 500, dissolved the Ekklesia, and started to execute citizens they regarded as political enemies. Among the tyrants were two prominent disciples of the city's most famous philosopher, Socrates—a reminder that the rise of democracy in Athens coincided with the birth of philosophy as a distinctive way of life.

As tensions flared in Athens, Socrates tried to stay above the fray, supposedly telling friends that only a shameful regime would deliberately murder large numbers of citizens. Among his followers were not only members of the tyranny like Critias and Charmides, but ardent democrats like Chaerephon, who had asked the Delphic oracle years before whether there was anyone wiser than Socrates. (The answer was no.)

Late in 404, a civil war broke out in Athens. The following spring, Critias was killed in a skirmish. Six months later, the Thirty Tyrants were driven from Athens, democracy was restored, and a political amnesty was decreed—a pioneering venture in public forgiveness and an effort to defuse the divisive, potentially destructive impulses that were never far from the surface in democratic Athens.

Unfortunately, the amnesty didn't stop enemies of Socrates from bringing charges in 399 against the old man, alleging that the putative seeker of wisdom was an arrogant dissembler, guilty of impiety and corrupting the youth. At his trial, Socrates defended himself against these charges by recalling his puzzlement that Apollo, speaking through the oracle of Delphi, had suggested that nobody was wiser than Socrates. Assuming, as a pious man would, that the god spoke truly, Socrates proceeded to question whomever he met about his knowledge of things. He discovered, as he told the jury, that most of his fellow citizens, even the greatest and most accomplished among them, were in fact unable to defend their beliefs about the best way to live, or the nature of a good society.

As he spoke, Socrates took evident pride in the fact that he had become someone *extra*ordinary—and his perceived haughtiness posed a real problem to jurors who expected a measure of deference to customary views and beliefs. (The city's democratic orators, besides defending the right of anyone to speak in the Assembly, routinely praised the value of consensus, or *homonomia*—literally, same-mindedness.) When he turned to the accusation that he had corrupted the young,

Socrates responded more sharply still, with taunts: "Do you know anyone who is less a slave to bodily desires than I am? Do you know anyone more free? . . . Could you plausibly regard anyone as more upright?"

Plato and Xenophon, two eyewitnesses who wrote accounts of the trial, agree that Socrates was defiant, even insolent in his self-defence, which wasn't helpful when some ordinary citizens already distrusted his air of superiority. The large jury of his peers—probably 501 citizens—found Socrates guilty by a slim margin. This verdict was perfectly legitimate by the norms of the city's democracy. But in the eyes of his philosophical followers, his trial and subsequent execution (by drinking a poisonous tea made of hemlock) was a grotesque miscarriage of justice—and an important piece of evidence in the case some of them would subsequently make *against* democracy.

The most important of these critics was Plato. In his dialogue the *Republic*, Plato shows Socrates in happier days, in prolonged conversation with two young friends, arguing that most people—"the many"— have "no knowledge of true being, and have no clear patterns in their minds of justice, beauty, truth" (in the Victorian paraphrase of Benjamin Jowett). Only a few people—those who love wisdom, the philosophers—have reliable knowledge and clear conceptions of justice, beauty, and truth. These observations lead Socrates, in the course of the imaginary conversation Plato depicts, to suggest that philosophers should become kings in a properly ordered polis, for (as Jowett puts it) "they are lovers of the knowledge of the eternal and of all being; they are lovers of truth and haters of falsehood; their desires are absorbed in the interests of knowledge."

Yet as every reader of Plato's dramatic dialogue knew, Socrates had been condemned at Athens, not crowned a king. Asked by his interlocutors in Plato's dialogue how a polis could ever treat a lover of wisdom unjustly, Socrates answers in a parable—striking images are a crucial part of Plato's power as a writer.

In this parable, Socrates asks his audience to picture a ship, and to imagine an owner at the helm, someone who "is bigger and stronger than everyone else on board, but he's hard of hearing, a bit short-sighted, and his knowledge of seafaring is equally deficient." The owner is a poor helmsman, and the sailors can plainly see his failings. They begin to quarrel among themselves about seizing control of the ship, with each of them supposing that he might make a better captain. Realizing they have strength in numbers, they corner the shipowner and try to force him to hand over the ship. Failing at first, they seek help from another eminent man of wealth and privilege on board, someone who is "clever at persuading or forcing the shipowner to let them rule." And when this silver-tongued man convinces the owner to hand over the helm to him, the sailors all cheer. Praising him (in Plato's words) as a "'navigator,' a 'captain,' and as 'one who knows ships,'" they dismiss anyone else as useless: "They don't understand that a true captain must pay attention to the seasons of the year, the sky, the stars, the winds, and all that pertains to his craft, if he's really to be the ruler of a ship." Even worse, Socrates concludes, if anyone on deck in such a fraught situation should claim that *he* knows how to navigate properly, by consulting the heavens, the mutinous sailors would surely jeer, and hurl insults, and call him a "stargazer, a babbler, and a good-for-nothing."

The charismatic captain in this parable is a demagogue. The unruly sailors represent the demos—and the stargazer is a philosopher, ridiculed and reviled instead of properly revered.

"The problem was that democracy pandered to desire," David Runciman remarks in a shrewd recent study, summing up some of Plato's many qualms about democracy: "It gave people what they wanted day to day, but it did nothing to make sure they wanted the right things. It had no capacity for wisdom, for difficult decisions, or for hard truths. Democracies were founded on flattery and lies. Democratic politicians told the people what they wanted to believe, not what they needed to hear. As Plato put it, they took their failings and dressed them up as though they were virtues."

III

ALCIBIADES—A WARD of Pericles, the prize pupil of Socrates, and a demagogue of the first rank (in both the neutral and pejorative sense of the term)—reportedly called the Athenian democracy an "acknowledged folly."

Despite this dim estimate of its value, democracy would endure for almost a century after the death of Socrates. As Thucydides remarked, "It was no light matter to deprive the Athenian people of its freedom"—surely one reason why Athenians quickly restored their democracy.

In the years that followed, democracy in Athens evolved and, in many respects, flourished. Its democratic institutions were refined and re-formed. If anything, the restored democracy of the fourth century seems to have produced ever more intensive participation by a dwindling number of full citizens. And even though the city had lost its empire, the regional power of the city remained considerable. Its continuing success has led a number of modern historians to argue that Athens by ancient standards was "a remarkably efficient State," if not quite the imperialist paradise imagined by Alfred Zimmern.

Throughout the fourth century, the city remained the most vital centre in the ancient world for scientific research and rival philosophical schools. In part as a result of this flowering of inquiry associated above all with the academy of Plato and the subsequent lyceum of Aristotle, we know much more about the Greek democracy in its final decades than we do about its functioning under Pericles, or during the Peloponnesian War.

The key piece of the puzzle appeared only in the final decades of the nineteenth century, when a papyrus scroll was discovered in Egypt containing the text we now know, somewhat misleadingly (since no Greek polis had a comprehensive written document similar to the Constitution of the United States) as *The Constitution of Athens*. (The Greek word *politeia*, sometimes translated as "constitution," refers to a community of citizens and how it is structured, via customary rituals and unwritten norms, as well as publicly posted laws.) This document, likely the work of one of Aristotle's students, though commonly attributed to Aristotle himself, and therefore included in modern editions of his complete works, dates from the end of the fourth century B.C.

Reading this document is a sobering experience for anyone

enchanted by the glories of Athens that Pericles depicted in his funeral oration. In her widely influential study *The Human Condition*—and in the context of praising Pericles and his oration—Hannah Arendt claims that the Greek "*polis* was supposed to multiply the occasions to win 'immortal fame,' that is, to multiply the chances for everybody to distinguish himself, to show who he was in his unique distinctness."

Inspired by Arendt, a series of armchair political philosophers in the decades since have sung the praises of Greek democracy for its putative embodiment of "the political," understood as a dramatic struggle staged for appreciative spectators, which would increase the chances that "a deed deserving fame would not be forgotten." At the same time, Arendt asserted that "the Greeks, in distinction from all later developments, did not count legislating among the political activities. In their opinion, the lawmaker was like the builder of the city wall, someone who had to do and finish his work before political activity could begin." In such an idealized conception, the essence of Athenian politics is taken to be lofty oratory and memorable confrontations between outstanding actors competing for glory.

The Constitution of Athens tells a different, and far less romantic, story about the everyday democratic meaning of "the political," and about the actual political practices prevailing in Athens from roughly 350 to 322 B.C.

III

PERHAPS THE MOST IMPORTANT public duty of every native-born Athenian man throughout this period was military service. In the second half of the fourth century, the city's ephebes—by now including every native-born Athenian boy over the age of eighteen—had to undergo several years of training, learning how to fight in armour and how to use the bow, the javelin, and the catapult. After a public display of his mastery of the martial arts, each citizen received a shield and spear as a gift from the city, and then was asked to patrol the countryside and man the city's guard posts, becoming a full-fledged citizen only after two years of mandatory military service. Once a citizen, a young man could participate in the city's Assembly (Ekklesia), but not yet the city's Council of 500.

The Council met every day except for festival days and an indeterminate number of days regarded as "inauspicious." In a typical year, the Council met about three hundred days. Meetings were normally held in a Council house, located in the southwest corner of the agora next to the city archive and a monument to the city's eponymous heroes, where public notices were posted. For roughly one month at a time, all of the councillors from one of the city's ten districts were treated as a standing committee in more or less permanent session and sharing the duty to watch over the Council chambers at night. Councillors all received a per diem.

The Council prepared the agenda for the Assembly and reviewed every matter to be put before the people. It audited the performance not just of the previous year's councillors, but of all city officials. It was in charge of awarding contracts for any public works (such as repair of the city walls, the erection of new temples, or the construction of new warships). It supervised all the other city boards, including those handling the city's finances; the health of the city's horses; the fitness of its armed forces; the provision of welfare to disabled Athenians; the integrity of the city's coinage and of its market weights and measures; the execution of criminals; and so on. The Council also received all envoys from foreign states—it was responsible for international relations.

The Council's agenda was in part fixed, requiring it to review at regular intervals the city's income and expenditures. Foreign policy had to be discussed at specified meetings. Ongoing review of major public works occurred at specific intervals. Voting was normally by a show of hands, and the results were estimated visually.

Being a councillor was (to put it mildly) a demanding task. It was especially onerous for citizens who lived outside the city walls and who had to travel on foot to and from daily meetings; for many, the per diem barely covered the cost of their food and lodging, if they chose to stay away from home. There is evidence that by the second half of the fourth century, some seats on the Council, when the population of Athens was declining, needed to be filled either by peer pressure or compulsory enlistment. Participation was obligatory (just as jury duty is today in many modern liberal societies).

Four days before the Assembly convened, according to the norms in effect at the time, the Council posted an agenda. Meetings of the Assembly began at dawn, so citizens from outside the city needed to be en route before sunrise. Attendants handed each participant a token, which was handed back when pay was distributed after the Assembly meeting was over.

The proceedings invariably began with a sacrifice. A pig was slaughtered and dragged around the Pnyx to purify the site with its blood. A herald gave a prayer, followed by a curse upon any participant who would seek to mislead the demos. He then asked, "Who of those above fifty years of age wishes to address the assembly?" Only after the Assembly had heard from its elders were other citizens invited to speak.

Meetings had to end by dusk, and proceedings could be stopped at any time by stormy weather, as rainfall was regarded as a bad omen. Questions of divine dispensations were taken very seriously; there is at least one attested case where the Assembly, unable to settle a dispute involving land use, sought the consul of Apollo at Delphi, and sent an embassy to consult the Pythia (Apollo, according to the oracle, advised leaving the land in question fallow).

Like the Council, the Assembly in the fourth century often had a fixed agenda. In those days, any citizen, if he chose, could charge under oath that an orator had improperly persuaded the Assembly to adopt a decree that was illegal (*paranomon*); if convicted by a popular jury, the decree was vacated and the orator found responsible for misleading the demos was fined. Any citizen could similarly impeach the conduct of any elected general or treasurer.

At the start of a new annual cycle of Assembly meetings, according to an account given by the orator Demosthenes (384–322), "the Herald having read prayers, a vote shall be taken on the laws, to wit, first upon laws respecting the Council, and secondly upon general statutes, and then upon statutes enacted for the nine Archons"—the ceremonial chief magistrates of the city, chosen by lot—"and then upon laws affecting other authorities." This meant that citizens annually could reconsider—and suggest revising—the laws governing the city.

Roughly once a month, the Assembly, according to a fixed agenda, voted on whether all officeholders were properly doing their jobs; they reviewed the state of the city's relations with the gods; they confirmed that the city had sufficient stocks of grain and that the homeland was secure militarily.

For some important matters, such as promulgating a new law or conferring an honorary citizenship, the Assembly required a quorum of six thousand at two successive meetings—so there was pressure to participate in this forum, too. And this was not the end of the pressure. In addition to the Council and the regular Assembly meetings, citizens had to staff up the juries of the courts. Every year, the city impanelled by lot six thousand potential jurors, who were all citizens over the age of thirty with no public debts. Jurors for a specific court case were drawn by lot from the bigger list. Juries varied in size, consisting of between 501 and 1,001 citizens. A number of courtrooms surrounded the agora, in order to process an escalating number of trials (caused in part by a growing number of commercial disputes in Aristotle's day, which the courts were expected to adjudicate). In the second half of the fourth century, scholars estimate that courts were in session between 150 and 200 days a year. Being randomly chosen as part of the city's annual jury pool in those years was almost as onerous as being randomly chosen to serve as a councillor.

Although some details of how the democracy worked in this period still remain obscure, this much seems clear: from 350 to 322, the era for which we have the most direct evidence, Athens had ensured equality of political access for all of its citizens by devising an astonishingly complex municipal government. "Never before or since in world history has such an elaborate network of political institutions been created and developed to run a very small and fairly simple society," claims the Danish historian Mogens Herman Hansen, perhaps the greatest modern expert on Athenian democracy.

IT SEEMS to have been true that this extraordinarily intricate form of amateur self-government largely worked—but making it work was a punishing task. The Cambridge historian Paul Cartledge calls it "participatory democracy with a vengeance." Aristotle's famous assertion that man is a political animal certainly applied to the citizens of fourth-century Athens.

Toward the end of the century, there was a proliferation of meetings. Chronic, potentially polarizing tensions between rival groups of citizens were "an inevitable cost of the democratic decision-making mode." The Swiss historian Jacob Burckhardt, in his prickly nineteenth-century lectures on Greek civilization, lamented the constant recourse to jury trials at Athens, and the city's "spirit of feverish litigation," not least as a means of political score settling, replete with grandstanding public speeches alleging crimes that were often amazingly ill-defined— the trial of Socrates for impiety being the most notorious example of this aspect of Athenian democracy.

By the time Aristotle's team compiled *The Constitution of Athens*, the active citizen population of Athens was perhaps half of what it had been under Pericles, making the demands of participation more all-consuming than ever. Under Pericles, the Athenians had created a closed community, with the rights of citizenship available to only a privileged (and dwindling) few—and that fact alone made the city increasingly vulnerable to conquest by outside forces.

This is not the place to recount the decline of Athenian democracy. Of the causes for its eclipse, perhaps the most important involved the rise of an expansive new imperial power to the north, Macedonia, which from 338 onward exercised effective hegemony over the entirety of Greece, including Athens. The kinds of moral flaws and lack of wisdom in a democracy stressed by Plato had little to do with the decline of Athenian independence (though his criticism had everything to do with the subsequent marginalization of democracy in the Western tradition of political thought).

Democracy in any case didn't disappear overnight. In Athens, the first step came in 321, when Antipater, Alexander the Great's successor as leader of Macedonia, imposed a minimum wealth qualification for holding Athenian citizenship. When the Macedonian Empire began to fall apart, it was replaced by a succession of regional multistate empires that competed to rule over vast swaths of territory. Meanwhile, for some years to come, some Greek cities, including Athens, maintained regimes that were nominally democratic, even when they were effectively ruled by local elites controlled by garrisons and governors who represented distant monarchs.

As Paul Cartledge has summed up the situation in the Hellenistic period, "the constitutional trend in political actuality was firmly toward various shades of oligarchy." Yet if only as an ideological fig leaf, "*demokratia*" continued to be used to describe Hellenistic Greek city-states that were neither monarchies nor tyrannies and had some degree of independence from relevant regional powers. Even more potentially confusing, this vague usage (Cartledge calls it a "calamitous verbal collapse") was extended in the first century A.D. by the application of the term *demokratia* to the Roman Empire of Augustus (perhaps on the grounds that Augustus claimed to preside over a "restored" Republic, or perhaps because he had assumed for life the title, and power, of a tribune of the common people, the *plebs Romana*). By the mid-second century A.D., Aelius, a famed orator, could declare, in the ode "To Rome," that "there has been established throughout the world alike a democracy—under one man, namely the best ruler and controller."

So "democracy" survived as a word for almost any type of ostensibly "popular" republic, however authoritarian or mixed with monarchic elements its constitution might be; just as the same word, much more rigorously defined by serious students of politics, survived as a word for direct rule by ordinary citizens, a form of government widely associated with the danger of mob rule.

At the same time, the memory of real democracy in its most radical forms in Athens was preserved in a variety of ancient texts. There it lived on not just as an object of systematic criticism, in the philosophical works of Plato and Aristotle, but also as an imagined community, preserved in the extant public speeches of demagogues like Pericles and Demosthenes.

Yet however vivid some of these oratorical paeans to "democracy," the equally vivid images of democratic disorder in Plato, combined with his sustained arguments against it as a reasonable form of government, would make an even deeper and much more lasting impression. What Alfred North Whitehead said about the European philosophical tradition applies with even greater force to the Western tradition of thought about politics: "the safest general characterization" of each "is that it consists of a series of footnotes to Plato."

III

AS A COLLEGE STUDENT in the sixties, I found Plato's conclusions deeply offensive—so repugnant, in fact, that I had to struggle to rise above my democratic prejudices and seriously engage the substance of his various arguments against popular self-rule. At the same time, inspired by the work of Hannah Arendt, and her romantic picture of the glory of public life in ancient Greece, I found myself yearning for a more active and direct form of democracy than that on offer in the United States. A wish for a more perfect democracy was part of what first inspired my interest in both radical activism and political philosophy. Faced with the scepticism of critics like Plato, I took heart from John Stuart Mill's argument, based in part on the example of Athens (and also the historiography of the great Victorian champion of Athenian democracy, George Grote), that participation in political life is, in itself, edifying, a "school of public spirit" in which citizens come to appreciate their common interests.

There is certainly something to the idea that participation in politics can forge a shared civic culture. But as the history of Athens (and other, subsequent democratic movements as well) shows, intense political participation can also breed conflict and polarization (what the Greeks called *stasis*), so that faction, sedition, even civil war are chronic threats. The case for such participation isn't as clear-cut as Mill implied.

And while the Athenian regime was certainly admirable in its capacity to draw all citizens equally into public affairs, it is impossible to ignore the many classes of people it simultaneously excluded from active citizenship. Even worse, these exclusions became more strict with the passage of time. The solidarity of the Athenian democracy came to depend, in part, upon claims of exclusivity codified in terms of consanguinity. In sharp distinction to the Romans, who extended the rights of citizenship to their allies and subjects as the empire grew, Athens maintained (with a few exceptions) its citizenship as a privilege open only to a chosen few.

Athenian-born women were largely kept out of the public eye, with the notable exception of participating in civic festivals and sacred rituals, and serving as the high priestess of Athena Polias. Resident aliens also played little role in public affairs, though some were allowed to make expensive contributions to the city (a source of status and not just a form of taxation).

The slave population was large, perhaps a third of the overall population of Athens at any time, and hugely important: some laboured under terrible conditions in the city's silver mines, others were skilled craftsmen, and still others were lucky enough to be trained functionaries. In fact, many administrative tasks under the democracy throughout its existence were relegated to *demosioi*, slaves owned by the city—public servants, literally—who supervised elections, maintained archives, tested the coinage, and served as clerks, accountants, street cleaners, even as policemen. But even as relatively privileged public servants, slaves had a vulnerability that citizens did not: if they failed to do their jobs properly, they could be whipped. (A stele unearthed in Athens in 1970 stipulates fifty lashes as the prescribed punishment for a public slave tasked with testing the currency who "does not sit at his post or test according to the law.")

In democratic Athens, any citizen was free to speak his mind when the people assembled—but that freedom coexisted with a drive toward unity and consensus, in a community where collective single-mindedness was prized as a demotic virtue, perhaps because sharp dissension was in practice such a chronic threat. A certain fear of nonconformity seems to have been one factor behind the guilty verdict of the citizen jury that tried the philosopher Socrates.

At the same time, Athens, in its heyday, was almost always at war. It wasn't as obsessed with cultivating the martial virtues as Sparta, where the army stood at the centre of civic affairs—but Athens was an aggressive regional power, and its recurrent mobilization of citizens to combat external enemies produced a distinctively democratic ideology, a vision of the soldier-citizenry as a band of brothers, of one mind and one purpose, its solidarity forged in combat.

In thinking about Greek democracy, one may choose to minimize such tensions and contradictions, and celebrate instead the extraordinary fact that all the citizens of Athens, at the height of its democracy, exercised virtually unfettered power, directly in the Assembly and the popular courts, and by random selection to staff up virtually all of the city's other offices.

By concentrating on the lofty rhetoric of Pericles, and the many cultural accomplishments of Athens in its prime, Mill and Grote, and later authors like Zimmern and Arendt, were able to inspire widespread admiration for the world's first democracy among educated readers. In this way, the revaluation of ancient Athens helped to turn democracy itself, against long odds, into a plausible, even praiseworthy, form of government, first in Europe and the United States in the nineteenth century—and subsequently throughout the world.

By then the French Revolution had made it clear that Athens would not be the last example of a democracy based on citizen-soldiers poised to shed blood. Fraternity, solidarity, and the kinds of virtues forged through conflict and struggle would prove alluring for a number of subsequent democrats of different persuasions.

At the same time, some of the most thoughtful modern proponents of democracy would press to make its promise of collective freedom dramatically more universal and inclusive—and, ideally, more pacific—than anything the Athenians had imagined possible.

A REVOLUTIONARY
ASSERTION OF POPULAR SOVEREIGNTY

LATE IN THE EVENING of August 9, 1792, church bells began to peal across Paris, to signal an imminent uprising. In front of the Hôtel de Ville, a palatial structure that housed the city's municipal council, a crowd gathered in the pale moonlight, filling the grand plaza where the French monarchy had long staged public executions.

Shortly after midnight, a large number of designated citizens deliberately mounted the steps to city hall, in order to occupy the council chambers. They represented a cross section of ordinary Parisians: clerks and shopkeepers, lawyers and surgeons, jewellers and cabinetmakers, water carriers and domestic servants. Most were "sans-culottes," labourers without fancy britches (or culottes), proud of their fighting mettle.

Declaring an "Insurrectionary Commune," the new occupants took charge of the National Guard and ordered the arrest of its commander, the Marquis de Mandat. Escorted down the steps of the town hall en route to prison, the nobleman was set upon by someone in the seething crowd and killed on the spot.

In his pioneering 1847 *History of the French Revolution*, Jules Michelet claimed that the people gathered that night were acting spontaneously, that "there was no other perpetrator of August 10 than public indignation, the anger caused by prolonged poverty, a feeling that invaders were approaching, and that France had been betrayed." But the historian Albert Mathiez, writing almost a century later, told a different tale: "No insurrection has ever been more openly prepared. They conspired in broad daylight. They declared what they hoped to accomplish."

And so these sans-culottes did. But because they had done so in their own voice, in local assemblies held throughout the city, the insurrectionists were also taking a leap into the unknown. Only one nationally prominent political figure, the imposing orator Danton, made a fleeting appearance at the Hôtel de Ville that night, but he was alone— and he promptly went back to bed.

There was blood in the air. The people of Paris knew that a Prussian army was marching toward the city, and they knew that these forces hoped to crush the French revolution that had begun in 1789. In response, militants in early August had already proposed an armed uprising to unseat King Louis XVI, the country's constitutional monarch, who was suspected of collusion with the invading army. But cooler heads had prevailed, tabling these petitions and giving the nation's Legislative Assembly a chance to deliberate at their next scheduled meeting, on the afternoon of August 9. The pause also gave the city's network of neighbourhood assemblies (or "sections") a bit more time to debate the future of the new republic—and to prepare for a possible insurrection.

By 1792, these assemblies had become to Paris what the Pnyx had been to classical Athens—laboratories of direct democracy, and a place where ordinary citizens met to wield political power directly. They had their roots in the local assemblies originally convened for elections to the Estates General in 1789. After the fall of the Bastille on July 14, 1789—the symbolic start of the French Revolution—these assemblies continued to meet, producing an impromptu network within Paris. In many neighbourhoods, Parisians who had assembled to form a local militia also began to discuss the forms in which popular sovereignty might best be realized in France.

The constitutional monarchy the French had adopted in 1791 had been designed, in part, to harness the power of the capital city's local assemblies. Under the new constitution, they were tasked with electing delegates to the Paris municipal government, or "Commune"—and to the newly formed Legislative Assembly, which met in Paris but represented the nation as a whole.

The right to vote was restricted to so-called active citizens, men owning a minimum amount of property. (In that era it was a truism that men with no property were too dependent on others to have a mind of their own, and too busy working to ponder public affairs.) The king, who no longer enjoyed absolute authority under the new constitution, retained the power to veto laws that had been passed by the Assembly (unless it overrode his veto at three consecutive sessions).

Despite the limited duties the new constitution gave the sectional assemblies of Paris, and a subsequent legislative decree that these assemblies should discuss only local affairs, activists in the capital continued to debate abstract political principles and matters of national concern. And by the summer of 1792, the Parisian sectional assemblies had emerged more unruly than ever.

By law, their meetings were open to all "active" citizens, regardless of their political views. In practice, by August 9, most Parisian sections had come to welcome even so-called passive citizens, those who were too poor to pay taxes—one reason why radical democrats had come to dominate in the majority of the sections.

For the Parisian insurgents, the great prophet of this fraught political moment was Jean-Jacques Rousseau, the Geneva-born sage who had died fourteen years earlier. "You trust in the present order of society without thinking that this order is subject to inevitable revolutions," Rousseau had written in *Émile*, first published in 1762: "The great become small, the rich become poor, the monarch becomes subject; are the blows of fate so rare that you can count on being exempted from them? We are approaching the state of crisis and the century of revolutions."

"Nobody has proposed a more just idea of the people than Rousseau, because he loved them," declared Robespierre, perhaps the most prominent proponent of democracy in France in these years; he was speaking on January 2, 1792, to the Jacobin Club, one of the voluntary civic associations that had sprung up like mushrooms throughout Paris. In these months, Parisians who were interested could easily learn the views of orators like Robespierre and philosophers like Rousseau by reading pamphlets and newspapers. Eighteenth-century Paris had a predominantly literate population, and radical journals had proliferated since the fall of the Bastille. By the start of 1792, almost every self-respecting political figure needed to have a print outlet of his own, and all the popular political societies, including the Jacobins, routinely published the major speeches of their members. Made famous by the widespread popular press coverage, Robespierre became a hero in the eyes of many militants, giving neighbourhood orators an example to emulate. In his January speech, Robespierre had gone on to quote Rousseau directly: "By itself, the people always want the good, but by itself does not always see it."

Inspired by such rhetoric, some in the Parisian sections grew impatient to force the issue of making all organs of the French government more genuinely "democratic or popular," as radical journalists had been demanding since the fall of the Bastille. Some also argued that ceding power to elected representatives was undemocratic, just as Rousseau had implied in the *Social Contract*, and as the ancient Athenians had believed as well. For the most militant among these activists, sovereignty resided not in a distant body of legislators but only in the primary, local assemblies, where the people met face-to-face. By the early summer of 1792, in some districts of Paris, the sectional assemblies had begun to meet daily, and not just to debate the principles of "the Immortal Rousseau."

Meanwhile, France's Legislative Assembly was torn between constitutional monarchists fearful of rocking the boat; moderate republicans in favour of gradual reforms; and an increasingly vocal group of avowed democrats demanding that ordinary citizens play a more direct role in making political decisions. Throughout the summer, the legislature had been sending mixed signals, veering between bold declarations and indecisive dithering. By the time August 9 arrived, the body was hopelessly divided; despite unrelenting pressure from the radicals in the sectional assemblies, the national Assembly narrowly voted to reject the Parisian petitions demanding that the king step down immediately.

That night, political activists convened in their neighbourhood assemblies throughout Paris to decide what to do next. As they met, couriers crisscrossed the city, to convey the results of votes occurring in the various sectional assemblies.

For example, at the Gobelins section, citizens gathered at 10:00 p.m. in the Left Bank church of Saint-Marcel. A series of speakers rose to demand the dissolution of both the Commune and the Legislative Assembly. If, as a majority now agreed, sovereignty belonged to the people themselves (and not to their king, nor to their elected representatives), then only an insurrection—an armed revolt—would assure that the people were truly sovereign. The Assembly duly dispatched three armed delegates to the Hôtel de Ville. (The Commune comprised 144 delegates, with the forty-eight official sections electing three delegates each.) At the same time, the Gobelins section sent a messenger to let other Parisian assemblies promptly know of their resolution.

As midnight approached, the designated citizens from the sectional assemblies began to arrive in threes at city hall. "Swift now, therefore," the nineteenth-century British essayist Thomas Carlyle wrote in his lyrical account of that Thursday night. "Let these actual old municipals, on sight of the full powers, and mandate of the sovereign people, lay down their functions; and this new hundred and forty-four take them up!"

When the insurgents en masse finally entered the chambers, they were challenged by one of the few sitting members present at that hour. His protest was sharply answered: "When the people place themselves in a state of insurrection," one of the new delegates replied, "they withdraw all power from other authorities and assume it themselves."

As the new Communards formally declared the next day, an "assembly of delegates from the majority of the sections" had gathered overnight "with full power to rescue the Republic." Popular sovereignty was "an indefeasible right, an inalienable right, a right that cannot be delegated." The insurrectionists had simply exercised their sovereign powers.

These modern-day democrats took political ideas very seriously—but many were also driven by sheer rage. As one eyewitness, a commander of a sectional battalion, recalled, events that night were "propelled by an impulse so violent that, wherever it arose, it was impossible to stop, or to anticipate the outcome."

Out of this explosive melee of political passions and interests there appeared a critical mass of people fiercely devoted to forging a radically egalitarian new form of self-government. For the first time since ancient Athens, direct democracy had become a concrete, collective goal—at least in the minds of the Parisian commoners defiantly convened that night at the Hôtel de Ville.

III

A NUMBER OF COMPLEX FACTORS lay behind the dramatic events that unfolded in Paris on August 9 and 10, 1792. Some of them involved recent events in France. But others involved more abstract factors, such as the idea of popular sovereignty, and the emergence of new ways of thinking about how to create a modern republic in eighteenth-century contexts as different as Britain's American colonies and the Franco-phone city-state of Geneva. This was Rousseau's hometown, and throughout the eighteenth century the Calvinist republic had experienced a series of sharp conflicts over the right of ordinary citizens to participate in its political institutions; armed revolts had erupted in Geneva in 1737, 1762, and then in 1783.

After the eclipse of direct self-rule in the ancient world, the idea of democracy had survived, barely, and mainly as a term of art deployed by legal scholars, generally in two contradictory usages. On the one hand, democracy became a virtual synonym for violent anarchy: as the influential Roman historian Polybius summed up his own views, "the licence and lawlessness" of democracy inevitably "produces mob rule," to complete a cycle through which all governments had to pass, going from best (monarchy) to worst (democracy, or rule by the many, turning into mob rule). On the other hand, Polybius, who claimed (not very plausibly) that the Roman Republic was his model, also argued that democracy had a potentially constructive role to play. He suggested that the most durable political regime would be a mixed constitution: a republic that combined the three pure forms of government (monarchy, aristocracy, democracy) into interlinked branches that would check and balance each other, enabling a well-ordered republic to navigate the winds of time "like a well-trimmed boat."

In the centuries that followed, and working with a conception of a good regime similar to that elaborated by Polybius, a tradition of republican thought emerged, based on the example of ancient Rome. The word itself derives from the Latin *res publica*, literally "public thing," or something held in common by many people. Used by Roman scholars as a Latin translation for the Greek word *politeia*, "republic" also was used to refer to the system of government that emerged in Rome following the expulsion of the kings in the sixth century B.C., and that had fallen apart in the first century B.C. with the rise of the Roman Empire under the emperor Augustus.

In the Renaissance, some theorists working within the republican tradition cautiously suggested that ordinary people might have an especially useful role to play, especially as watchdogs and as sol-diers. Because they were jealous of their freedom, they would be vigilant spectators of executive and administrative conduct, on guard against malfeasance. The very passions of the people, which could generate a certain *esprit de corps*, could also be harnessed for the enhancement of a republic's military might. The Florentine author Machiavelli, dreaming of a resurgence of Italian glory in the Renais-sance, was eager to exploit popular ardour: "The best armies are those of armed peoples," not paid mercenaries. Some modern schol-ars have even argued that one can find in his work a justification for a kind of "Machiavellian democracy."

At the same time, republican writers tended to agree that the chief danger to a mixed constitution came from the democratic element, because of its tendency to degenerate into anarchy. Machiavelli warned that the people, left to their own devices, were "promoters of licence." Alger-non Sydney, an English republican beheaded for expressing treasonous political views in 1683, vigorously denied being a proponent of pure democracy. So did the French Enlightenment philosopher Montesquieu, who pointedly worried about the "spirit of extreme equality" he as-sumed was typical of democracies.

Even in the United States, in the wake of a war against colonial rule by a distant monarch, and in the context of expansive new asser-tions of the legitimate power of the people, serious political theorists gingerly handled the idea of democracy, if they acknowledged it at all. Still, some Americans, swept away by popular enthusiasm, began to conflate the ideal of a free republic and democracy, not unlike some of the writers of late antiquity. It was in order to avoid such confusion that James Madison, the chief architect of the U.S. Constitution, took pains to explain that the framers had meant to create a (mixed) repub-lic, not a (pure) democracy.

In the context of conventional republican theories about the supe-rior value of mixed forms of government, the political writings of Jean-Jacques Rousseau came as a shock, largely because of the auda-cious way he redefined sovereignty in terms of democracy. Before

Rousseau, "sovereignty" had implied brute force, empire, and the ability to command: in the learned political treatises of Jean Bodin and Thomas Hobbes, it had primarily defined the dominion of monarchs, not the power of a people. After Rousseau, the prerogative of kings had become an unambiguous byword for democratic self-rule, as readers of the *Social Contract* in his native city of Geneva immediately understood.

He had been born in 1712. His father was a watchmaker and his mother died in childbirth. A voracious reader, he consumed the heroic *Lives* of the Greek and Roman statesmen by Plutarch, the *Republic* of Plato, and the romantic eighteenth-century epistolary novels that his father enjoyed reading as well. Self-taught, Rousseau mastered the key works in the Western tradition of political thought, paying special attention to the republican tradition, and the works of Hobbes, Locke, and Montesquieu. But Rousseau, unlike those authors, grew up in a small city-state, one among a number of fiercely independent Swiss city-states that had a tradition of direct self-government (denizens of the Alps were also renowned for their martial virtues, one reason why Swiss Guards were employed by the French monarchy to protect the king).

Geneva was an anomaly in eighteenth-century Europe, a Protestant city-state in the midst of Catholic kingdoms, its borders confined, its population no more than twenty-five thousand people—and its form of government an unstable amalgam of aristocratic and democratic elements. The democratic element was the city's General Council, consisting of the male heads of households that were long established in the city—excluded were children, women, resident aliens, and male heads of households more recently settled in the city. About fifteen hundred citizens were entitled to attend the General Council's annual meeting.

But in Rousseau's day, political power in Geneva effectively belonged not to the General Council but to a much smaller group consisting of four executives, called Syndics, and a Small Council with twenty members. The Syndics were elected at a General Council meeting from a slate of eight candidates picked by the Small Council; and the members of the Small Council were elected by the wealthiest citizens organized in a Council of Two Hundred; new members of the Council of Two Hundred were in turn appointed by the Small Council.

The resulting regime had been formally decreed an "aristo-democracy" by civic officials in 1734. Scoffing at the neologism, the proponents of giving more power to ordinary citizens argued that "our government is purely democratic"—and in 1737, these dissenters staged an abortive insurrection to demand strengthening the powers of the General Council.

Rousseau is superficially circumspect about democracy in the *Social Contract*. In one famous passage, he remarks that a democracy is a form of government suited only to gods, not mere mortals. But Rousseau also notes in passing "the peculiar advantage of a democratic government," which "can be established in reality by a simple act of the general will."

According to Rousseau, all human beings have a free will, expressed in whatever wants and interests an individual may choose to pursue. The general will, in contrast, designates a much smaller number of wants and interests that all the individuals in a group happen to share; in some contexts, these common interests can move each one of us to say "we," and to act in accordance with that identification. For example, Rousseau asserts that people generally want to be treated with respect in institutions that enhance, rather than inhibit, their autonomy: "If one seeks what precisely comprises the greatest good of all, which ought to be the end of every system of legislation, one will find that it comes down to these two principal objects: *freedom* and *equality*."

In principle, the general will is neither universal nor inborn, but instead is a potential—call it solidarity or fellow feeling—that is developed only through association with others. Although in a genuine community the general will, like the feeling of "We want," is a familiar phenomenon, in other, less cohesive societies, it may appear as a more remote ideal, associated with a dutiful sense that "I ought" to be concerned with my fellows, whatever my spontaneous inclinations.

Rousseau goes on to define various aspects of the body politic that embodies a general will, "which its members call State when it is passive, Sovereign when active . . . As for the associates, they collectively take the name the people; and individually are called Citizens as participants in the sovereign authority, and Subjects as subject to the laws of the State." The only legitimate state, according to the stringent criteria of the *Social Contract*, is a Republic in which the Citizens are Sovereign, and the laws are formed according to the general will.

These were incendiary ideas—especially in Geneva, where Rousseau was implicitly allying himself with democrats who wanted the ordinary citizens to exercise more political power. Shortly after the *Social Contract* was published, the Small Council, in consultation with legal experts, declared that the book's contents were "*destructive* of society and *of all government*, and very dangerous for our Constitution." Geneva's magistrates issued a warrant for Rousseau's arrest and ordered that all copies of the book be seized.

Rousseau was defiant. In 1764, he defended his political theories in a work addressed explicitly to the citizens of Geneva. "The democratic constitution," he now wrote, "has up till now been poorly examined. All those who have spoken of it either have not understood it, or have taken too little interest in it, or have an interest to show it in a false light." Some, raised on the classical image of Athens, "imagine that a democracy is a government where the whole people is magistrate and judge," only to be repelled by the prospect of anarchy; others, who have always been "subjected to princes," see "freedom only in the right to elect leaders"; they have been given the false impression that "whoever commands is always the sovereign," when in fact the only legitimate sovereign is a people animated by a general will. "The democratic constitution is certainly the masterpiece of the political art," Rousseau concludes, "but the more admirable its artifice, the less it belongs to all eyes to see through it."

After the publication of this fierce democratic broadside in

Geneva, events there spun briefly out of control, as a slight majority of the ordinary citizens refused to vote for a single Syndic from the slate offered that year by the Small Council. It took several months before a tenuous calm was restored.

Rousseau subsequently retired from political theorizing, exiled himself to England, and eventually died in 1778—but Geneva remained a political tinderbox. In 1782, after the ordinary citizens tried to expand unilaterally the power of the General Council at its annual meeting, the city's chief magistrate declared that the acts of the Council would no longer be considered binding. In response, armed citizens took to the streets and took into custody members of the city's ruling class.

Alarmed by this turn of events, the rulers of neighbouring France, Sardinia, Berne, and Zurich mustered armed forces to enter the city, suppress the rebellion, and restore Geneva's lawful rulers to power. Observing events on the spot was Jacques-Pierre Brissot, who would subsequently emerge as a proponent of democracy during the French Revolution. And from afar, Mme Roland, a Rousseau enthusiast who would also subsequently emerge as a prominent radical, exclaimed that "virtue and freedom find refuge only in the hearts of a handful of honourable men; a fig for the rest and for all the thrones of the world!"

III

ONE FRENCH MINISTER in 1782 warned that Geneva's rebels showed the dangers of Rousseau's abstract argument that "sovereignty lies with the people, who alone can give it or take it away." At the same time, the Genevan uprising, coming in the wake of the American Revolution, heartened French republicans and offered them a precedent when the people of France rose in rebellion in 1789.

On May 5 of that year, King Louis XVI, under pressure from a growing number of disaffected Frenchmen, had opened the nation's Estates General for the first time since 1614, bringing together elected delegates from the clergy, the aristocracy, and the "third estate," representing commoners. On June 20, the members of the third estate, with support from a number of parish priests, took an oath not to disperse until they had given France a new constitution. On July 9, bowing again to popular pressure, the king announced that the Estates General would be transformed into a National Constituent Assembly, to begin an orderly transition to a constitutional monarchy. On July 14, a crowd of Parisians stormed the Bastille, a medieval state prison, to protest the king's abuse of power—and to hunt for weapons. On August 4, the Constituent Assembly declared the abolition of feudalism. A few weeks later, delegates passed the Declaration of the Rights of Man and Citizen, proclaiming that "men are born free and remain equal in rights."

In the months that followed, France entered a tense and protracted period of political negotiations. The uneasy peace was broken on the night of June 20–21, 1791, when King Louis XVI and his retinue, anticipating that a new constitution would drastically curtail his authority, attempted to flee Paris. The escape had been planned with the help of royalist officers and troops that had gathered near the frontier with the Austrian Netherlands, in order to launch a counter-revolution. The king was quickly captured and forced to return to Paris, where he was confined to the Tuileries Palace, under virtual house arrest. In the months that followed, fear gripped the capital, as it became clear that war with Austria and Prussia was a real possibility. The majority of representatives in the National Constituent Assembly were nevertheless willing to forgive Louis for his treachery, in part out of fear that abolishing the monarchy would open the door to a widening of the citizenry to include male residents who were too poor to pay any taxes. In September 1791, an elected Constituent Assembly tasked with drafting new laws for France presented a republican plan for a constitutional monarchy to the king, who reluctantly approved it.

Elections held according to the restricted franchise stipulated in the new constitution produced a new Legislative Assembly consisting of 745 members, many of them young and with no previous political experience. In Paris, meanwhile, members of the city's political elite— including some key delegates to the Legislative Assembly, such as

Brissot and his friend Condorcet, an eminent philosopher already well-known as an expert on voting procedures—were growing more militantly democratic. The views of such leaders were in turn widely disseminated in Paris through a burgeoning number of political clubs. The largest and most influential of these clubs, the Society of the Friends of the Constitution, was renamed in 1792 the Society of the Jacobins, Friends of Freedom and Equality (the new name derived from the monastery of the Jacobins, where the club met).

By then, the Jacobins had forged a national network of some six thousand affiliated clubs, with branches in cities from Marseille to Rouen. To start, club members shared a general *esprit révolutionnaire*, a patriotic *élan* with widespread appeal. Historians estimate that "as many perhaps as one adult French male in six or seven was at some moment committed to Jacobinism, an extraordinary figure for the time, and one that prefigures the mass political commitments of our own day." Like the Parisian sectional assemblies, the network of Jacobin clubs functioned as local laboratories in direct democracy.

The leading members of the Parisian Jacobin club at first held varied political views. Pragmatists like Condorcet were active alongside political puritans like Robespierre and cunning careerists like Danton. As time passed and battle lines became more clearly drawn between royalists and democratic republicans, the views of the club's dominant members grew fiercer and its national appeal narrowed, even as its political power in Paris slowly expanded.

That winter, Brissot and Condorcet, previously staunch defenders of constitutional law and order, began to qualify their views in the face of ongoing agitation by the sans-culottes in the Parisian sectional assemblies. Writing in the *Chronique de Paris* on February 21, 1792, Condorcet argued that "so long as a revolution is not complete, respect for the law depends upon the state of the people's confidence in its representatives and executive agents, and the sole means of giving power to the law is to secure this confidence and maintain it."

In the weeks that followed, some members of the Jacobins, led by Brissot and Condorcet, tried to convince their colleagues that the Legislative Assembly should declare war on the Holy Roman Emperor in a preemptive strike, assuming (correctly) that the royal family was still secretly scheming with foreign forces. Other members of the Jacobins, led by Robespierre, argued that without the prior formation of a true people's army, consisting entirely of citizen volunteers and led by officers who were not holdovers from the *Ancien Régime*, a war would simply empower a fighting force that hold monarchist views.

When Queen Marie Antoinette's brother, the Holy Roman Emperor Leopold II, began to muster his troops on the French frontier in April, Brissot's fears seemed to be vindicated. If only for the sake of appearances, the king felt compelled to declare war on Austria. Yet when the Legislative Assembly in turn resolved to raise a people's army consisting of twenty thousand volunteers, or *fédérés*, pledged to protect Paris, the king balked and vetoed the idea.

A huge demonstration followed. On June 20, 1792, a crowd of pike-wielding sans-culottes marched first to the Legislative Assembly and then to the Tuileries Palace, where they found a side door they could enter. Mounting stairs with a cannon in tow, and breaking through locked doors with their pikes, the crowd cornered the king with cries of *"Vive la nation!"*

"Oui," the king agreed, *"vive la nation!"* "Prove it," a protester shouted, holding out a red liberty cap, a popular emblem of revolutionary commitment. The king donned the cap. Another protester demanded he drink a toast to his visitors and handed him a bottle of wine. "People of Paris," the king said, "I drink to your health and that of the French nation." The protesters then dispersed—but the political atmosphere was now toxic.

Condorcet had become unabashed in his praise of the sans-culottes: "Each day," he exclaimed, "public opinion grows more enlightened and expresses itself more vigorously." He welcomed the events of June 20, calculating, along with Brissot, that the threat of a popular uprising might hasten a peaceful collapse of the monarchy. Drafting an aggressive message demanding that the king choose between his subjects and the nation's foreign enemies, Condorcet persuaded the Legislative Assembly to publish it. Robespierre publicly called for the dismissal of royalist generals. In an operatic gesture, Brissot and his allies in the Assembly persuaded the delegates to open its doors on July 1, and to invite ordinary Frenchmen to watch their lawmakers in action—the government was now under the surveillance of the sovereign people! The next day, the Assembly worked around the king's veto by inviting the *fédérés* from all regions of France to visit Paris in order to celebrate Bastille Day: delegates agreed to pay the troops' expenses, and to provide lodging as well.

On July 6, the king informed the Assembly that Prussian forces were advancing toward Paris.

On July 11, the French Legislative Assembly issued a proclamation that the country was in danger, and that all political organs of the republic were to remain in constant session. The Parisian National Guard was called to arms. The first *fédérés* from Marseille arrived in Paris with their famous marching song (which would become the French national anthem). Fresh volunteers rushed to join the citizen soldiers—nearly fifteen thousand Parisians enlisted within a few days. The Legislative Assembly decreed that all citizens should be supplied with weapons. Sectional assemblies meeting day and night welcomed the poorest of "passive" citizens to join their meetings and to grab a weapon, too, just in case. The city was now an armed camp, packed with soldiers and citizens brandishing muskets and pikes.

On July 25, an ultimatum had arrived from the advancing Prussian armies, the so-called Brunswick Manifesto, warning against attacks on the king and promising that any rebels would face "an exemplary and unforgettable act of vengeance."

While Brissot urged calm and adherence to constitutional norms, Robespierre had other ideas. On July 29, he delivered a major speech to the Jacobins, titled "Wrongs and Resources of the State."

Acknowledging the views of the sans-culottes in the sectional assemblies, he questioned the legitimacy of the Legislative Assembly and called for new elections, with the stipulation that no current deputies could be reelected (Brissot, who was a current deputy, promptly quit the Jacobins in protest). At the same time, Robespierre justified this scheme in terms of the inalienable sovereignty of the people: "Where then to find love of the homeland and the general will if not in the people itself? Where to find arrogance, intrigue and corruption, if not in the powerful bodies that substitute their particular will for the general will, and that are always tempted to impose their authority on those who entrusted it to them?" In this context, Robespierre unswervingly upheld "the truth of the thunderous anathema" pronounced by Rousseau against the very idea of representation. Rousseau had famously declared that "the instant a people chooses representatives," a sovereign people "is no longer free, it no longer exists"—and Robespierre concurred, though in carefully qualified terms. "It follows," Robespierre said, "that the people is oppressed whenever its mandataries act independently of it." Robespierre was here observing a scruple of revolutionary rhetoric: by referring to all delegates as "mandataries," everyone was reminded that none of them were independent representatives but rather served only at the pleasure of the people, according to a mandate that could be revoked at any time. Robespierre concluded that "the primary assemblies have the power to evaluate the conduct of their representatives, and they are able to revoke it," if any had abused the people's trust.

Throughout Paris, debate raged in the sectional assemblies. In the Section Roi-de-Sicile (soon to be renamed Droit-de-l'Homme), located in the Marais district, moderates tried to outwit Jean Varlet, a militant who favoured direct democracy and the redistribution of wealth (along with the priest Jacques Roux, he wore the epithet Enragés, the "enraged ones," as a badge of pride). The political manoeuvring in this sectional assembly gives a vivid sense of how direct democracy in practice worked in Paris in these tense days.

On the night of August 5, Varlet had introduced a motion to dethrone the king: "The country is in danger; these terrible words meant that we are betrayed." He went on to argue that the people, after deposing Louis XVI, should, among other things, convoke the sectional assemblies and take the unprecedented step of introducing universal manhood suffrage (it should be noted that the Enragés hoped to quickly give women more political power too—women played a leading part in the group's activities). Varlet's motion carried, along with a motion to convey the results of sectional deliberations to other sectional assemblies.

But moderates in the Section Roi-de-Sicile fought back. The following night, they showed up in numbers. One of them implied that the previous night's meeting had been illegitimate. Although the neighbourhood contained 2,000 active citizens, only 100 to 130 had participated in the voting, and some of those included nonresidents. This speaker also charged the radicals with trying to intimidate the constitutional monarchists, in order to keep them from attending meetings, so that radicals could jam through their own resolutions without opposition. The next day, moderates forced the section's president, a radical, to resign; he was replaced with a constitutional monarchist.

On the eve of the planned uprising on August 9, both sides arrived at the Section Roi-de-Sicile with the outcome in doubt. The section's new moderate president tried to block a vote by abruptly adjourning the evening session and going home with the official register of proceedings. Ignoring his directive, the radicals stayed in session and elected a new president. Belatedly, at 3:00 a.m., on August 10, the sectional assembly voted to send three delegates to join the insurrectionists already gathered at the Hôtel de Ville.

III

AS THE SUN rose on another unseasonably hot and humid day, Paris was teeming with people, many of them drowsy thanks to the thrum of drums and pealing bells throughout the previous night, when the Parisian sections had seized control of the Commune. In preparation for an armed approach to the king's quarters, the *fédérés* in the streets around the Tuileries joined battalions of sans-culottes from the sections. This stage of the insurrection had been planned, in part, by a forty-three-member committee of *fédérés*, led by a five-man "Secret Directory of the Insurrection."

National Guards who had previously been loyal to the monarchy began to switch sides. The king and his ministers were by now largely isolated and without any real protection, apart from the Swiss Guards who stood ready to defend the monarchy to the death.

Anticipating an assault on the Tuileries and hoping to avoid bloodshed, a sympathetic municipal official early in the day had warned the king that Paris was in arms. He convinced the royal family to seek refuge in the Legislative Assembly, a short walk from the Tuileries, where a handful of representatives were still in session in the Salle de Manège, a repurposed indoor riding academy.

After the king had departed from his palace, and even though the majority of the National Guards stationed at the Tuileries now joined the insurrection, the Swiss Guards stood their ground. Efforts at a peaceful surrender of the palace ended with pushing and shoving—and the Swiss opening fire. *Fédérés* and sans-culottes fell in numbers, and the insurgents were forced to retreat.

But the insurrection by now had force on its side. As the Swiss Guards prepared to stand down under belated orders from the king, *fédérés* and sans-culottes stormed the palace, quickly creating a mountain of corpses in the entrance. Some of the Swiss Guards leapt from windows in an effort to escape; others fled as a unit toward the Champs-Élysées. They were pursued by soldiers and sans-culottes wielding muskets and pikes, their red uniforms making them easy targets (and also making targets of *fédérés* who happened to be wearing red, so indiscriminate was the crowd's murderous rage).

As one eyewitness to the slaughter in the Tuileries later recalled, "I remained . . . until four o'clock in the afternoon, having before my eyes a view of all the horrors that were being perpetrated. Some of the men were still continuing the slaughter; others were cutting off the heads of those already slain; while the women, lost to all sense of shame, were committing the most indecent mutilations on the dead bodies from which they tore pieces of flesh and carried them off in triumph . . . Toward evening I took the road to Versailles . . . [and] crossed the Pont Louis Seize, which was covered with the naked carcasses of men already in a state of putrefaction from the intense heat of the weather."

The most radically democratic phase of the French Revolution thus began with a carnival of atrocities.

III

THE HISTORIAN Simon Schama has argued that the "bloodshed was not the unfortunate by-product of revolution, it was the source of its energy." In effect, the threat of violence gave ordinary citizens an unfamiliar, and therefore intoxicating, power to challenge constituted authority. If Schama is correct—and I believe he is—then previous scholars have been wrong to imply that the ardent desire of ordinary people for public freedom can be separated, in fact, from their willingness to use force in its pursuit.

In any case, the entire episode certainly casts light on what another modern historian has aptly called "the uneasy coincidence of democracy and fanaticism present at the birth of modern politics."

At this moment of its eighteenth-century rebirth, this is what democracy looked like.

III

ON THE NIGHT of August 10, with fires smouldering in the Tuileries Palace and the stench of death still in the air, Robespierre addressed the Jacobins club. He had been leery of the planned uprising, fearing it would fail. Like Brissot, Condorcet, Marat, and most of the other well-known tribunes of the French people, he had kept himself out of harm's way during the previous twenty-four hours. But now that the revolt, against all odds, had proved successful, Robespierre, like the other popular orators and journalists, was eager to seize back the political initiative.

There was only one path forward, Robespierre proclaimed before his fellow Jacobins: the Commune had to urge the French people "to make it absolutely impossible for its mandataries to harm the cause of liberty." Robespierre suggested the dispatch of delegates to every one of the eighty-three regions of France, to explain the situation in Paris, and to garner support for dissolving the Legislative Assembly. He was, in effect, advocating a coup d'état under the cover of a democratic revolt:

> The solemn manner in which [the people of Paris] proceeded toward this great action was as sublime as were their motives and objectives . . . They organized it with a harmony that only the friends of freedom can display. It was not a pointless riot, provoked by a few trouble-makers; it was not a conspiracy shrouded in mystery; they deliberated in full view, before the nation; the day and plan of the insurrection were posted publicly. It was the people as a whole that exercised its right. It acted as a sovereign who despises tyrants too much to fear them, and who is too sure of his power and the holiness of his cause to stoop to conceal his intentions.

Other political leaders, recoiling from the slaughter they had just witnessed, were more cautious in their response. After this unexpected turn of events, Brissot, who had been an ally of the sans-culottes weeks before Robespierre had rallied to their cause, was anxious to restore some semblance of law and order as quickly as possible. So was his colleague Condorcet, arguably the most gifted legal mind of them all.

Sharply disagreeing with Robespierre, both argued that the new Commune should allow the current Legislative Assembly to survive, so long as it was willing to organize fresh national elections. The purpose of these elections would be to establish a convention tasked with creating a new, truly democratic constitution, to replace the mixed, but still monarchic, constitution of 1791.

Those few members of the Legislative Assembly still brave enough

to risk coming to work under these new circumstances agreed with understandable alacrity to the compromise proposed by Brissot. So did a
majority of the sans-culottes in the Commune and the Parisian sectional assemblies.

The stage was now set for what Condorcet and Brissot hoped would be
sober deliberations over what democracy might mean in a modern state
like France.

III

THE FRENCH CONVENTION met for the first time on September 21,
1792. The delegates convened shortly after the September Massacres,
another episode of indiscriminate slaughter, this one leaving thousands
of people pulled from Parisian prisons dead, on the unfounded suspicion that they were traitors waiting to join royalist forces (most of the
victims were in fact prostitutes and petty criminals).

The context was harrowing—and the challenges facing the Convention
were daunting. A new constitution that was genuinely democratic would
have to square a circle, somehow reconciling the demands of the sectional
assemblies for a direct expression of popular sovereignty with the
needs of governing a large nation that consisted of citizens holding
diverse—and even divergent—views about what a good society should
look like.

France in 1792 was overwhelmingly a rural society of peasants,
and many were more or less happily embedded in customary communities regulated by traditional habits and religious beliefs. Even in Paris,
the second-largest city in Europe (after London), the activists in the
sections comprised a self-selected minority of the city's population: although many Frenchmen participated in one of the country's new political clubs at least once in this period, modern historians estimate
that on average only a tiny fraction of eligible citizens (15 percent at most,
5 percent more often) participated regularly in the Parisian sectional
assemblies, and that "even major political issues could only rarely stir
more than a hundred or so citizens out of their political apathy in any
section."

And these were not the only challenges. The very idea of creating a durable framework of laws had just been called into question by the Parisian sans-culottes themselves. Having already nullified one republican constitution through an armed insurrection that they believed was a legitimate expression of direct popular sovereignty, how could the sans-culottes settle for anything less than the right to revolt at will?

And yet how could the rest of France endorse such an outlandish demand from a comparatively small group of armed democrats, when sovereignty properly belonged to the people of France as a whole, according to the very political logic the sans-culottes themselves ostensibly embraced?

On October 11, 1792, the Convention formed a committee to draft a new democratic constitution for France. Among the members were Brissot; the Abbé Sieyès, who had played a leading role in drafting the prior constitution; Danton; and Bertrand Barère, an ally of Robespierre.

But the undisputed intellectual leader of the group was Condorcet, who had already outlined political mechanisms (in his 1785 "Essay on the Application of Mathematics to the Theory of Decision Making") that would rationalize the drafting of laws for the public good, as Rousseau had tried to do in the *Social Contract*.

Marie-Jean-Antoine-Nicolas de Caritat, *ci-devant* Marquis de Condorcet, was unique among the revolutionary leaders. He was a permanent secretary of the French Academy of Sciences, a fellow of Britain's Royal Society, and a member of the French Academy—all in addition to his activities as a lawmaker during the revolution. A mathematical prodigy, he was also a speculative philosopher equally comfortable with Cartesian metaphysics and the theory that all knowledge is derived from sense experience. A methodological individualist in the tradition of Adam Smith and his mentor, the French economist Turgot, he was a proponent of "social mathematics" as a source of enlightened public policy, a pioneer in the analysis of collective decision-making processes, "the godfather of modern probability theory"—and also an early advocate of equal rights for women and the abolition of slavery. He held optimistic views about the potential capacities of ordinary human beings, but his faith in human perfectibility was tempered by what the Victorian British writer and statesman John Morley described as his "preeminent distinction," a "religious scrupulosity, which made him abhor all interference with the freedom and openness of the understanding as the worst kind of sacrilege."

He had been born in 1743 to a cavalry officer and a devout mother who turned him over to the Jesuits to be educated from the age of eight. In a biographical essay read to the Academy of Sciences in 1841, his eulogist summed up two surprising results of this "extraordinary" confluence of circumstances: "In politics a total rejection of any idea of hereditary prerogative; in matters of religion, scepticism pushed to its extreme limits." Impassioned by abstract ideas, he was outwardly reserved—a "volcano covered with snow," his friend D'Alembert quipped.

Temperamentally averse though he was to anarchy and bloodshed, Condorcet was quick to defend the results of the sans-culottes insurrection: "Men who, like the French, love true liberty, who know that it cannot exist without an entire equality, and who acknowledge the sovereignty of the people," he wrote shortly afterward, "ought to approve the revolution of the 10th of August," an event in which "a considerable portion of the people, combining by spontaneous impulse and addressing themselves to a legal assembly of the whole," took care to ensure that "the natural and primitive rights of man" would be "scrupulously respected."

III

THERE WAS WIDESPREAD AGREEMENT in the Convention about what a modern democratic constitution should look like. The delegates' first act had been to abolish the monarchy. Everyone agreed that a modern democratic state must be unicameral, that is, built around a single national legislature, with no division of powers. Everyone conceded that there would need to be some mechanism to lodge the power of the sovereign in the delegates, and almost everyone agreed that these delegates should not be American-style "representatives" (entrusted with full power for a fixed period by a vote), but mandataries, enjoying a contingent mandate that could be revoked at any time by the sovereign people. Everyone agreed that citizenship must be unrestricted by any kind of property qualification. They agreed that the executive and judiciary should be strictly subordinate to the legislature. They also agreed that the new constitution should uphold human rights, equality, and the sovereignty of the people. And almost everyone assumed that the constitution would need also to embody in some way the principles of Jean-Jacques Rousseau, by establishing a real institutional framework for expressing the nation's general will.

There were nevertheless some important disagreements among the members of Condorcet's committee. There was no consensus about whether or not to temper the extraordinary power currently wielded by the Parisian sectional assemblies. Some Jacobins favoured the status quo, while Condorcet and his allies advocated constitutional reforms that would create a more equitable distribution of political power throughout the nation. A majority disagreed with Condorcet about offering women full citizenship; nor did the majority share his view that the death penalty should be abolished.

Condorcet's approach to Rousseau was idiosyncratic. Where Rousseau spoke of the general will, Condorcet in 1785 had preferred to use "the common reason" as his key criterion for establishing what was politically right. Unlike Condorcet, Rousseau was notoriously suspicious of the power of subtle reasoning to obfuscate and rationalize unjust institutions. But Rousseau also appreciated the relevance of "common reason" in the context of elaborating his own principles of political right in the *Social Contract*. In an obscure but important passage in that work, Rousseau had, like Condorcet, suggested that his own criterion of political right might admit of a mathematical formulation: "Take away from these . . . wills the pluses and minuses that cancel each other out, and the remaining sum of the differences is the general will."

Condorcet had gone much farther in his "Essay on the Application of Mathematics to the Theory of Decision Making," offering an argument for the wisdom of the multitude, known today as the "Condorcet Jury Theorem." Condorcet took for granted Rousseau's premise, the goodwill of the common people; the problem was showing why a majority of them would be wise in the aggregate. According to Condorcet's mathematical argument, a group of ordinary people voting on a yes-or-no question are liable more often than a single person, however well educated, to arrive at a "true" decision, as long as three conditions are met: (1) individual voters are generally better than random at choosing true propositions (a condition that obviously suggests the importance of public access to reliable information and improving the capacity of ordinary citizens to reason clearly); (2) everyone votes independently of others; and (3) everyone votes sincerely and not strategically. One counterintuitive implication of this mathematical argument was that the larger the group voting, the more likely it was to arrive at a judicious outcome.

Rousseau himself had oscillated wildly between efforts to bring some measure of reason to bear in public life and his deep suspicion of smooth talkers able to produce apparent reasons for almost anything. Far more emphatically than Condorcet, Rousseau also respected the role that sentiments and the passions played in public life. Rousseau's ambivalence about reason would eventually reappear—with a vengeance—in the Convention's debates over Condorcet's draft constitution, which represented a remarkable attempt to institutionalize what one modern writer has called "the wisdom of crowds."

III

ON JANUARY 21, 1793, thousands of Frenchmen flocked to the largest square in Paris, once the Place de Louis XV, but renamed the Place de la Révolution (and eventually, in a gesture of reconciliation, renamed Place de la Concorde). The crowd had gathered on that wintry day to watch their former king face death. Louis stoically mounted the scaffold, and, after protesting his innocence, was strapped onto a board and pushed under the guillotine that had been installed at the centre of the square. After the blade fell, the executioner pulled the king's severed head from a basket and held it aloft, blood dripping, for all to admire. As one eyewitness recalled, tens of thousands of spectators roared their approval and tossed their hats in the air: "I saw people pass by, arm in arm, laughing, chatting familiarly as if they were at a fête."

A few weeks later, on February 15, Condorcet had a draft to share on behalf of the constitutional committee with his colleagues in the Convention, which was meeting at the Salle de Manège. The former riding academy was a space ten times as long as it was wide, with a high, vaulted ceiling. Banquettes in six tiers ran the length of the hall, ranged on both sides of the central podium, with the delegates arranged, depending on their political views, to either the left or the right of the podium (this is the origin of the distinction between left and right in modern politics). An upper deck with more seats offered space for the public to view the proceedings, and the rafters were often packed with sans-culottes who jeered and cheered, not unlike the ordinary Greek citizens who had regularly gathered at the Pnyx in ancient Athens.

Condorcet began by laying out the challenge the Convention was facing:

> To form a constitution for a territory of twenty-seven thousand
> square leagues, containing twenty-five millions of inhabitants,
> which constitution, wholly founded on the principles of reason
> and justice, shall secure each citizen in the enjoyment of his
> rights; and to combine the various parts of this constitution,
> so that the necessary obedience to the laws, and the
> submission of the will of individuals to the general will, shall
> be the result; and so that the extent and sovereignty of the
> people, with equality between man and man, and the exercise
> of natural freedom, shall be left in their full force; to
> accomplish all this is the task we are required to perform.

Because Condorcet was hoarse that day, he had to ask Barère to deliver most of his prepared speech to the Convention. In order to ensure that citizens were constantly reminded of their own sovereign power, the committee proposed instituting a nested set of assemblies, starting at a local level, proceeding to a regional level, and issuing in a National Assembly. But it also stressed the importance of "private societies," like the Jacobins, where men, having had time to read and reflect on current affairs, could refine their political views through face-to-face interaction. And it similarly stressed the freedom of the press: "No man should be deprived of any means of information, and each should be free to use such means at pleasure." (Elsewhere Condorcet had also made it plain that the provision of universal instruction in schools was, in his view, another necessary precondition of any viable modern democracy.)

Trying to strike a balance between robust popular participation and the production of rational laws, Condorcet's prepared text stated that "it would be equally dangerous for the people either to refuse to delegate their power, or in any manner to abandon that power."

On the one hand, "primary assemblies," convened locally, would be granted the power to discuss whatever they liked. Any citizen would have a right "to propose, that his primary assembly should demand any law, whatever, to be submitted anew to examination" by his community. If enough primary assemblies concurred, then the issue—even if it involved rewriting the constitution itself—must be discussed by regional assemblies. If enough regional assemblies concurred, then the issue must be addressed by the National Assembly. "Should the majority" of primary and regional assemblies "require a convention, the National Assembly will be obliged to call one. Its refusal to convoke the primary assemblies is, therefore, the only case in which the right of insurrection can be justly executed."

To ensure the ongoing, democratic legitimacy of these institutions, Condorcet's draft called for a periodic national constituent assembly that could meet, in order to submit "the constitution to reform, at a determined epoch, independent of any request from the people." (In later years, Thomas Jefferson famously lamented that the Americans had neglected to include similar provisions for making ongoing improvements to their Constitution.)

On the other hand, Condorcet took pains to point out that no primary assembly in itself could possibly claim sovereign powers, for such "sovereignty can only appertain to the whole."

He also thought that insurrections should be rare, not a routine occurrence, as they were threatening to become in Paris. Constant armed uprisings jeopardized public safety. Even more alarming, the centralization of these revolts in the capital city undermined the democratic principle of equality of political access, by giving the Parisian sans-culottes much more political power than citizens in other cities and rural regions. Such disproportional influence was "contrary to that equality between the parts of the whole, which the rights of nature, justice, the common good, and the general prosperity, so powerfully require."

At one point, Barère, reading Condorcet's prepared remarks, reminded his listeners that the committee's proposals were not unprecedented: democracy "is no new institution," he remarked. "It was established and long subsisted in the republic of Athens."

Barère concluded by reiterating the committee's conviction that "a constitution expressly adopted by the citizens, and including the regular means of correcting and changing itself, is the only one by which a people, understanding their rights, jealous of preserving, after having lately recovered them, and still fearing they may be lost, can be subjected to permanent order."

III

CONDORCET'S DRAFT of a democratic constitution, and the speech justifying it, are both remarkable documents. But inside the Convention, the committee's work met with a frosty reception. The details of Condorcet's proposal were both subtle and complex. Given the low rates of participation in the Parisian sectional assemblies, it was not self-evident how many Frenchmen, if given the opportunity, would actually want to participate regularly in primary assembly meetings, in the calm and deliberative manner that Condorcet was clearly hoping to facilitate through his proposed constitution.

One of the most radical delegates, Marat, the self-proclaimed *ami du peuple* (people's friend) and a man of bloodthirsty instincts—he had defended the September Massacres in print—immediately grasped that the constitution's new, nationwide network of primary assemblies had been explicitly designed to diminish the concentrated power of the Parisian sectional assemblies. "Everything the sectional assemblies do so well voluntarily," Marat complained, the new constitution would turn into an onerous duty in the primary assemblies. He went on to deplore the draft's "monstrous vices" and to denounce Condorcet and his friends as a "criminal faction." (By this point, measured deliberation was not a salient feature of the Convention's meetings.)

The delegates prevaricated, by ordering that Condorcet's plan be published and distributed throughout France; by dissolving the committee that had drafted it, on the grounds its work was done; and then by delaying debate for two months, so that alternative proposals could be prepared and distributed before debate over the draft constitution resumed.

The political situation in these months was grave, with deteriorating economic conditions, ongoing popular unrest in Paris, and resistance to revolutionary taxation provoking a bloody uprising in the rural region of the Vendée, even as French troops suffered a series of reversals abroad, fighting in Holland and Belgium.

The Convention had become the scene of a pitched power struggle between rival factions, and the constitution itself was a bone of contention. Radicals like Robespierre, Saint-Just, and Marat vehemently questioned the democratic good faith of Condorcet and his allies. (As one modern historian has quipped, "The power of ideas can inflame ideas of power.")

Inside the cavernous Salle de Manège, some participants in these debates began to articulate an authoritarian conception of the emergency means necessary to attain an ultimate goal everyone nominally agreed on, a regime in which the "sovereignty of the people, with equality between man and man, and the exercise of natural freedom, shall be left in their full force."

Meanwhile, the Parisian sans-culottes were by now regularly taking democracy into the streets—and into the halls of the National Convention, where militants monitored their mandataries and submitted petitions demanding cheaper bread, equalization of income, and the arrest and swift punishment of aristocrats suspected of hoarding grain.

By April 17, when the Convention resumed debate over the constitution, Condorcet found himself isolated politically. His pleas for the Convention to ratify the February draft constitution were met with invective and ad hominem attacks on him as an aristocrat. A week later, Saint-Just, the most dashing of the deputies elected to the Convention, homed in on Condorcet's treatment of the general will, which he found to be too "intellectual." Rousseau, he reminded his audience, had "written from the heart," whereas Condorcet was a cunning casuist, angling to keep himself and his cronies in power.

The debate over the constitution continued, but was constantly interrupted, as delegates were forced to deal with an increasingly brutal civil war in the Vendée and daily petitions from the Parisian sections, never mind the jockeying for power inside the Salle de Manège.

On May 10, Robespierre addressed the Convention. The challenge faced by every great legislator, he declared, is "to give to government the force necessary to have citizens always respect the rights of citizens and to do it in such a manner that government is never able to violate these rights itself." Rarely had this challenge been met; as Rousseau had shown, history was generally a saga of "government devouring sovereignty," and of the rich exploiting the poor. "The interest of the office holder" is always a "private interest," whereas "the interest of the people is the public good." In order to ensure that "the interest of the people" will prevail, Robespierre urged the Convention to pay a per diem to ordinary citizens to enable them to participate in political meetings (just as Athens had done in the fourth century B.C.). He urged the Convention to "render to individual freedom all that does not belong naturally to public authority, and you will have left that much less of a prize for ambition and imperiousness. Above all, respect the freedom of the sovereign in primary assemblies."

Such safeguards—many of them already included by Condorcet in his draft constitution—still did not strike Robespierre as sufficient. Elected officials must be constantly in the public eye, and for this purpose France needed some additional means for participation in politics, over and above the institutions outlined by Condorcet. And while it was obviously impossible for the people of France to assemble as a whole, as the people of Athens had assembled, Robespierre proposed, as an approximation to the ideal, that the republic build "a vast and majestic edifice, open to twelve thousand spectators," who in this way would monitor meetings of the National Assembly. "Under the eyes of so great a number of witnesses, neither corruption, intrigue nor perfidy dare show itself; the general will alone shall be consulted, the voice of reason and the public interest shall alone be heard."

Hoping to find a democratic way forward, Condorcet replied three days later. Acknowledging the criticisms of his draft, he suggested that the Convention set itself a deadline, promising to convene primary assemblies in six months, on November 1. By then, the people would either have a completed constitution to consider ratifying, or they would be free to elect a new group of delegates, to convene a new National Convention that could try its collective hand at tackling the challenge of formulating a properly democratic constitution.

His colleagues ignored this idea—and it was the last time Condorcet publicly addressed the French people.

III

ON MAY 31, 1793, the sans-culottes again seized control of Paris, just as they had on August 10 the prior year, but this time in concert with radicals in the Convention led by Robespierre. On June 3, the Convention, besieged by armed citizens, capitulated to a list of popular demands, including the arrest of Condorcet and twenty-eight other delegates accused of political misconduct.

The purge completed, the new leaders of the Convention produced a new draft constitution in a week, obtained the virtually unanimous approval of the delegates, and sent it on to the primary assemblies of the French people for their approbation. This text was a simplified version of Condorcet's original draft, with a few revolutionary revisions—most notably, a new passage proclaiming insurrection to be "the most sacred of rights, and the most indispensable of duties."

Although the Jacobin constitution was quickly ratified in a popular referendum by 1,784,377 votes out of approximately 1,800,000 votes cast by eligible citizens (that is, all adult Frenchmen regardless of wealth or property), it was never implemented. Instead, it was set aside indefinitely on October 10, 1793, when a "Revolutionary Government," endowed with extraordinary powers to repress "counterrevolutionaries," was declared—a declaration that marks the formal beginning of the Jacobin Reign of Terror.

The outcome was ironic. What had begun as an earnest effort to institute the most democratic form of government feasible in a large modern state instead produced three unforeseen results.

The first was the de facto transformation of France in the autumn of 1793 into a one-party state, controlled by a small clique of Jacobins. Led by Robespierre, this clique in effect had asserted the need to create a kind of dictatorship, in the original Roman sense, of investing a person or a group with supreme authority during a crisis, the regular rule of law being suspended until the crisis had passed.

A second consequence would be the result, in part, of experiencing the Jacobin dictatorship. In the years that followed, there emerged a group of French politicians and theorists who wished to set explicit limits to expressions of popular sovereignty, in order to protect individual liberties. The emergence of this new and more sceptical approach to the potential value of a modern democracy may be called properly "liberal" in its concern with protecting not just civil liberties but also freedom of conscience—and it coincided with a rejection of some of Rousseau's core concepts. Years later, Benjamin Constant pointed out how Rousseau's conception of popular sovereignty inadvertently facilitated tyrannical results:

> The people, Rousseau says, are sovereign in one respect and subject in another. But in practice, these two relations are always confused. It is easy for the authority to oppress the people as subject, in order to force it to express, as sovereign, the will that the authority prescribes for it . . . When sovereignty is unlimited, there is no means of sheltering individuals from governments. It is in vain that you pretend to submit governments to the general will. It is always they who dictate the content of this will, and all your precautions become illusory.

But the final, and perhaps most ironic, outcome of the French Revolution was the triumph of a new conception of "representative democracy." To the most prominent political theorists of the eighteenth century, including Montesquieu, the phrase would have seemed an oxymoron. Like the ancient Greeks, Montesquieu regarded the election of representatives to be an aristocratic, not a democratic practice, as democracy entailed a direct access to political offices, preferably through random selection.

Yet now a critical mass of politicians, activists, jurists, and authors began to view the election of representatives to be preferable to, and a necessary check on, the unruly excesses of a purely direct democracy. In the context of the American Revolution, the phrase had appeared as early as 1777—though only in private correspondence. Condorcet himself had tried to balance the powers of primary assemblies with the need to delegate power, via elected regional assemblies, to a national assembly of mandataries who could legitimately represent the general will of the entire French nation.

And Thomas Paine, one of Condorcet's allies in the Convention—after the *journée* of August 10, he had been made an honorary citizen of France and subsequently elected as a delegate—had been even more explicit about the benefits of a representative democracy in *The Rights of Man*. Originally published in English in two parts, the first in 1791, the second in February 1792, this paean to revolutionary values was quickly translated into French and a number of other European languages. And in part two, Paine welcomed the French Revolution's political outcome as a triumph—not for simple democracy but for "the representative system."

"Simple Democracy was society governing itself without the aid of secondary means," Paine explained. "By ingrafting representation upon Democracy, we arrive at a system of Government capable of embracing and confederating all the various interests and every extent of territory and population; and that is also as much superior to hereditary Government, as the Republic of Letters is to hereditary literature."

Two years later—in the improbable context of a "Report on the Principles of Public Morality" that commends terror as "the mainspring of popular government" in the midst of a revolution—Robespierre himself came to a similar conclusion even more emphatically: "A democracy is not a state where the people, continually assembled, regulate by themselves all public affairs, and still less one where one hundred thousand portions of the people, by measures that are isolated, hasty and contradictory, would decide the fate of the whole society." Properly understood, Robespierre avers, "democracy is a state where the sovereign people, guided by laws that are their work, do by themselves everything they can do well, and by means of delegates everything that they cannot do themselves." Modern democracy may perish, not just from "the aristocracy of those who govern" but also from "contempt on the part of the people for the authorities that they themselves have established."

This is a complete about-face from the ultra-democratic views Robespierre had championed in his speech on the draft democratic constitution in 1793. And even though the passage occurs in a speech justifying his government's recourse to frightful violence, these comments, so similar to those of Tom Paine, suggest an emerging consensus among professed democrats in favour of this previously unknown hybrid regime, an indirect or representative democracy.

III

ROBESPIERRE'S SPEECH was a warning to the sans-culottes. The indigenous sovereignty of the people, he now argued, had to be replaced, first by a transitional dictatorship to defend the new republic, and then by a representative democracy in which the people, through elections, would hand over power to a government of the "just and wise."

When Robespierre was arrested a few months later, on July 27, 1794, the tocsin was sounded, but few sans-culottes rallied to his side. By slowly but surely alienating a growing number of ordinary Parisians, he had destroyed the original basis of his power. His execution the following day marked the end of the Terror in France and also the effective end, in that epoch, of any serious effort to institute a truly self-governing democracy in France.

III

CONDORCET'S FATE was even more harrowing. Facing arrest after the insurrection of May 31, 1793, he had gone into hiding. In these months, the architect of the world's first modern democratic constitution had every reason to despair: he knew perfectly well that his fondest hopes for an enlightened regime of political freedom had been hijacked by Robespierre and a few other fanatics of virtue. But even in his clandestine chambers, he was able to give voice to his wildest hopes, by writing his "Sketch for a historical picture of the progress of the human mind"—a defiant declaration of secular faith that would become his last will and testament.

Condorcet was finally cornered ten months later in Clamart-le-Vignoble—an innkeeper's suspicions were aroused by his hungry guest's order for a twelve-egg omelette. Arrested by the police and transferred to a prison, Condorcet died twenty-four hours later—whether by suicide or murder will never be known.

Condorcet was just one of countless political victims in these years. Hundreds had perished in the uprising of August 10, 1792, and more than a thousand during the September Massacres a month later. In the months that followed, some seventeen thousand people were executed after a trial, the king and queen the most prominent among them. Perhaps another twenty thousand suspects—including Brissot, Danton, and Condorcet, among other political leaders—were left dead with less formality during the Jacobin Reign of Terror.

But it was the pious Catholic peasants of the Vendée who suffered most. In the autumn of 1793, after the Jacobin coup, the new republic's conscripts, on orders from Paris, embarked on a murderous rampage, indiscriminately targeting civilians as part of a campaign to avenge the bloody royalist uprising in that remote west-central French province. Before this pioneering venture in "total war" was over, almost 250,000 people, many of them innocent men, women, and children, had perished in a premeditated slaughter.

The French Revolution had produced a new understanding of democracy—and a hecatomb on a grand scale.

THREE

A COMMERCIAL
REPUBLIC OF FREE
INDIVIDUALS

E VEN THOUGH MOST PEOPLE today associate democracy with America—and even though an eminent American historian has plausibly claimed that democracy is "America's most distinguishing characteristic and its most significant contribution to world history"— it remains a fact that most of the leaders of the American Revolution, including George Washington, John Adams, and James Madison, didn't think of themselves as democrats, either in theory or in practice. Those among them who knew about ancient democracy doubted its relevance to the American experience: Republican Rome was their model, not Periclean Athens. Distrusting the capacity of ordinary citizens to be self-governing, most of them favoured instead creating a hybrid regime, without a king or a hereditary ruling class but with only limited input from commoners, who were expected to pick among their betters in periodic votes to elect a "natural aristocracy" (as John Adams called it), a meritorious elite, comprising men of virtue and talent, who would govern on behalf of all, with a dispassionate regard for the common good.

Benjamin Rush, a signatory of the Declaration of Independence, summed up the founding generation's conventional wisdom in typically crisp language: "All power is derived *from* the people," he averred—but political power is not seated *in* the people: "They possess it only on the days of their elections. After this, it is the property of their rulers, nor can they exercise or resume it, unless it is abused."

Such convictions differed sharply from the democratic ideas championed by radicals at the height of the French Revolution. But once enshrined in the Constitution ratified in 1788, this characteristically guarded American approach to popular sovereignty made elections a crucial feature of the new regime—and struggles over the right to vote a focus of subsequent efforts to ensure that *all* Americans, regardless of race, gender, or wealth, felt they had standing in a republic of equals.

At the same time, the new republic had from the start to reckon with the "moral and political depravity" of race-based slavery. "I tremble for my country when I realize that God is just," Thomas Jefferson wrote in 1781; slavery was a system, he acknowledged, that inexorably turned slaveholders like himself into "despots" and his bondsmen into his bitter enemies.

Jefferson in 1776 had articulated the new nation's most daring political demand—for the right to collective self-determination, on the premise that all men are created equal. But efforts to realize this demand would be "played out in counterpoint to chattel slavery, the most extreme form of servitude," as the American scholar Judith Shklar sharply remarked. "The equality of political rights, which is the first mark of American citizenship, was proclaimed in the accepted presence of its absolute denial. Its second mark, the overt rejection of hereditary privileges, was no easier to achieve in practice, and for the same reason. Slavery was an inherited condition"—and its consequences haunt America still.

The discrepancy between the nation's professed ideals and the reality of chattel slavery, combined with a sharp focus on voting as the most important means of political engagement, wasn't the only distinctive feature of the new republic. Also important was the concurrent rise in America of the conviction that free labour and free trade were crucial guarantors of civic freedom. Appreciating what Adam Smith had called "the human propensity to truck, barter, and exchange one thing for another," some American advocates of free institutions looked primarily to "society," rather than government, in hopes of creating a commonwealth of self-reliant individuals—a vision eloquently expressed by Thomas Paine in *Common Sense*, a pamphlet that crystallized American popular opinion in the winter of 1776 and paved the way for the nation's formal Declaration of Independence later that year.

III

TOM PAINE CAME from a humble British background. Before immigrating to America in 1774, he had worked as a corset maker, a sailor, a shopkeeper, and an excise officer. Settling in Philadelphia, Paine became the editor of *The Pennsylvania Magazine: or, American Monthly Museum*. The new periodical contained a blend of news, feature pieces, poems, philosophical essays in English, foreign works in translation, and lists of vital statistics. The first issue included a profile of Voltaire, a piece on the beavers of North America, and an essay on suicide, among other articles; the vital statistics included current prices in Philadelphia for butter and spirits, and beef and pork. Thirty-eight years old at the time, Paine contributed anonymous poems, pieces on natural science, and signed political commentary, the latter giving him a crash course in the debates of the day.

Since the Battles of Lexington and Concord in April 1775, North America's British colonies had been at war with Great Britain, though there was no consensus yet on the war's aims. Some wanted to renegotiate onerous new taxes and restrictions on trade; others hoped to relax or lift London's administrative control of the colonial state governments; still others argued for a formal declaration of independence. A "Continental Congress," composed of delegates from the thirteen British colonies in North America, had been meeting in Philadelphia since May 1775. In July, George Washington had assumed command of the Continental Army. Ever since independence had become a real possibility, the American press had been filled with speculation about the political future. By the end of the year, there were thirty-eight newspapers in the mainland colonies, and interested readers could also consult political posters and pamphlets that started to circulate hand to hand.

Priced at two shillings and published anonymously "by an Englishman" in January 1776, the forty-seven-page *Common Sense* instantly stood out amid this roiling wave of commentary. Paine's style was simple and his tone impassioned. An argument in favour of independence, the pamphlet was also an attack on traditional republican views of good government. Rejecting the British model, Paine advocated instead a simple government, consisting of a unicameral legislature elected by a broad franchise of citizens; he also advocated frequent elections to ensure that the people controlled the government and not the other way around. This was a far cry from the complex kinds of constitution with limited franchises favoured by most patriotic writers at the time. In Massachusetts, John Adams hastened to refute Paine with a learned essay, *Thoughts on Government*, which defended the value of a mixed constitution for most states. But by then, Paine's broadside had sold more than a hundred thousand copies in the colonies and was on its way to becoming an international bestseller (it was one of the first such political texts to be so widely distributed).

Common Sense wasn't the only important piece of political prose to appear in America in 1776. Six months after the appearance of Paine's pamphlet, the Continental Congress on July 4 formally issued a Declaration of Independence and sent the text to the printers. The declaration was largely the handiwork of one of the congressional delegates, thirty-two-year-old Thomas Jefferson. The owner of a tobacco plantation and the master of a large number of slaves, Jefferson was a polymath: an amateur architect, a widely read man of letters, and an aspiring statesman who had already become well-known for his outspoken views about independence from Great Britain. He embodied a terrible paradox: as the historian Edmund Morgan put it, "Virginians may have had a special appreciation of the freedom dear to republicans, because they saw every day what life was like without it."

Where Paine had praised a simple form of government directly accountable to its citizens, the Declaration, a much briefer work, invoked a small number of transcendent ideas: "We hold these truths to be self-evident, that all men are created equal, that they are endowed by their Creator with certain unalienable Rights, that among these are Life, Liberty, and the pursuit of Happiness.—That to secure these rights, Governments are instituted among Men, deriving their just powers from the consent of the governed."

As one modern reader has argued, Jefferson's text exemplifies, in its terseness and directness of address, a new "art of democratic writing." A revolutionary aide-mémoire, its key lines were as memorable by design as anything in Paine's *Common Sense*. Even more important, its ideals offered a profound moral challenge, one that Americans, including Jefferson himself, have struggled to meet. As Abraham Lincoln remarked on the eve of America's Civil War almost a century later, Jefferson and the other signatories of the Declaration "meant to set up a standard maxim for free society, which should be familiar to all, and revered by all; constantly looked to, constantly labored for, and even though never perfectly attained, constantly approximated, and thereby constantly spreading and deepening its influence, and augmenting the happiness and value of life to all people of all colors everywhere."

It is worth stressing how different the content of such American rhetoric was from that prevalent in ancient Athens. Both the Declaration and *Common Sense* (and Abraham Lincoln's oratory) assume that government is subordinate to "the consent of the governed." The idea of "consent"—understood as voluntarily acceding to what another person or institution proposes or desires, as opposed to compulsory submission—didn't exist in the classical world. Both Paine and Jefferson also assume that governments grow out of associations of consenting individuals who stand apart from and exist prior to the appearance of a state—a characteristically modern view of politics (though similar views were not completely unknown in antiquity).

Interestingly enough, the word "democracy" is nowhere to be found in the Declaration. Nor does it appear in *Common Sense*.

Despite the political edge to his pamphlet, Paine focused most of his energy on praising what later writers would call not simply "society," but "civil society"—a term that denotes not just voluntary associations and nongovernment organizations but also the kind of structured social world created by the spontaneous interactions and market transactions between individuals, each one following his or her own interests in an effort to achieve a modicum of happiness. (In English, the word "individual" to refer to a single person doesn't appear until the start of the seventeenth century, and the notion of "individualism" doesn't appear until the 1830s, most notably in volume two of Tocqueville's *Democracy in America*, first published in 1840.)

"Our plan is commerce," Paine declared in *Common Sense*. America should become "a *free port*. Her trade will always be a protection." Under just laws, the spread of markets, he argued, helped ordinary people to become more rational and autonomous agents—and in this way helped to produce a generally more prosperous and dynamic society. The exchange of goods is civilizing, Paine argued in *Rights of Man*: "It is a pacific system, operating to cordialize mankind, by rendering nations, as well as individuals, useful to each other." Trade should be expanded freely, for "if commerce were permitted to act to the universal extent it is capable, it would extirpate the system of war, and produce a revolution in the uncivilized state of governments."

Paine regarded production, exchange, and consumption as naturally harmonious: "Society is in every state a blessing, but government, even in its best state, is but a necessary evil." Commerce could produce an independent network of associations that would check the corrupting power of the state: "Society is produced by our wants, and government by our wickedness," he wrote in *Common Sense*. "The former promotes our happiness *positively* by uniting our affections, the latter *negatively* by restraining our vices. The one encourages intercourse, the other creates distinctions."

This was recognizably the same kind of potentially beneficent social order that the Scottish philosopher Adam Smith had described, also in 1776, in *The Wealth of Nations*. And it was this new world of enlightened self-government and commercial progress that Paine and Jefferson jointly championed as part of the revolutionary claims they both made on behalf of "common sense" (just as Condorcet had stressed the power of "common reason").

Still, reading *Common Sense* in conjunction with the Declaration, it's hard to miss a tension between the two texts. Commerce may unleash the productive powers of the labouring individuals it connects through free trade—but it also risks creating disparities that might undermine the "self-evident" truth of the assertion that "all men are created equal." Paine in time acknowledged the tension himself, advocating various public policies to lessen inequality, including an estate tax to fund a onetime cash grant to every person over the age of twenty-one, and an annual pension to everyone over the age of fifty.

III

DESPITE A COMMON MISCONCEPTION, the American Revolution was not a bloodless affair. Sixty thousand British loyalists were driven into exile, and the war caused proportionately more deaths than any other American conflict apart from the more famous Civil War of 1861–1865.

Still, as John Adams once remarked to Thomas Jefferson, the real revolution "was in the minds of the people," and it is possible to track some of its most consequential results in the pamphlets, newspapers, and official records of the new republics, which registered the progress of public opinion. During the course of this quiet conceptual revolution, positive references to democracy in America slowly but surely grew more frequent.

For example, in 1777, Alexander Hamilton had privately praised the new constitution of New York as a prudent and "representative democracy, where the right of election is well secured and regulated & the exercise of the legislative, executive and judiciary authorities, is vested in select persons, chosen *really* and not *nominally* by the people." These were remarkable words—Hamilton was typically sceptical of popular participation in politics, later writing that "the rich and the well-born" deserve "a distinct permanent share in the government."

Other isolated honorific usages of democracy had appeared even earlier in British North America. For example, in 1641, a meeting of Rhode Island's General Court of Election ordered that "the Government which this Bodie Politick doth attend unto in this Island, and the Jurisdiction thereof, in favour of our Prince is a DEMOCRACIE, or Popular Government; that is to say, It is in the Powre of the Body of Freemen orderly assembled, or the major part of them, to make or constitute Just Lawes, by which they will be regulated, and to depute from among themselves such Ministers as shall see them faithfully executed between Man and Man." In 1717, the word "democracy" appears prominently in John Wise's famous pamphlet, *A Vindication of the Government of New-England Churches*, a defence of Congregationalist Church government on the grounds that "the Primitive Constitution of the Churches was a Democracy."

By then, secular authority in New England had in part devolved from the state to the local government of villages and hamlets, where citizens sought to reach consensus in face-to-face town meetings—a radical expression of popular sovereignty, though Americans, even after the Revolution, "would still grope for terms in which to describe this new fact of the dispersal of effective authority."

In 1776, Americans proclaiming their independence from England had convened a series of extralegal conventions to draft new state constitutions—setting an example the French were to follow in their own Revolution. In the case of the Pennsylvania constitution of 1776, designed to enshrine the sovereignty of the people in practice as well as theory, Americans even created a document that, in its unicameral legislature, use of rotation, and stipulation that the people at large ratify all bills passed by the state's General Assembly, suggests nothing so much as a native American antecedent to Condorcet's proposed French constitution of 1793 (in part because Condorcet knew of, and admired, the Pennsylvania document).

Still, striking though some of these experiments in self-governing institutions were, the idea of democracy did not, for a variety of reasons, gain much traction in America before the 1790s. After America had won its freedom from Britain, there was a widespread tendency among the political class to use "republic" and "democracy" as synonyms. Many of them began to confuse republicanism per se with a highly qualified defence of a more "democratical" mixed regime, with its monarchical element eliminated, and a right to vote carefully extended to men with a minimum amount of wealth. While the question "How much democracy?" was crucial in this context, addressing it directly became peculiarly difficult, given the low regard in which democracy as a pure form was generally still held.

As a result, the Americans who drafted the constitution of 1787 broadly agreed that the power of the people, properly understood, was virtual, and that any attempt by them to claim it more directly, as in a simple democracy, could be rebuffed by citing the legitimate authority of the legislature and its duly elected representatives. Even more telling, the franchise in the Constitution was, to start, narrow by design: among the excluded were women, slaves, indigenous people, and adult white males who did not own land. Only a small percentage of Americans cast ballots in the first national elections for president.

Trying to forestall any possible confusion between democracy and republicanism, James Madison, the chief architect of the American Constitution, took pains in the *Federalist Papers*, published in 1787 and 1788, to distinguish the federal government's proposed new constitution with its intricate checks and balances, which were praiseworthy, from pure democracies, "which have ever been spectacles of turbulence and contention." Speaking in the Massachusetts convention in defence of Madison's plan for the federal government, Fisher Ames similarly warned that "a democracy is a volcano, which conceals the fiery materials of its own destruction."

Still, words like "democracy" remained slippery. Partisans tried to twist the meaning of keywords to their own ends, depending on the political context. For example, when James Wilson, who had helped Madison draft the Constitution, addressed the Pennsylvania state convention to debate the document, he disingenuously reassured his more radical compatriots that the new federal plan simply *was* a democracy:

> In giving a definition of the simple kinds of government known
> throughout the world, I had occasion to describe what I meant
> by a democracy; and I think I termed it, that government in
> which the people retain the supreme power, and exercise it
> either collectively or by representation. This Constitution
> declares this principle, in its terms and in its consequences,
> which is evident from the manner in which it is announced.
> "We, the People of the United States."

Wilson had been an outspoken critic of the Pennsylvania constitution of 1776. And despite his peroration a decade later, he hadn't changed his stripes at all; he subsequently helped draft a new state charter for Pennsylvania that, when adopted in 1790, narrowed the franchise and introduced extensive new checks on popular political participation, modelled on those in the federal Constitution.

III

THE NEW AMERICAN CONSTITUTION was ratified in 1788. But it wasn't long before an even more pointed public debate over the value of democracy in America erupted—this time in response to current events in France.

Though news travelled slowly in those days, on sailing ships and horseback, Americans soon enough learned that Parisians had stormed the

Bastille on July 14, 1789. Thomas Jefferson, at the time serving as U.S. ambassador to France, prepared an eyewitness account to send to John Jay, the secretary of foreign affairs, in Washington. In his report, Jefferson calmly described how the crowd had poured into the Bastille, freed prisoners, seized weapons, killed the fortress's governor and lieutenant governor, and then cut off their heads, mounted them on pikes, and "sent them through the city in triumph to the Palais royal."

The butchery didn't dampen Jefferson's sympathies for the revolutionary cause. "I say," he wrote to James Madison shortly afterward, "the earth belongs to each of these generations during its course, fully and in its own right. The second generation receives it clear of the debts and incumbrances of the first, the third of second, and so on. For if the first could charge it with a debt, then the earth would belong to the dead and not to the living generation."

At the peak of the American interest in France, between 1792 and 1794, American booksellers offered English editions of the various French constitutions, works by Condorcet, the speeches of Robespierre, something called "Morality of the Sans Culottes . . . ; or, The Republican Gospel"—and, of course, Tom Paine's bestselling apologia, *Rights of Man*, the first prominent text in English to praise "representative democracy" as the best feasible form of modern government.

A number of American newspapers published pieces in translation from the most radical of the Parisian papers. When Jacques-Louis David presented his portrait of Marat to the French National Convention, readers in Philadelphia heard about it. The ratification of the Jacobin Constitution in 1793 was—literally—front-page news in America. Robespierre's major speeches were translated with remarkable alacrity, and printed, in their entirety, in major urban daily papers.

On January 24, 1793, radical republicans in buttoned-down Boston saluted the French Revolution with a daylong carnival of food, drink, and festive speeches. In the morning, a throng of men wound through the city displaying a "Peace Offering to Liberty and Equality"—a roasted ox with the tricolour on one gilded horn, and the stars-and-stripes on the other. From rooftops and windows, women and children watched, waved, and roared their approval. In the afternoon, the American patriot Samuel Adams presided over a public banquet in Boston's Fanueil Hall, flanked by a statue of Lady Liberty, displaying the 1789 French Declaration of the Rights of Man and Citizen:

ARTICLE I—Men are born and remain free and equal in rights. Social distinctions can be founded only on the common good.

ARTICLE II—The goal of any political association is the conservation of the natural and imprescriptible rights of man. These rights are liberty, property, safety and resistance against oppression.

ARTICLE III—The principle of any sovereignty resides essentially in the Nation. No body, no individual, can exert authority that does not emanate expressly from it.

After washing down their barbecued "peace offering" with a hogshead of punch, the republican celebrants raised a purse for the release of local prisoners, so that all of Boston's citizens could "breathe the air of liberty."

In the midst of the republican euphoria that winter and spring appeared Edmund Charles Genet, the first envoy from the new French Republic. Arriving in Charleston on April 8, 1793, "Citizen Genet" plunged recklessly into American politics, trying to embroil America in France's European war, portraying himself with unfeigned enthusiasm as the prophet of a universal political regeneration.

So great became the political ferment in the weeks after Genet's arrival that Thomas Jefferson, now back in the United States, marvelled that "all the old spirit of 1776 is rekindling."

"What an age of WONDERS and REVOLUTIONS!!" exclaimed another eyewitness. "Subjects turned into citizens; citizens turned soldiers; peasants turned rulers; palaces turned to prisons; kings turned to dust; . . . the people turned inquisitive . . ."

Such sentiments found an organized outlet in a number of

American democratic clubs and democratic-republican societies that suddenly began to sprout up. Local in orientation, often linked with armed militias, and always friendly to France, these voluntary political associations, which Citizen Genet naturally went out of his way to encourage, were concentrated along the eastern seaboard and western frontier. Since there were more than forty widely scattered clubs in all, generalizations are risky—the societies varied considerably in size, aims, and appeal. The most important one, in Philadelphia, at one point listed 320 members: it was Genet himself who had suggested the Philadelphia group call itself a "democratic" society. Most of these clubs met monthly; members were carefully screened, and "apostasy from Republican principles" was grounds for expulsion. Composed of artisans, sailors, and small farmers on the one hand, and merchants, shop owners, and journalists on the other, the members were generally self-made men, united by zeal for the democratic spirit of the French Revolution.

Despite their enthusiasm for the French Republic, American democrats regarded themselves as upholding, above all, the ideals of 1776. Their aims were simultaneously sociable, deliberative, and educational. They hoped to create voluntary associations animated by a shared enthusiasm for true republican virtues—and also love for the *American* republic, its laws and its constitution. Like the Jacobin clubs throughout France, the American societies were determined "not only to discuss the proceedings of Government, but to examine into the conduct of its officers in every department."

But the American democrats were, literally, conservative: memories of their own glorious revolution were still fresh in their minds. Wishing to renew and revivify the revolutionary tradition in America, they pointed out that the Fourth of July, unlike Bastille Day in France, was too rarely celebrated with appropriate panache. To make plain their own patriotism, in 1794 the New York Democratic Society helped turn the Fourth of July into a proper republican fête, replete with a parade featuring militia companies, members of the General Society of Mechanics and Tradesmen, democratic club members, the state's governor—all preceded by a procession of French Jacobins, marching two by two, singing "La Marseillaise."

Like their counterparts in France, the most radical members of the American political clubs regarded "the different members of the government" as "nothing more than agents of the people." "The government," declared the New York Democratic Society, "is responsible to the sovereign people"—and the sovereign had an obligation to remain active. "Self-interest, the great moving principle of men in power, has operated to paralyze the American people," warned "An American Sans Culottes" in 1794: "The people ought to regulate the proceedings of government," so that it will have "no other rule than the general will."

"We have too long been amused and misled by names," wrote a correspondent in the *National Gazette*. "The new constitution [of 1787] has introduced such a Babel-like confusion into our language, that I fear it will be long, perhaps too long, before the people will be able to come to a right understanding." Many terms—"popular sovereignty," for one—"have changed their meaning since 1776," observed this writer. "If our rapid progress in refinements does not meet with a speedy check, the language of Common Sense will be totally discarded in our country, and the Rights of Man considered chimerical."

Under attack, radicals now defiantly embraced "democracy" as their preferred form of government. "I am, sir, a true Democrat," declared one correspondent in the pages of the *General Advertiser* in the spring of 1794. "Thanks to Gallia's sans culottes, they gave me an opportunity of appearing a patriot." "I pronounce them all Democrats where I come from," wrote "An Old Yankee" farmer that same year.

Though few Americans ever belonged to the clubs, many read about them in the republican papers, and still more heard the new talk of democracy in the taverns and coffeehouses and local assemblies where public affairs were discussed. By popularizing a political lexicon purged of "Babel-like confusion"—and restoring Tom Paine's plain talk of 1776 and 1792—the American democrat of 1794 hoped to win back a vocabulary (and a republican constitution) that he feared was being surreptitiously hijacked by "masked aristocrats."

The targets of such rhetoric didn't warm to being cast as a menace to the republic. In his annual message to Congress delivered in the autumn of 1794, President Washington criticized the democratic societies for breaching the limits to political participation that had been carefully laid out in the federal Constitution. The societies, warned Washington, were "self-created." To be "self-created" was to fall beyond the pale of the law: the implication, familiar from tracts of the 1780s, was that voluntary political associations should be banned as illegally organized factions that posed a threat not just to public order but also to the proper exercise of popular sovereignty, at periodically held elections, when *all* citizens could freely participate in choosing their representatives. Ironically, the American political elite had by now itself begun to divide into more or less clearly defined "factions"—the Federalists of Washington and John Adams versus the Democratic Republicans of Thomas Jefferson and James Madison, each faction denouncing the other as a divisive threat to the common good.

Washington delivered his speech at a time when news of the Jacobin terror in France and the Whiskey Rebellion in Pennsylvania—a revolt over federal excise taxes on liquor—had made freshly plausible old fears about democracy. Sooner or later, argued a weighty tradition, democracy, unless wisely tempered in a prudently mixed constitution, would produce—inevitably, ineluctably—mob rule. That Washington suspected radical democrats of helping to foment the Whiskey Rebellion only made this line of thought more compelling, despite the fact that most of the democratic clubs in fact had passed resolutions condemning the armed insurrection as "unconstitutional."

Though an effort to censure them narrowly failed to win congressional support, the clubs slowly faded from view, their fighting spirit sapped by their failure to defeat John Jay's controversial treaty with England in 1795, their enthusiasm for the French Revolution dampened by continuing revelations about the bloody horrors of the

Jacobin dictatorship. (Some clubs in the slaveholding states of the South fell apart when it was discovered that Edmund Genet belonged to the Société des Amis des Noirs, Society of the Friends of Blacks, a group of mainly white antislavery Frenchmen, founded in 1788 by Brissot.) In this dispute over the new republic's political lexicon, the Federalists in effect won the battle, by mobilizing their own base of partisan support—but they lost the war, in part by legitimizing the mobilization of ordinary people to settle disputes among rival elite factions.

III

IN THE PRESIDENTIAL CAMPAIGN of 1800, Thomas Jefferson brought what was now called the Democratic-Republican Party to power, and in this way also brought democracy—at least as a word—into the mainstream of American politics. As Walter Lippmann observed a century later, "The American people came to believe that their Constitution was a democratic instrument, and treated it as such. They owe that fiction to the victory of Thomas Jefferson, and a great conservative fiction it has been. It is a fair guess that if everyone had always regarded the Constitution as did the authors of it, the Constitution would have been violently overthrown, because loyalty to the Constitution and loyalty to democracy would have seemed incompatible."

Instead, support for democracy and fealty to the Constitution gradually came to be conflated. And the peaceful defeat of the Federalists in 1800 made possible the subsequent triumph of a uniquely American kind of democratic culture: rooted in a shared distrust of big government, combined with a paradoxical reverence for its written Constitution, and devoted as well to free enterprise, commerce, and self-reliant individualism as pillars of a free society. This political culture was nourished by dissenting religious traditions and communitarian local practices such as the New England town meeting—but at the same time it was sustained by coercive policies at the state level that regulated everything from marriage to the availability of alcohol, and established restrictive criteria for citizenship and suffrage. Southern states were free to take a dramatically different approach to the question of chattel slavery than that taken in the North.

Even as great urban centres rapidly formed on the East Coast, the Western territories belonging to the United States expanded even more dramatically in the first half of the nineteenth century. By European standards, and despite the aristocratic pretensions of its founders, America evolved a relatively coarse political culture, and one in which even the poorest citizens over time felt increasingly free to mock authorities and attack privileges. It was liberal in the protections it accorded to private property, broadly understood (as James Madison wrote) to embrace "every thing to which a man may attach a value and have a right," including his political opinions, his religious beliefs, and "the free use of his faculty and free choice of the objects on which to employ them."

As one anonymous poet of this new world of politics summed up the American idyll as the eighteenth century drew to a close, "In America, . . . [every man] will with pleasure view the happiness of a free people, enjoying all the sweets of a pure democratic government: he will see every man enjoying his own property unmolested, choosing his own rulers, enacting his own laws, and the uncontrolled master of his own actions."

Within a generation, something like this reverie had become a reality for a growing number of primarily white citizens of the United States. In most of the new states, civil society was strong, just as Tom Paine had hoped, while the federal government was comparatively weak. Unlike similarly large European nation-states at the same time, the federal state did not require heavy taxation to support a military establishment (that came later, in twentieth-century America); its policing powers, to start, were relatively modest as well. And because the franchise was broadened only slowly; because political power was localized state by state, town by town; because the United States was far less populous in the 1830s than it would become by the start of the twenty-first century; and because by law in many states women, slaves, indigenous peoples, and even a number of white men too poor to pay taxes, were *still* excluded from political participation—most of the remaining white men lucky enough to be full-fledged citizens would, in those days, have had *some* direct experience in public affairs.

III

FOR THE FIRST TWO GENERATIONS of the American Republic, "all the presidents had been statesmen in the European sense of the word," the British scholar James Bryce remarked in his landmark study, *The American Commonwealth*, first published in 1888; they were "men of education, of administrative experience, of a certain largeness of view and dignity of character." Washington, John Adams, Thomas Jefferson, James Madison—these were just the sort of public-spirited "natural aristocrats" the founders had hoped would become the new republic's leaders and serve as a moderating influence on popular passions. Defending the powers of the presidency in the new American Constitution, Alexander Hamilton wrote, "It will not be too strong to say, that there will be a constant probability of seeing the station filled by characters pre-eminent for ability and virtue."

But as Bryce ruefully acknowledged in a chapter titled "Why Great Men Are Not Chosen Presidents," all this changed with Andrew Jackson. To contemporary admirers, Jackson was "at the head of the Democracy of the world, fighting its battles, and stemming the tide of selfish interest combined with unprincipled ambition." To critics, he was a classic demagogue, a boorish commoner who pandered to the rabble and epitomized "the democracy of numbers."

Jackson was born in South Carolina in 1767 in a log cabin on the state's western frontier. Raised by God-fearing Scots and Irish kinsmen, he served as an adolescent soldier in the Continental Army, and barely survived imprisonment by the British in 1781. After studying law and qualifying for the bar in 1787, he moved to Tennessee, where his fortunes changed dramatically. (By then all of his immediate family members were dead, victims of the war, or cholera, or smallpox.)

He married into a prominent local clan and became a protégé of the territorial governor, serving as attorney general in 1791. After Tennessee won statehood in 1796, he became the state's first representative in the U.S. Congress, and then, briefly, an interim U.S. senator. In these years, he was an outspoken Francophile and ardent champion of the Rights of Man. But his most indomitable political passion was hatred: for monarchy, for aristocracy, for privileged elites, and, above all, for Indians.

Returning to Tennessee, he worked as a circuit-riding justice of the state's superior court and also began to angle for a post in the state militia, hoping to make his mark as a military man. At the same time, he started to build a personal fortune, eventually becoming the slaveholding master of one of the largest cotton-growing plantations in Tennessee.

Jackson is sometimes celebrated for his rural roots and unvarnished manners—but in many ways, he better embodies the upwardly mobile ethos of "the planter, the farmer, the mechanic, and the laborer" who form, in one of Jackson's more lyrical formulations, "the bone and sinew of the country." Like Tom Paine, Jackson hymned the virtues of commerce and worried that an unresponsive federal government was a major threat to the full fruits of free labour.

The War of 1812 turned Jackson, almost overnight, into a national hero. At the Battle of New Orleans, he led the American forces that turned back a far larger British army—a victory achieved, ironically, two weeks after the war had formally ended with a peace treaty signed in Ghent, Belgium.

In the following generation, as the country added new states to the West, many states abolished or lowered property qualifications that had restricted the right to vote. But the process was uneven. And in some states, old barriers remained and new barriers were erected, as public officials tried to channel the democratic currents sweeping through politics.

Jackson was now the most renowned American general since George Washington—and an archetypal self-made man. Given command of the U.S. Army in the South, Jackson and his troops defeated a wing of the Creek nation at the Battle of Horseshoe Bend in 1814.

Between 1816 and 1820, Jackson helped force treaties on the Cherokees, Choctaws, and Chickasaws; in 1817, acting on his conviction that whites and Native Americans could never coexist peacefully, Jackson arranged for the Cherokees to surrender two million acres of land in Tennessee, Georgia, and Alabama, and to move west of the Mississippi. He became a leading proponent of a national policy of Indian resettlement, America's unique contribution to the art of "ethnic cleansing." After serving several months as the military governor of the Florida Territory, Jackson retired briefly to Tennessee, before winning a seat in the federal Senate in 1822.

Two years later, in a five-way presidential contest, Jackson won a plurality (42 percent) of the popular vote but lost the presidency in a subsequent election in the House of Representatives to his rival John Quincy Adams. The defeat piqued his ambition—and helped to crystallize the positive meaning of democracy in America.

Like his father and other distinguished members of the founding generation—and unlike Andrew Jackson—John Quincy Adams held that while "democracy is the oxygen or vital air" of a government, it is "too pure in itself for human respiration." In 1828, Adams ran for re-election as a "National Republican," while Jackson ran as a "Democrat." By splitting Jefferson's Democratic-Republican Party in two, Jackson confirmed that "democracy" from now on would be an unambiguously honorific term in the American political lexicon—and also would define the aspirations of one of America's two major parties (alongside the resurrected Republican Party that Abraham Lincoln led to victory in 1860).

In those days it was considered crass for a candidate himself to hold rallies and address huge crowds of noisy supporters. But Jackson turned his quest for the White House into a true "campaign"—a military term of art for a coordinated attack on an objective, introduced into politics by a military man. Marches and coordinated media and fund-raising were all elements of Jackson's presidential campaign of 1828—and so was the marshalling of outrageous lies and various forms of character assassination, disseminated through the mass media of the day, the daily newspapers. A certain image of the candidate was conveyed in the popular press: the hero of New Orleans as an outsider able to clean up political corruption and champion the interests of the little man, not the entrenched elites. Jackson became an icon of democracy. Casting a vote for him was turned into a kind of civic sacrament, reaffirming the sovereignty of the people.

One result of this quasi-liturgical marshalling of votes was a notable increase in the number of citizens voting, more than four times the number who had voted in 1824. Despite this uptick in turnout, a golden age of perceived self-rule could, as in ancient Athens, be built on a surprisingly narrow conception of who counted as a member of the putatively sovereign people. The overall number of eligible voters in America was growing—but in a nation of nearly thirteen million people, only about one million white men cast votes in the 1828 presidential election.

Americans at the time nevertheless perceived the outcome as a great victory for democracy. And subsequent historians have tended to agree. One has called the election a "mighty democratic uprising," while another has observed that "soaring turnouts among white men reinforced the impression of the People governing." In the years that followed, democracy became "so crucial to America's nation-building process that rhetorically America and democracy became inseparable, almost interchangeable."

Despite President Jackson's cavalier disregard for the rule of law—he simply ignored the Supreme Court's 1832 decision (in *Worcester v. Georgia*) holding that the Cherokee Indians constituted a nation with sovereign rights—his reputation as a great American democrat only grew with the passage of time. By the turn of the twentieth century, in the eyes of the preeminent progressive historian Frederick Jackson Turner, he was the very epitome of an era, designated by the phrase "Jacksonian Democracy," and associated by Turner with the belief that "the self made man had a right to his success in the free competition which Western life afforded." (It didn't hurt that Alexis de Tocqueville had visited America when Jackson was president—he briefly met the great man—so that his famous *Democracy in America* at first glance supported the idea that "Jacksonian democracy" was somehow central to the American experience.)

Still, if one reads modern biographies, one is struck by the discrepancy between what Jackson, based on the evidence, seems actually to have accomplished in the way of democratizing reforms, and the disproportionately large role he assumes in American lore (at least the lore I was taught growing up about this putative hero of the common man).

Jackson did advocate term limits on officeholders and rotation in office, and he also urged Americans (without success) to abolish the Electoral College, one of the most flagrantly undemocratic elements in the Constitution. Yet in instituting what he called "rotation," putting term limits on civil servants, Jackson also made it easy to appoint his own allies and friends instead, creating what critics called a spoils system. And by transforming himself into a cynosure for the explicitly democratic hopes of ordinary citizens in his presidential campaigns, Jackson laid the basis for an imperial presidency.

The result was perverse: by mobilizing commoners against an entrenched elite (just as democratic leaders had done in Athens), and by trying to turn the quadrennial vote for the most powerful figure in the federal government into a national plebiscite (institutions and practices unknown in the polis), this personification of egalitarian aspirations came to wield executive powers that perforce risked overshadowing the political initiatives of the ordinary citizens who had chosen him as their tribune.

Frederick Jackson Turner recognized the essential paradox: "Jacksonian democracy flourished, strong in the faith of the intrinsic excellence of the common man, in his right to make his own place in the world, and in his capacity to share in government. But while Jacksonian democracy demanded these rights, it was also loyal to leadership as the very name implies. It was ready to follow to the uttermost the man in whom it placed its trust, whether the hero were frontier fighter or president."

III

ON JUNE 30, 1831, after spending a week at Sing Sing, a prison with nine hundred inmates in Ossining, New York, two young Frenchmen, Alexis de Tocqueville and Gustave de Beaumont, made their way up the Hudson River via sloop and steamboat to Albany, the state capital. The two scions of aristocratic families had persuaded the French government to send them on an official mission to study the new republic's penal system. Both had previously worked at the tribunal at Versailles, Beaumont as a deputy public prosecutor, Tocqueville as an apprentice judge. They had arrived in America on May 9, landing at Newport, Rhode Island, and immediately travelling to New York City, where they had stayed for more than a month.

A few days after arriving in Albany, Tocqueville experienced a kind of epiphany—and it happened, appropriately enough, on the Fourth of July.

Early that morning, Tocqueville and Beaumont had been wakened by an artillery explosion, the firing of guns, and the ringing of church bells, as Albany prepared to celebrate America's Independence Day. Shortly afterward, local dignitaries knocked on their hotel door, to implore the two startled guests to join them in a parade and public ceremony.

At 10:00 a.m., the local newspaper, the *Albany Argus*, reported, the procession began. It was led by a militia escort, followed by a few ageing local veterans of George Washington's army in a carriage, and then the lieutenant governor and the chancellor of New York State, with Tocqueville and Beaumont walking between them. (The officials were Democrats and supporters of President Jackson.) Behind the two Frenchmen marched the Fire Department, the Association of Printers, and the Albany Typographical Society, along with a float featuring a real printing press that was producing real copies of the Declaration of Independence, to hand out to bystanders, followed by a series of benevolent societies and industrial associations marching in formation.

The march ended with a gathering at the city's Methodist church. After a benediction by a minister, a magistrate read with deliberate gravity the entire text of the Declaration of Independence. A young lawyer then gave a short sermon on the majesty of freedom. The ceremony ended with the performance of a choral hymn to liberty, set to the tune of "La Marseillaise" and accompanied by a single flute that played a ritornello after each couplet:

Child of the skies—Jove's peerless daughter—
Birthright of men—soul of the free!
Through seas of blood, o'er fields of slaughter
Thy march has been, must ever be.
Though tyrants aye that march impeded,
And superstition spread o'er all
Thy cheerful smiles, her midnight pall,
Still from thy path thou'st ne'er receded.
(Chorus) Then onward be thy way,
Unstayed thy progress be,
Empires and thrones shall own thy sway
Triumphant Liberty!

Beaumont found the spectacle slightly ridiculous. But he was nonetheless impressed, writing in a letter home that "there is more brilliance in our ceremonies; in those of the United States there is more truth."

Tocqueville was particularly moved by the reading of the Declaration of Independence:

A profound silence reigned in the meeting. When in its
eloquent plea Congress reviewed the injustices and tyranny of
England we heard a murmur of indignation and anger
circulate about us in the auditorium. When it appealed to the
justice of its cause and expressed the generous resolution to
succumb or free America, it seemed that an electric current

made the hearts vibrate. This was not, I assure you, a theatrical performance. There was in the reading of these promises of independence so well kept, in this return of an entire people toward the memories of its birth, in this union of the present generation to that which is no longer, sharing for the moment all its generous passions, there was in all that something deeply felt and truly great.

Tocqueville concluded that democracy in America wasn't a sham; it was (as the British writer David Runciman has put it) "more like a true religion. Faith was the lynchpin of American democracy. The system worked, Tocqueville decided, because people believed in it."

In Albany, Tocqueville saw America's political piety in action. And in *Democracy in America*, he acknowledged how its civic religion, rooted in a Protestant form of "Christianity that can best be described as democratic and republican," served as a powerful brake on the potential wildness of self-reliant self-rule. "Thus, even as the law allows the American people to do anything and everything, there are some things that religion prevents them from imagining or forbids them to attempt."

III

WHEN THE FIRST VOLUME of Tocqueville's *Democracy in America* was published in 1835, it was an instant success, first in France, then in England, and finally in America as well.

According to Tocqueville, democracy denoted not merely a form of government but, in addition, and more important still, a new kind of society, in which the principle of equality was pushed to its limits. In America, Tocqueville wrote, men "can be seen to be more equal in fortune and intelligence—more equally strong, in other words—than they are in any other country, or were at any other time in recorded history." (Tocqueville had a genius for hyperbole.) "Democracy does not give the people the most skilful government," he conceded, "but what it does even the most skilful government is powerless to achieve: it spreads throughout society a restless activity, a superabundant strength, an energy that never exists without it, and which, if circumstances are even slightly favourable, can accomplish miracles."

Tocqueville is often regarded as an uncanny prophet, and he certainly wasn't bashful in his generalizations. He was certain, for example, that "the dogma of popular sovereignty" had taken firm root in America during the Revolution: "All classes enlisted in its cause. People fought and triumphed in its name. It became the law of laws." Tocqueville's evidence for this was the peaceful spread of "universal suffrage," which he equated with "the most democratic forms" of the American governments, both state and federal. "Once a people begins to tamper with the property qualification," removing that barrier to the suffrage, Tocqueville also predicted, "it is easy to foresee that sooner or later it will eliminate it entirely. Of the rules that govern societies, this is one of the most invariable."

Still, throughout the first half of the nineteenth century, the effective extent of the franchise dramatically varied from state to state. This irregularity was a by-product of American federalism. And where property restrictions remained, the response could be dramatic and even violent—as could be seen in one of the strangest episodes in antebellum America, Rhode Island's democratic uprising of 1842.

III

IN 1776, most American states had organized conventions to establish new forms of state government, and most of the resulting constitutions had been ratified in some sort of popular vote. Rhode Island, however, had retained the royal charter granted by King Charles II of England in 1663. In its day, this charter had been a model of progressive governance, with a relatively large enfranchised population, despite a modest property qualification. But by the 1830s, in the context of rapid industrialization and the Democratic Party's exaltation of the common man, pressure was mounting to extend the right to vote to the state's growing number of landless labourers, many of them poor Irish immigrants.

In 1840, with presidential campaigns for both the major political parties deploying the barnstorming techniques pioneered by Andrew Jackson, the percentage of citizens voting in a presidential election sharply rose, to over 70 percent of those eligible in a majority of the states. (Supplying free liquor at rallies helped boost the popular passion for politics in those days.)

In Rhode Island, by contrast, the turnout in 1840 had been less than 40 percent of eligible voters. In an effort to excite more interest in politics among those eligible to vote, and in hopes of instituting universal manhood suffrage as a good way to accomplish this, local democrats formed a new organization, the Rhode Island Suffrage Association.

The most prominent of its leaders was Thomas Wilson Dorr. The son of a prominent Providence family, he was an Exeter and Harvard man who had repudiated his patrician pedigree and championed instead the creation of a new republic of equals within his home state.

The Suffrage Association was decentralized in its organization, local in its orientation—but radical in its ultimate aims. Ignoring restrictions laid out in the royal charter, Dorr and his allies declared that the people of Rhode Island had every right to organize a constitutional convention of their own, in keeping with the conventions held in most other states in 1776.

On July 4, 1841, the Suffrage Association held a large rally in Providence to announce the convening of a "People's Convention" that would be open to *any* male residents over the age of twenty-one, blacks included. (In 1840, blacks comprised about 3 percent of Rhode Island's population.) The delegates would be selected at local meetings.

The idea of a People's Convention caught on. But it turned out that a great majority of the state's most zealous democrats opposed extending the franchise to black men. Opposition was especially fierce in Newport, which in the eighteenth century had been a major hub of the Atlantic slave trade. When the People's Convention met that autumn, the delegates voted by an overwhelming majority to limit the franchise to white men.

It is telling that the new People's Constitution cast doubt on Thomas Jefferson's famous assertion that "all men are created equal." The events in Rhode Island gave a preview of the increasingly bitter American debate over slavery and race—a debate that would be provisionally resolved only by the Civil War, and the leadership of Abraham Lincoln, who almost single-handedly turned the opening lines of the Declaration of Independence into an inviolable set of core principles that guaranteed civil rights to *all* Americans, regardless of race. Lincoln's own laconic, and completely unconventional, definition of democracy—a term he normally avoided because of its association with a political party he opposed—is noteworthy: "As I would not be a slave, so I would not be a master. This expresses my idea of democracy. Whatever differs from this, to the extent of the difference, is no democracy."

On December 1, 1841, the People's Party organized a referendum on the People's Constitution, which dramatically extended the right to vote to all white men. A clear majority of Rhode Island's eligible citizens, more than fourteen thousand people, ratified the document—an overwhelming victory, despite a boycott of the vote by opponents.

The sitting governor and formally elected state assembly had naturally ignored both the People's Convention and the new People's Constitution, both of which were illegal under the colonial charter. Throughout the first months of the new year, supporters and opponents of the People's Constitution marched in demonstrations, debated in pamphlets, and appealed for political support from outside the state.

Dorr and his allies argued that the state's people were merely exercising their sovereign power to establish a legitimate form of government. Opponents warned that their illegal acts had put a powder "magazine beneath the fabric of civil society," which they might explode "without warning."

The chief justice of the Rhode Island Supreme Court intervened on the side of law and order, cautioning that any effort to implement the People's Constitution risked reproducing the bloodshed of the French Revolution. The official state assembly chosen under the charter's franchise passed laws imposing penalties on anyone who presided at a meeting or ran for office under the People's Constitution, and further decreed that anyone assuming office under its auspices would be guilty of treason.

Dorr plunged ahead. His People's Party staged elections under the expanded franchise established by the People's Constitution. The illegal vote produced a new people's state assembly and a new people's governor—Thomas Wilson Dorr. And on May 3, 1842, Dorr choreographed his own inauguration in Providence. After marshalling in front of Hoyle's Tavern near Federal Hill, the people's volunteer militia led a procession of thousands on foot, followed by representatives of the different trades on horseback. "Even the most conservative estimates placed the number of those present at more than 20 percent of the city's population; others thought it exceeded 40 percent." Rhode Island was now "a house divided."

The bizarre situation in Rhode Island—which seemed to have two different elected governors and two different state assemblies—attracted national attention. Moderates decried the potential for anarchy, while Andrew Jackson in private endorsed the right "of the people" to "alter and amend their system of government when a majority wills it." Outsiders, including Daniel Webster, the U.S. secretary of state, intervened in an effort to broker a compromise between Dorr and the official state government. At the same time, radical Democrats, particularly in New York City, were inciting Dorr. On a visit to the city, he was presented with a sword that Andrew Jackson had used during one of his Indian campaigns and urged to go home and fearlessly fight the good fight. Emboldened, Dorr and his confederates began to plot an armed assault on the state arsenal, in hopes of forcing the duly elected governor and assembly to stand down.

What followed was pure farce. Dorr's health was fragile at best, and his mastery of the martial arts nonexistent. Defying the state's threat of sanctions, Dorr returned to Rhode Island on May 15. A small-*d* democrat with a weakness for pageantry, he paraded through Providence again, this time with a gleaming sword at his side, riding in an open-air coach pulled by a team of four white horses and escorted by three hundred armed men followed by a large crowd of supporters.

Assuming power, the people's governor convened the people's state assembly. He began to fire off official letters, including one to the U.S. Senate, signing it "Thomas Wilson Dorr Governor of the State of Rhode Island and Providence Plantations."

Two days later, some of Dorr's men raided a Marine Corps armoury in downtown Providence, seizing two cannon that had been confiscated from the British at the Battle of Saratoga in 1777. They brought the guns to Dorr's headquarters on Federal Hill, where, in a show of force, they were aimed at the city below.

Alarmed allies and friends pleaded with Dorr to get a grip. Night fell. Delayed but undaunted, Dorr and his troops at last slowly marched, lugging along the British cannon, through a damp fog toward the arsenal in the west end of the city. By then, word of the planned assault had spread, and the state was able to muster a large force to defend the arms depot. When Dorr's men arrived, the loyalists—including Dorr's father, who abhorred his son's madness—refused to surrender.

The rebels wheeled their ordnance into position and hastily aimed the antique pieces. In the chaos, both weapons were fired, perhaps on Dorr's command. The powder flashed, but the big guns failed to discharge. The arsenal's defenders were left staring as Dorr and his men melted back into the night, leaving the cannon behind.

This botched assault left the outlaws isolated and on the run. Conceding defeat, Thomas Wilson Dorr a few weeks later fled the state and took refuge in New Hampshire under the protection of a sympathetic Democratic governor—thus sparing Rhode Island an improbable civil war over the right to vote.

III

STILL, EVENTS IN PROVIDENCE showed how intense the American struggle over the right to vote could be—and gave a preview of battles still to come.

It is often assumed that suffrage had become all but universal for white men in the 1830s and 1840s—but that assumption is a bit misleading. Although the franchise on the whole had been broadened in the 1820s, a growing number of immigrants and the looming crisis over slavery spurred the introduction of *new* barriers on the franchise, targeting specific groups. As Alexander Keyssar has shown in his definitive study, *The Right to Vote*, "these barriers were expressions of the nation's reluctance to embrace universal suffrage, of the limits to the democratic impulses that characterized the era."

The situation varied greatly from state to state. For example, in Pennsylvania, in rules newly adopted in 1838, only white men were eligible to vote, if, and only if, they had paid state or county taxes during the previous two years. In Virginia in that decade, a white man was eligible to vote if, and only if, he had owned land for six months prior to the election or could prove some other material assets (for example, a "leasehold estate, with the evidence of title recorded two years before he shall offer to vote, of a term originally not less than five years, of the annual value or rent of twenty dollars"). In North Carolina in the 1830s, there was no property qualification for a white man to choose a candidate for the House of Representatives, but a freehold of at least fifty acres was required to vote to choose a candidate for the Senate.

And that was not the end of the limits on the right to vote. Rhode Island, in the constitution of 1842 it passed in the wake of the Dorr rebellion, became the first state to grant suffrage to African Americans; the new charter eliminated property qualifications to vote but excluded "those convicted of bribery or of any crime deemed infamous at common law, until expressly restored to the right of suffrage by act of General Assembly." The state's new constitution also excluded "paupers, lunatics, persons non compos mentis, persons under guardianship."

Many states also maintained residency requirements to vote that excluded white men who were students from out of state, soldiers in the federal army, or men living in almshouses. In the United States, astonishingly enough, the use of poll and other taxpaying prerequisites for voting were outlawed at the federal level only by the Twenty-fourth Amendment to the Constitution, passed in 1964.

And then there was the colour line. For example, in New York before the Civil War, a "man of colour" could vote, but only if he had been in possession for at least one year of "a freehold estate of the value of $250 over and above all debts and incumbrances charged thereon." There was no such property qualification for white men.

The young Frederick Douglass, an escaped slave who had already emerged as one of the most stirring abolitionist orators in New England, had aggressively campaigned *against* the People's Constitution in Rhode Island, precisely because of its exclusion of blacks from the franchise. Six years later, in 1848, Douglass was one of the few men to participate in the women's rights convention at Seneca Falls, New York, organized by local Quakers and the pioneering feminist Elizabeth Cady Stanton. Stanton and Douglass were longtime allies; they were both abolitionists, and both supported women's right to vote. In 1866, Douglass gladly joined the Equal Rights Association that Stanton had launched.

But within a few years, they split bitterly over the Fifteenth Amendment to the Constitution, which in 1870 would grant black men the right to vote. Douglass himself wished that the amendment had outlawed qualification tests for the franchise, and had also extended the vote to women, but he was a pragmatist, and he was willing to support the amendment on offer.

Furious that women were being left behind, Stanton opposed the amendment. She predicted that giving black men the vote would "culminate in fearful outrages on womanhood." As the most recent biographer of Douglass, David Blight, drily remarks, "The imagined demon of the black rapist crawled into the suffrage debate, courtesy of the leader of the women's rights crusade." In her fury, Stanton even argued that "it is better to be the slave of an educated white man, than a degraded, ignorant black one."

As Stanton feared, it would take fifty more years for American women to gain the franchise. They won the right to vote only with the passage of the Nineteenth Amendment in 1920.

By then, many states, especially in the South, had introduced legislation designed to roll back, in practice, the ability of blacks to vote, by adopting poll taxes, literacy tests, lengthy residence requirements, elaborate registration systems and, eventually, party primaries restricted to white voters. In this period, felony disenfranchisement also became widespread.

Some of these restrictions were challenged successfully by the American civil rights movement of the 1950s and 1960s, and overturned. For the first time since Reconstruction, black men and women won municipal, state, and federal elections. Still, new barriers to blacks voting were subsequently put into place. As a result of an extraordinary increase in America's prison population, the number of black men who have suffered felony disenfranchisement has dramatically risen in recent decades.

Even as struggles continue over the right to vote, the *percentage* of eligible voters actually voting has fluctuated even more wildly throughout American history. For example, the percentage of eligible voters who participate in American elections is lower in the second decade of the twenty-first century than it was in the mid-nineteenth century. And current American rates are far below levels of voter participation in other contemporary democracies around the world. Voter participation in America also remains extremely uneven: older and wealthier people vote in far larger numbers than those who are young or poor. Unequal voter turnout produces unequal political influence.

Most of these problems could be solved simply if the United States chose to follow Australia, Belgium, and a number of South American countries in making voting compulsory (just as jury duty, paying taxes, and primary education are compulsory in America). In his presidential address to the American Political Science Association in 1996, the Dutch scholar Arend Lijphart argued that the United States should seriously consider treating the franchise not simply as a right but as a civic duty: "Its advantages far outweigh the normative and practical objections to it."

But given the historic resistance of many Americans to compulsory rules of any kind—and given a recurrent fear that ignorant citizens will

embrace venal demagogues running on disingenuous policy platforms—it is highly unlikely that voting will ever become obligatory in
the United States.

Instead, proponents of political participation will have to keep
struggling to make it easier, rather than harder, to register to vote, just as
candidates seeking election will have to continue investing time and money
to convince supporters to turn out to vote—making the United States a
seriously limited democracy by its own preferred political criterion for
defining the term.

III

IN VOLUME 2 of *Democracy in America*, first published in France in
1840, Tocqueville had intuited that America's *culture* might well prove
more significant than its political institutions for determining the future
of democracy in America. "I see an innumerable multitude of men,"
Tocqueville icily observed, "alike and equal, circling around in pursuit of
the petty and banal pleasures with which they glut their souls. Each one
of them, withdrawn into himself, is almost unaware of the fate of the
rest . . . I have thought that this brand of orderly, gentle, peaceful slavery which I have just described could be combined, more easily than is
generally supposed, with some of the external forms of freedom . . .
Under this system, the citizens quit their state of dependence just long
enough to choose their masters and fall back into it."

Tocqueville's worries about conformism proved misleading. In those
years, the United States had already begun to elaborate a distinctively
clamorous style of public culture, with opera houses, Shakespeare's
plays, and legitimate theatre flourishing alongside such mass-marketed
diversions as dime novels, minstrel shows, and lectures aimed at a working-
class public. As America's historic commitment to a commercial society
solidified, an emergent culture industry made it both possible—and
profitable—to market cultural artefacts that strove to satisfy the otherwise
frustrated yearnings of ordinary Americans to be regarded as free and
equal individuals, with cultural tastes as valid and worthy as those of
any European aristocrat.

This nascent demotic American culture emerged as an unacknowledged legislator of the American heart, helping to shape public opinion. In midcentury America, it was popular novels and public lectures and minstrel shows that most vividly expressed common yearnings and equally consequential popular ambivalences—about class, about race, about Puritanism. Because they were more attuned to the psychic discords of American national identity, the producers of America's demotic culture were able to play a leading role in articulating conflicting desires, fears, and dreams that were barely expressible in the realm of electoral politics.

Consider, for example, the paradoxical convergence in antebellum America of popular interest in the northern states in Ralph Waldo Emerson, Harriet Beecher Stowe, and the minstrel show—a cultural convergence that helped set the stage for the Civil War and the subsequent abolition of slavery.

Emerson became the architect of a popular philosophy for the new nation by lecturing on the Lyceum circuit of organizations that sponsored public events meant to promote "the universal diffusion of knowledge" to the general public. As the prophet of a new secular gospel of "self-reliance" (not so different from that preached by Nietzsche in Europe a generation later), Emerson provided a quasi-religious sanction for the American cult of individualism—this, in essence, is what the American critic Irving Howe meant when he described Emersonianism as America's characteristic "ideology" (one that fosters what another cultural critic derided as "the herd of independent minds").

From the start, this Emersonian ideology was in tension with puritanical religious and moral commandments. "I do not wish to expiate but to live," preaches Emerson in "Self-Reliance." "If I am the Devil's child, I will live then from the Devil."

Insofar as America's public culture has assumed an Emersonian cast, it has often turned inward. The self-reliant individualist is wary, on principle, of the moral and political convictions and conventions that circulate in society at large. Redemption is to be sought not in obedience to the laws and adherence to outward forms but rather in the elaboration of "a new degree of culture"; it is through the novelty of his creative life that the self-reliant individualist may hope to "instantly revolutionize the entire system of human pursuits."

A key implication of this worldview was its express disdain for conventional forms of politics. "Some fetish of a government, some ephemeral trade, or war, or man, is cried up by half mankind and cried down by the other half, as if all depended on this particular up or down," declared Emerson in one of his most famous lectures, "The American Scholar." "The odds are that the whole question is not worth the poorest thought."

But this is not the whole story. After all, there were moments when Emerson himself rose above his own inclination to contemplative quiescence. Throughout the 1850s, after the passage of the Fugitive Slave Law, he denounced the law and urged others to flout it. And in 1859, after John Brown's apocalyptic raid on Harpers Ferry, Emerson provoked a minor uproar when he declared that Brown's execution would "make the gallows as glorious as the cross."

When the self-reliant Emersonian does descend into the cave of politics, it is by preference in the form of civil disobedience, no matter how violent—as witness the representative figures of Thoreau, whom Emerson had mentored, and of John Brown, the archetype of all later transcendentalist political outlaws.

Emerson in these years also expressed his admiration for Harriet Beecher Stowe's novel *Uncle Tom's Cabin* not only for its abolitionist sentiments but also because "it is read equally in the parlor and the kitchen and the nursery of every house." Through a dramatization of the conflict between the evil of slavery and the redemptive power of Christian love, Stowe meant to touch, and so transform, the sentiments of a large and mixed public that included countless members of the northern working class.

The product of a rare kind of enthusiasm (in the literal sense: she felt inspired by God), Stowe's novel did, in fact, "instantly revolutionize the entire system of human pursuits" in antebellum America. After its publication in 1852, *Uncle Tom's Cabin* went on to become one of the bestselling books in the world, eventually selling more copies in America in the nineteenth century than any other work except the Bible.

A paradigmatic product of America's nascent culture industry, the novel produced a flood of consumable artefacts meant either to capitalize on its popularity, or to amplify its abolitionist message, or both. There were Uncle Tom dioramas, engravings, gift books, card games, figurines, plates, silverware, and needlepoint. Poems and songs about Tom appeared. Above all, his story was dramatized throughout America in minstrel shows, which offered a parody of African American experience, featuring singers, dancers, and comedians, usually white people, always performing in blackface.

Minstrelsy was America's first major contribution to the emergent global entertainment industry (Stephen Foster, a midcentury composer of minstrel songs, was the first major American popular musician to achieve global fame, through the international sale of sheet music). In later decades, as the minstrel tradition was reinvented by a variety of black performers, it produced the musical and melodramatic basis for almost all subsequent forms of African American musical entertainment, from ragtime to blues to jazz (the great tenor saxophonist Lester Young cut his teeth in a black minstrel show).

But in the beginning, the minstrel shows were the sole province of white folk. White performers "blacked-up" to amuse the same kind of white northern working-class audience that had flocked to hear Emerson's lectures and to read *Uncle Tom's Cabin*. As one modern scholar put it, "blackface was their bohemianism"—an essential reinforcement, now racially coded, of the anti-Puritan impulses already at play in the Emersonian dispensation.

For several fateful years, *Uncle Tom's Cabin* in its various incarnations—as a novel, as kitsch, as minstrel entertainment—defined the cultural climate of the northern United States. Years later, the novelist Henry James recalled his youthful trips to watch the martyrdom of

Uncle Tom reenacted on the minstrel stage. "We lived and moved at that time, with great intensity, in Mrs. Stowe's novel," James wrote. The book, he continued, "knew the large felicity of gathering in alike the small and the simple and the big and the wise, and had above all the extraordinary fortune of finding itself, for an immense number of people, much less a book than a state of vision."

To be able to communicate a "state of vision" is an astonishing feat under any circumstances. That the convergent popularity of Emersonian nonconformism, Stowe's novel, and the minstrel show accomplished this feat before the Civil War is beyond dispute. That the public in the North could now *see* black slaves as figures of sympathy transformed the grounds on which political debate could move forward. As one prominent aficionado of minstrelsy, Abraham Lincoln, purportedly quipped when he met Harriet Beecher Stowe in 1862, "So this is the little lady who made this big war."

Still, there were obvious limits to what a writer like Stowe could accomplish. Weeping at her depiction of Uncle Tom's suffering is not an act comparable to joining others in a struggle to abolish racial injustice. A fantasy of racial justice can provoke a demand for real racial justice—or it can serve as a palliative substitute, covering up a lack of real political justice by allowing isolated citizens to satisfy a certain desire for compassion and justice in fantasy, not in reality. Indeed, as the entire history of the United States confirms, nonconformism and defiant individualism can flourish while entrenched racial prejudices are left in place—and the quest to create a more inclusive democratic society languishes.

III

IN THE WAKE of the Civil War, Walt Whitman, America's self-declared "poet of democracy," was living in Washington, D.C., where he was a clerk for the attorney general. A decade earlier, in the first edition of *Leaves of Grass*, Whitman had exalted America's democracy as he had experienced it inwardly, as a kind of sublime pantheism, egalitarian in substance and cosmic in scope:

Whoever degrades another degrades me . . . . and whatever is
   done or said returns at last to me,
And whatever I do or say I also return.

Through me the afflatus surging and surging . . . . through me the
   current and index.

I speak the password primeval . . . . I give the sign of democracy;
By God! I will accept nothing which all cannot have their
   counterpart of on the same terms.

"In all people I see myself," he wrote elsewhere in *Leaves of Grass*, "none more and not one a barleycorn less, / And the good or bad I say of myself I say of them."

The war, however, had chastened Whitman and left him feeling more ambivalent than ever about the depth of his democratic faith, in part because he now had deeper doubts about the capacity of ordinary people to measure up to his rapturous vision: "The people! Like our huge earth itself, which, to ordinary scansion, is full of vulgar contradictions and offense, Man, viewed in the lump, displeases, and is a constant puzzle and affront."

During Whitman's time living in Washington, the city's black population had exploded. In January 1866, Congress, which was still in the hands of radical Republicans, passed a new voting statute for the District of Columbia, granting virtually all males over the age of twenty-one the right to vote, without regard to race, property, or educational background. Two years later, black voters turned out in force to help elect a new mayor of Washington, Sayles Jenks Bowen, a radical Republican who was also a civil rights activist. The night of Bowen's victory, Washington's streets filled with revellers, as Whitman wrote to his mother:

We had the strangest procession here last Tuesday night,
about 3000 darkeys, old & young, men & women—I saw them

all—they turned out in honor of *their* victory in electing the
Mayor, Mr. Bowen—the men were all armed with clubs or
pistols—besides the procession in the street, there was a
string went along the sidewalk in single file with bludgeons &
sticks, yelling & gesticulating like madmen . . . they looked
like so many wild brutes let loose—thousands of slaves from the
Southern plantations have crowded up here—many are
supported by the Gov't.

The poet who had once boasted that he could "contain multitudes"
now, in private, expressed disgust at dark-skinned compatriots who
were intoxicated by their first taste of political power.

At the time Whitman wrote this acerbic letter, he was struggling to
write an ambitious essay that would confute the critics of America's
great experiment in self-government. Hoping to measure up to, and take
the measure of the British prose writer he most admired, the increasingly dyspeptic Thomas Carlyle, he titled the book *Democratic Vistas*. It
began briskly:

I will not gloss over the appalling dangers of universal
suffrage in the United States. In fact, it is to admit and face
these dangers I am writing. To him or her within whose
thought rages the battle, advancing, retreating, between
Democracy's convictions, aspirations, and the People's
crudeness, vice, caprices, I mainly write this book.

Whitman goes on to deplore the country's crass materialism and
lament the ignorance of most people. At the same time he hymns the
glories of a "perfect individualism," the true "purpose of democracy," the
"doctrine or theory that man, properly trained in sanest, highest freedom, may and must become a law, and series of laws, unto himself, surrounding and providing for, not only his own personal control, but all
his relations to other individuals, and to the State."

This passage articulates a sentiment I can recognize within

myself—I was raised to revere Walt Whitman, in part because my father admired his poetry and devoted more than one academic monograph to analysing his work. But what a strange vision!

In Whitman's hands, democracy is no longer a form of government. It is a kind of prophecy, a voice raised to keep faith with a future to which our shared past has committed us, and it is a supreme fiction, made up of portents and warnings, exhilaration and fear, as if the common man could live on the bread of faithful speech. America's democratic vistas provoke wonderment, not unlike what Jay Gatsby experienced gazing at the green light at the end of Daisy Buchanan's dock in F. Scott Fitzgerald's 1927 novel *The Great Gatsby*. For Whitman, democracy was (to borrow Fitzgerald's words) an "orgastic future that year by year recedes before us. It eluded us then, but that's no matter—tomorrow we will run faster, stretch out our arms farther . . ."

But this is what democracy in America often seems like: an elusive fantasy, forever out of reach, forever unrealized, even as its most eloquent bards, trapped in their own prejudices, are "borne back ceaselessly into the past."

FOUR

A STRUGGLE FOR POLITICAL AND SOCIAL EQUALITY

O N MAY 7, 1839, fifty-two men, sporting ribbons and marching in pairs, escorted a wagon draped with Union Jacks as it wound through the streets of London. All of them were delegates to a General Convention of the Industrious Classes, each one elected by at least twenty thousand British people, most of them otherwise disenfranchised, many of them active in demonstrations demanding political reform. The delegates were escorting a petition with the text of a "People's Charter," bearing the signatures of more than one million people.

In the months leading up to this moment, three hundred thousand citizens had rallied in support of the Charter on Kersal Moor in

Manchester; two hundred thousand people had assembled in Birmingham; and one hundred and fifty thousand in Glasgow.

The Charter conveyed six demands: the right to vote for all men over the age of twenty-one; a secret ballot; the repeal of property qualifications to serve as a member of Parliament; payment for serving as an MP; the creation of electoral districts of equal size; and annual elections for Parliament, to produce a more democratic form of government.

Each demand had been ratified by the fifty-plus delegates to the General Convention of the Industrious Classes, which first convened on Monday, February 4, 1839, at a coffeehouse in Charing Cross. The delegates included shoemakers, newspaper editors, booksellers, printers, a barrister, a draper, a stonemason, a pub owner, trade union leaders, a physician, a pearl button manufacturer, a typesetter, tailors, a handloom weaver, a grain dealer, a tea merchant, a wood carver, a thimble manufacturer, a tobacconist, a lamp manufacturer, a Methodist preacher, and an Anglican vicar. A number of these people were too poor to have the right to vote for members of Parliament.

The Reform Act of 1832 had dramatically extended the franchise in the United Kingdom—but property qualifications continued to be imposed, and the electorate in 1839 amounted to some eight hundred thousand eligible voters in a country with a population of fourteen million men, women, and children. Disenfranchised workers had watched as more prosperous citizens won the right to vote—and had concluded, logically enough, that one cause of their relative poverty was their own lack of the same right. "Reasoning from effect to cause," the first historian of the movement wrote, "there is no marvel that they arrive at the conclusion—that their exclusion from political power is the cause of our social anomalies." Universal manhood suffrage became the overriding aim of all Chartists—but for many, it was also a means to redress the wretched conditions of a working class that had left the land to labour in the northern textile factories or the coal mines scattered through the United Kingdom from Bristol to Clyde.

A few Chartists had even more radical goals in view, notably the delegates from the London Democratic Association, who were pressing the Convention to demand more direct forms of democratic self-government. "No man is too poor to unite with us," the London Democratic Association had declared at its 1838 founding. "On the contrary, the poorer, the more oppressed, the more welcome."

These London Chartists revered the Parisian insurrection of August 10, 1792—It was on this date In 1838 that the London Democrats had founded their association. Treating the Jacobin constitution of 1793 as sacred scripture, they idolized Robespierre, and wished to resurrect, in a British context, his efforts to introduce "a new social order into society, based on equality of rights and purity of morals." They deplored that the French government in 1795, after the execution of Robespierre, had produced a new constitution with restrictions on the franchise and on the capacity of ordinary citizens to participate in politics; and they applauded the response of Gracchus Babeuf, an avowed democrat who founded a secret society of armed insurrectionists. Before Babeuf was arrested, put on trial, and executed, he was preparing to overthrow the French government, restore the Jacobin constitution of 1793, and implement the right of every man to "the enjoyment of an equal share in all property."

Perhaps the most eloquent of the London radicals was the "schoolmaster of Chartism," Bronterre O'Brien, the son of a wine and spirit merchant who had grown up in County Longford, Ireland. A polymath able to read and speak English, Latin, Greek, Italian, and French, and notorious as well for his hard drinking habits, O'Brien had become radicalized by working in London for the publisher Henry Hetherington, the editor of the *Poor Man's Guardian*, and a delegate himself to the 1839 Chartist Convention. In 1836, Bronterre had rendered into English Philippe Buonarroti's detailed 1828 account, *Babeuf's Conspiracy for Equality*, which Hetherington published as a book along with supporting documents, including the full text of the Jacobin constitution of 1793.

When the Chartists unveiled the People's Charter in 1839, it was with the pomp and ceremony owed a similarly consecrated text. The flag-draped wagon in London bore a monumental scroll that weighed a third of a tonne. When fully unfurled, the petition was three miles long. Its preamble was blunt: "We perform the duties of freemen; we must have the privileges of freemen. Therefore, we demand universal suffrage. The suffrage, to be exempt from the corruption of the wealthy and the violence of the powerful, must be secret."

Arriving at their destination, the Chartist delegation handed over the petition to Thomas Attwood, a sympathetic Member of Parliament and a founder of the Birmingham Political Union, a key node of Chartist organizing in the Midlands. With some trepidation—since Attwood, a banker by trade who was also a well-known critic of classical economics, personally deplored the drift toward revolutionary rhetoric at the Chartist Convention—the MP had promised to present the petition in the House of Commons. But that very day, May 7, the prime minister, Lord Melbourne, a rich landowner and political moderate, announced his intention to resign, provoking a parliamentary crisis that wasn't resolved for several weeks and delayed formally presenting the petition.

On June 14, when the People's Charter was belatedly transported to Westminster, one reporter described the astonishing scale of the document: "It appeared to have the circumference of a carriage wheel, and was rolled solidly round a straight axle, supported by transverse uprights at each end." According to the official parliamentary record, "loud laughter" greeted the appearance of the petition, because of its "gigantic dimensions"—it required twelve men to lift and carry the scroll into the House chamber. Attwood, after unspooling the document to place one end on the clerk's table, addressed his fellow MPs, and made a formal motion:

> that it might please their honourable House to take the
> petition into their most serious consideration, and to use their
> utmost endeavour to pass a law, granting to every man of
> lawful age, sound mind, and uncontaminated by crime, the
> right of voting for Members to serve in Parliament; that they
> would cause a law also to be passed, giving the right to vote

by the ballot; that the duration of Parliaments might in no case be of greater duration than one year; that they would abolish all property qualifications, to entitle parties to sit in their honourable House; and that all Members elected to sit in Parliament, should be paid for their services.

The motion was tabled, and debate on its merits deferred to a later date.

In the interim, the Chartists moved their Convention from London to Birmingham, in order to discuss in friendlier surroundings what, if any, "ulterior measures" to consider taking, should Parliament (as seemed likely) reject their petition. "Ulterior measures" was a euphemism for armed struggle, and this was a topic of heated debate among the Chartists: a number favoured using only "moral force," while others were willing to countenance the use, in some circumstances, of "physical force."

After prolonged deliberation, the group's leaders had collectively agreed on a list of approved tactics, including a reassertion of "their old constitutional right" to defend themselves, if necessary, with armed force. They had also endorsed the possibility of observing "a sacred month," a set period of time that would oblige all Chartists "to abstain from their labouring during that period, as well as from use of all intoxicating drinks." For many Chartists, temperance was seen as a prerequisite for personal as well as political self-government, and observing a "sacred month" seemed a suitably God-fearing way to launch a general strike. At the same time, the most militant members of the movement hoped to find some way to provoke a violent response from the state, in hopes that armed conflict would outrage people and help swell the ranks of the movement, while also ensuring that most participants were in fighting mettle.

When word came that Parliament would soon start debate on the petition, magistrates in Birmingham, anticipating the worst, banned large meetings and enrolled several thousand special constables, augmented by battalions of police from London. In response, the most militant Chartists settled into what would become a pattern—pike manufacture, the purchase of firearms, and secret drilling.

On July 12, the House of Commons at last met to argue the pros and cons of the Chartist petition. The prominent Whig and future Liberal Party leader Lord John Russell (a courtesy title accorded to this younger son of a duke, as he wasn't yet a peer in his own right) was vehement in his objections, comparing the Chartists to the most bloody-minded Jacobins during the darkest days of the French Revolution, and disputing, rather curiously, the democratic standing of the document. There were between five and six million adult males in England, Lord Russell noted, and the number of signatories to the petition was merely 1,280,000 adult males: how could this self-selected minority pretend to represent the majority of adult males? The debate united the two main parliamentary factions—conservative Tories and moderate Whigs—in firm opposition. By a vote of 235 to 46, Parliament rejected Attwood's motion.

Learning of the Charter's defeat, a crowd assembled in Manchester; when police tried to disperse it, they were met with force. A pitched battle ensued, with several houses burned and looted. Similar riots occurred throughout the country.

It was unclear what would happen next. Should the Chartist Convention remain in session? Should it try to put itself forward as a rival source of political power? One Chartist suggested as much at a mass meeting outside Manchester, held in August 1839: "I owe the British Government no allegiance but what I am obliged to give it. I declare, that I will obey the Convention; nor death nor hell shall prevent me from being obedient to them. They are my Government. I had a hand in chusing them."

Britain's Seditious Meetings Act of 1817 complicated matters. This act had outlawed all meetings of more than fifty people called "for the purpose . . . of deliberating upon any grievance, in church or state," unless the meeting had been convened by an authorized state official, or advance notice had been given to local authorities. The act also made it illegal for societies to correspond with each other, or for individuals to correspond with societies. The rise of national newspapers with an overt political slant, like the Chartists' widely read weekly broadsheet, *The Northern Star*, enabled the group to circumvent the last provision by publishing accounts of local meetings and letters from readers. It was nevertheless virtually impossible for Chartists to coordinate the activities of local branches without constantly risking arrest.

Between January 1839 and June 1840, the British government detained nearly five hundred Chartists, resulting in two hundred and fifty prison sentences, and six death sentences that were commuted at the last moment. The more Chartists the government arrested, the more preoccupied the movement became with freeing its prisoners, which diverted time and energy from the movement's constitutional agenda— and also tempted militants to risk "ulterior measures."

Like the Jacobins in France in the 1790s, the Chartists claimed to represent *all* the people, and they promised to defend the "nation" as a whole against a closed elite that controlled politics and the economy. These promises were, in a strong sense, *democratic*—but their methods were increasingly revolutionary and hinged on the actions of a relatively small minority of committed militants.

In the long run, the Chartists promised a restoration of harmonious social relations—but they simultaneously raised the prospect of a civil war. While some members of the middle class had been sympathetic to instituting universal manhood suffrage, most were averse to a movement that aimed to topple the government. In the months that followed, and despite generating some moments of spectacular disruption, including a large but abortive uprising in Wales in November 1839, and a massive but equally abortive general strike in 1842, Chartism slowly began to fall apart as a plausible strategy for democratizing British politics. The swift suppression by the state of uprisings and strikes, combined with dwindling support among the voting middle class for the radicals, destroyed any possible illusion that Chartism represented the general will of the British people—even though it had raised the hopes of millions of their compatriots for a more democratic organization of society and politics.

III

AT A BANQUET held on September 22, 1845, one thousand democrats from different nations gathered in London to celebrate the founding of the French Republic, as decreed by the Convention on that date in 1792. Thus came into being the Fraternal Democrats, a new international association organized by Julian Harney, a Chartist journalist who had participated in the General Convention of the Industrious Classes six years before. In the eyes of Harney and his associates, Europe was facing a protracted and epochal struggle, between advocates of democracy on the one hand, and the autocratic rulers of the Habsburg, Romanov, and Ottoman Empires on the other. Besides promoting the exchange of information among the different democratic groups in Europe, Harney's new association offered aid to the city's political refugees. By then, London was home to a large number of exiled German, French, Polish, Russian, and Italian radicals of various creeds and convictions.

One of Harney's allies in this venture was Karl Schapper, a burly German typesetter and veteran insurrectionist who had stormed the Frankfurt police station in 1832, escaped from prison, and finally settled in London. In exile he became friendly with the Italian insurrectionist Giuseppe Mazzini, and also with Auguste Blanqui, an ardent French revolutionary who advocated a temporary dictatorship as the best means to realize a democratic republic of equals. Like Blanqui, Schapper fancied secret societies; like Harney, he regarded himself openly, if rather vaguely, as a "communist," a word that had gained currency in English as a description of Babeuf's economic programme.

In a speech on the first anniversary of the group's founding, given after a toast to "the Sovereignty of the People," Harney explained that a government "elected by, and responsible to, the entire people, is our political creed. We believe the earth with all its natural productions to be the property of all; we . . . therefore denounce all infractions of this evidently just and natural law as robbery and usurpation . . . We condemn the 'national' hatreds which have hitherto divided mankind, as both foolish and wicked; foolish, because no one can decide for himself the country he will be born in; wicked, as proved by the feuds and bloody wars which have desolated the earth, in consequence of these national vanities." Given these views, it is no wonder that Harney was soon in contact with a German exile of similar convictions.

At the time, Karl Marx was based in Brussels, Belgium, having been expelled from France in 1845, under pressure from the Prussian government. Born to an assimilated Jewish barrister in 1818 in Prussia's province of the Lower Rhine, Marx had studied law at the University of Berlin and philosophy at the University of Jena; after receiving his PhD in 1841 for a dissertation on ancient Greek materialist philosophers, Marx became a journalist, moving to Paris in October 1843, after the Cologne newspaper he briefly edited was banned by the Prussian government.

In exile and unemployed, the young Marx plunged into a crash course of reading books on the French Revolution, while he was re-reading perhaps the greatest single work of systematic political philosophy in the nineteenth century, Hegel's *Philosophy of Right*. At the same time, he started to compose his thoughts about what he was reading, in both a series of private notebooks and a few short essays he published at the time.

It was in these months that Marx began to develop a distinctive outlook on the dynamics of modern social change. Like Hegel, he believed that freedom was an emergent result of a historical evolution that was complex and "dialectical"; like the French liberal historian Adolphe Thiers, whom he read at this time, he conjectured that the key to this evolution under contemporary conditions was class conflict; and like Thomas Carlyle in his apocalyptic account *The French Revolution*, Marx represented the labouring class as a historical agent seething with violence, "a still barely moving yet faintly stirring Enceladus," as the historian Gareth Stedman Jones has put it, "who might suddenly arise from the fiery deep, as he already had in France, toppling the flimsy superstructures of . . . civilization in his wake." (In the *Aeneid* of Virgil, as in Carlyle's prose, Enceladus represents a mythic Greek giant sleeping beneath Mount Etna in Sicily, whose arousal caused the volcano's periodic eruptions.)

As his writings from these early years reveal, Marx was ambivalent about democracy. On the one hand, he privately remarked that Hegel had forced his vision of the modern state into a Procrustean bed of monarchic prejudices: in this context, Marx asserted that "democracy is the solved *riddle* of all constitutions," because in a democracy "the constitution appears as what it is, the free product of men." On the other hand, Marx felt that democracy was not an end in itself but only a means toward the ultimate aim of fully realizing human freedom in a peaceful society of equals. He argued that the French revolutionaries had simply tried to aggregate the views of "egoistic, independent individuals," without addressing the economic barriers to enabling "the real, individual man" to organize "his own powers as *social* powers," so that these powers were "no longer separated from his *political* power."

In other words, realizing an egalitarian community of truly emancipated individuals—a goal Marx shared with almost all the radical democrats—required putting an end to the exploitation of workers, not just drafting a new constitution. As one scholar of Marxism put it, "In order to bring true democracy to life it is necessary to remove the poisonous fumes of capitalism that asphyxiate it." Without the abolition of capitalism, even ostensibly democratic political institutions would remain under the effective control of the rich and powerful, leaving ordinary citizens at a dreadful disadvantage in the coming violent conflict Marx foresaw between two great, hostile classes, the proletariat and the bourgeoisie.

But Marx's problems with a purely political focus went deeper still. Though in keeping with Rousseau's democratic principles, the political effort to transform the free will of individuals into the general will of a self-governing people had encouraged a reckless voluntarism—the belief on the part of some French revolutionaries that willpower alone could forge a new social order. "*Robespierre* saw in great poverty and great wealth only an obstacle to *pure* democracy," Marx complained.

But this was only to be expected, Marx continued, as (according to Rousseau), "the principle of politics is the will. The more one-sided and thus the more perfected *political* thought is, the more it believes in the *omnipotence* of will, the blinder it is to the *natural* and spiritual *limits* on the will, and the more incapable it is of discovering the source of social ills." For Marx, the most important cause of social ills lay in the organization, not of government, but rather of the economy. Only the fullest development of the forces of production, placed under the control of associated free individuals instead of a few wealthy capitalists, could create a new world of abundance, a true commonwealth. This analysis was one of the reasons that Marx repudiated conspiratorial insurrectionists like Babeuf and Blanqui—just as it persuaded some former insurrectionists, like Julian Harney, to adapt instead Marx's more painstaking and public strategy of preparing the workers themselves to develop an understanding of objective economic conditions, as a precondition for assuming control of the means of production.

Yet even Marx conceded the need for at least one "*political act*" of will: a great collective act of "*overthrow* and *dissolution*," a revolution that would destroy the existing order. That was one reason why in Brussels he was involved with a clandestine political organization, the Communist League, which eventually became allied with Harney's Fraternal Democrats.

But once the destruction of the old order was complete, "where the proper *aim* and *spirit* of socialism emerges, there socialism throws the *political* hull away." In other words, he speculated that an economy organized on egalitarian principles would, eventually, be able to do without the hierarchical methods of command and control characteristic even of representative governments like that of the United States. (As his friend and frequent collaborator Friedrich Engels later put it, the state would "wither away" in a communist society.)

By 1845, Marx had abandoned his original plan to write a *Critique of Politics and Political Economy*. He concluded that an analysis of capitalism would suffice.

III

LONDON'S FRATERNAL DEMOCRATS briefly brought together a varied group of revolutionaries and reformists from a number of European countries. But differences within the group soon became apparent. Fraternity was hard to sustain among the revolutionary sects vying for preeminence in the late 1840s.

The Communist Manifesto that Marx and Engels published in 1848 is a case in point. Though the authors spared Harney and his friends (in part because they hungered for a prominent ally in England), the two Germans issued a series of blistering attacks on now obscure socialist authors and their programmes. Comprising a third of the *Manifesto*, these passages suggest that only the party of Marx and Engels possesses the correct solution to all of the world's most pressing social and economic problems.

The result was ironic: the *Manifesto* predicted an end to all social divisions but clinched the argument with a barrage of insults aimed at rival groups. Such divisive rhetoric guaranteed a bitter contest on the avowedly democratic left between different political parties, many of them claiming to move closer to the goal of creating a republic of equals comprised of emancipated individuals—but all of them clashing aggressively over the best path forward. At the same time, rival political groupings—conservative, monarchic, and middle class—were also, with similar sharpness, competing for the support of individual citizens.

In effect, the appearance of revolutionary workers' parties in Europe "achieved the result of structuring the political system as a means of expression of social conflict," as the French social theorist Marcel Gauchet has observed, stressing a paradox: "Democratic society, at its most profound, is one of conflict, but one in which there is no one who does not dream of social unity (however they may conceive of it)."

III

SURVEYING THE STATE of European politics in 1847, Giuseppe Mazzini celebrated "the democratic tendency of our times, the upward

movement of the popular classes, who desire to have their share in political life," as "a page of the world's destiny, written by the finger of
God." The reference to God wasn't metaphorical. Mazzini believed that he,
along with his fellow democrats, were "labouring that the development
of human society may be, as far as possible, in the likeness of the divine society":

> The law of God has not two weights and two measures:
> Christ came for all: he spoke to all; he died for all. We cannot
> logically declare the children of God to be equal before God
> and unequal before men. We cannot wish our immortal spirit
> to abjure on earth that gift of liberty which is the source of
> good and evil in our actions . . . We protest, then, against
> all inequality, against all oppression, wheresoever it is
> practised; for we acknowledge no foreigners; we recognize only
> the just and the unjust . . . This forms the essence of what men
> have agreed to call the *democratic movement*.

Mazzini had been born in the Republic of Genoa in 1805, a decade before the Congress of Vienna dissolved the venerable city-state
and awarded all of its territory to the Kingdom of Sardinia. Since the
golden age of the Northern Italian city-states of the fifteenth and sixteenth centuries, the Italian-speaking peoples inhabiting the Apen-
nine Peninsula had been subordinated by neighbouring nation-states,
its different regions carved up among Spain, France, and Austria. Its
peoples lived at the mercy of outside forces, without any right to self-
determination, or, in most places at most times, any share of political
power.

The child of a Jacobin father and a Jansenist mother, Mazzini tried
to reconcile the democratic principles of his father with the austere
faith of his mother, coming to champion a distinctive view of the modern democratic movement. Instead of zealously defending the political
principles of Rousseau or the economic programme of communists like
Marx, he came to view modern democracy in much loftier terms: as the

advent of a new form of life, organized around a redemptive new social gospel of shared duties and just institutions that might, through concerted action, exalt all human beings within a global community of independent nations, uniting humankind in a living, universal faith, reborn in a "Rome of the People" (not of the pope). Mazzini illustrates perfectly how many modern democratic movements toward self-government had, in fact, become inseparable from explicitly *national* movements toward the collective self-determination of a people with unique shared customs and beliefs.

In 1827, Mazzini had travelled to Tuscany and joined the Carbonari, a secret network of revolutionaries active in Italy in the first decades of the nineteenth century. In this way he first met Filippo (aka Philippe) Buonarroti. A Pisan noble (and a distant relative of Michelangelo), Buonarroti had participated in various insurrections during the French Revolution, surviving to write the classic chronicle *Babeuf's Conspiracy for Equality*. He was a living link between the Paris Commune of 1792 and the British Chartists, the German communists, and the militants in the Carbonari, one of the many conspiratorial groups of young men he organized in these years, as sleeper cells ready to impose an ideal democracy, by force if necessary.

Buonarroti initiated Mazzini into the romance of secret societies. But the older man was wary of his new recruit's passion for religious rhetoric. Mazzini in turn rejected Buonarroti's glorification of violence. In 1831, Mazzini broke away to found his own secret society, Young Italy, which took as its motto "God and the People." Its primary goal was to unite Italy as "One, Independent, Free Republic." Mazzini also hoped that a democratic revolt in Italy might trigger a European-wide wave of insurrections that would produce a league of democratic nations with its capital in Rome.

By the time Mazzini published his essay on democracy in Europe, he had been arrested, served time in prison, and then moved from Geneva to Marseille before settling in London. There he met the other exiled democrats and revolutionaries of his day from Poland, Germany, and Russia. The hopes of this saving remnant were quickened by the outbreak of revolution in Sicily in January 1848, followed by a spectacular series of democratic revolts demanding universal manhood suffrage in Paris, in Berlin, in Vienna—and finally in Rome, where Mazzini was made a citizen and welcomed as a patriotic hero a few weeks after the pope had fled and a new Roman republic had been declared.

The new republic didn't last long. At the behest of the pope, France sent troops to conquer the city. The other democratic revolts, almost all of them demanding the creation of representative political institutions, had met similar fates, in part because it had become clear that most people didn't yearn for democracy, as Mazzini did, as a sacred end in itself; nor was there any evidence, as he fervently believed, that the democratic movements of his day formed "a page of the world's destiny, written by the finger of God." In Italy and elsewhere after the optimism of the European Spring of 1848 there stood restored monarchies almost everywhere. Only in France, where all men in 1848 were granted the right to vote after a protracted struggle in the wake of the French Revolution over the extent and terms of the franchise, did universal manhood suffrage survive.

Mazzini, in defeat more famous than ever, returned to London and continued to write and speak out on behalf of the democratic cause, elaborating his distinctively edifying social views, much to the irritation of critics like Marx and Engels, who deplored his pious idealism. Mazzini in turn attacked Marx and Engels for their naïve conviction that a baptism by violence might create an emancipated new world of peace and harmony. Mazzini instead imagined a great evolutionary expansion in the capacity of the human species "to have more love, more feeling for the beautiful, the great, and the true . . . Democracy says to us—'If you wish to attain it, let man commune as intimately as possible with the greatest possible number of his fellows.'"

III

IN THE AFTERMATH of the abortive revolts of 1848, the European democratic movements, already divided, began to fracture further. Undaunted in defeat, republican insurrectionists like Blanqui continued to work toward the violent overthrow of the old order. More moderate insurrectionists like Mazzini eschewed civil war in principle, hoping, after a brief popular revolt, to form a new republic peacefully around a common language and a quasi-religious faith in universal brotherhood. Marx and his followers accepted the need for a revolutionary uprising but stressed the need to educate the working class, and also to create a new international organization, so that workers of the world could learn from one another and find ways to coordinate a global class struggle. In between these poles stood a variety of other political tendencies and parties: some national democratic republican parties broadly shared the political aims of Blanqui and Mazzini but rejected their recourse to secret societies and insurrection. In stark contrast, anarchist groups rejected the creation of a new republic in principle, with some, inspired by the French theorist Proudhon, organized around plans for associations of small producers that would supplant the centralized state, while others, led by Mikhail Bakunin, embraced revolutionary violence as the only means to destroy the state and inaugurate a communist association of spontaneously interacting free and equal individuals.

In 1864, Marx, along with Blanqui, Bakunin, and followers of Proudhon, established the first International Working Men's Association. Meanwhile, newly created national trade unions tried to win material gains for their members, and various socialist parties tried to win seats in their country's national assemblies, in order to introduce legislation to realize more egalitarian political, social, and economic arrangements.

The tensions among these different aspects of the social democratic movement of the last half of the nineteenth century were manifold. Nationalist sentiments were stirred by popular demands for self-determination and the emergence of viable nation-states with increasingly more broad-based representative political institutions. Republicans, some Jacobins in France, and Giuseppe Mazzini defined democracy not as "the mere liberty of all," as Mazzini wrote, "but Government freely consented to by all, and acting for all." They hoped to create legitimate republics with universal manhood suffrage and freely chosen leaders who might help a sovereign people form "a common union in pursuit of a common object." Cosmopolitan ideals waxed and waned as efforts to build transnational forms of solidarity had to compete with more local attachments. Some democrats were focused, like Mazzini, on creating the best possible national constitution, with sturdy political institutions; others wanted ultimately to destroy the modern state as incompatible with true self-government. The anarchists suggested eschewing all forms of institutional authority, and Marx and his followers also anticipated that the state would eventually disappear—but only after a transitional period, when the powers of the state would be mercilessly deployed to root out the enemies of a free society.

III

ALMOST ALL OF these political tendencies were represented in the most significant democratic uprising in Europe in the late-nineteenth century, the Paris Commune of 1871—the accidental outcome of a misguided military campaign.

In 1870, Bonaparte III, emperor of the French since 1852, had been goaded into war by the Prussian chancellor Bismarck, who used the war to consolidate a unified German nation-state. When news reached Paris that Bonaparte and some eighty thousand French soldiers had surrendered to the Germans on September 2, 1870, a popular uprising in Paris led to the collapse of Bonaparte's Second Empire, the declaration of the Third French Republic, and the creation of a new Government of National Defence. The city's National Guard was mobilized and armed to help defend the capital; as had happened in 1792 and 1848, Paris became a hotbed of radical democratic agitation.

That autumn, German forces encircled Paris—at the time the largest city in continental Europe, with almost two million inhabitants—cutting off its access to food and other supplies. With Paris on the brink of starvation, and followers of Blanqui inside the city threatening insurrection, the Government of National Defence signed an armistice with Prussia in the Hall of Mirrors at Versailles on January 26, 1871, with special terms for Paris: the Germans would not occupy the capital, nor would the National Guard be immediately disarmed, in hopes of preserving law and order in the City of Lights.

A new provisional French republican government was formed, led by Adolphe Thiers, the historian and veteran liberal politician. On February 8, 1871, a national election (in which all male citizens could vote) returned a conservative majority to the new French National Assembly, then meeting at Versailles. Meanwhile, Thiers negotiated with the Parisian National Guard to surrender the cannon that still commanded the heights of Montmartre and Belleville.

In the national election, the capital as a whole had favoured mainly moderate republicans. But the situation was tense, with thousands of decommissioned soldiers roaming the streets of Paris looking for food and shelter. A good many Parisians detested the terms of the armistice Thiers had signed. Fearing for their safety, a number of wealthy families decamped to the countryside. And the National Guard refused the new government's request to turn over their arms.

In the early hours of March 18, the Versailles government ordered a sneak attack on the city's cannon. Government troops quickly gained control of the ordnance but had to wait for teams of horses to haul the cannon away. As they waited, the sun rose over Montmartre and Belleville, and residents awoke to platoons of heavily armed soldiers on their doorsteps. One eyewitness, Prosper-Olivier Lissagaray, described what happened next:

Women were the first to act. Those of the 18th March, hardened by the siege—they had had a double ration of misery—did not wait for the men. They surrounded the machineguns, apostrophized the sergeant in command of the gun, saying, "This is shameful; what are you doing there?" The soldiers did not answer. Occasionally a non-commissioned officer spoke to them: "Come, my good women, get out of the way." At the same time a handful of National

Guards, proceeding to the post of the Rue Doudeauville, there found two drums that had not been smashed, and beat the rappel. At eight o'clock they numbered 300 officers and guards, who ascended the Boulevard Ornano. They met a platoon of soldiers of the 88th, and, crying, *Vive la République!* enlisted them to defect from the government and join the people. The troops fraternized everywhere with the crowds that had collected at the first alarm. By eleven o'clock the people had vanquished the aggressors at all points, preserved almost all their cannon, of which only ten had been carried off, and seized thousands of chassepots. All their battalions were now on foot, and the men of the faubourgs commenced unpaving the streets.

Barricades of cobblestones sprang up as crowds of people streamed toward the Hôtel de Ville to celebrate joyously. Here was a moment when, as one participant later put it, a "great and sublime movement" had appeared, causing those swept up in it to "break out of their habits and set their sights on a new ideal." People from every walk of life suddenly found themselves transformed into a delirious community of equals. "One returns from such exaltations as one would awake from a dream, but what remains is the exquisite memory of a moment of intoxication; you've had the illusion of fraternity!"

The provisional government of Thiers ordered its troops to retreat. The next day, the National Guard Central Committee announced elections in Paris to form a new city government. Thus began the Paris Commune of 1871—the fruit of an adventitious uprising.

But from the start, the leaders of the Commune faced a virtually impossible challenge as they tried simultaneously to form a new municipal government, draft new policies to regulate the economy and society, and raise an armed force able to wage and win a civil war with a hostile but duly elected provisional government. There was also a continuing threat of Prussian intervention, should circumstances deteriorate.

Paris held elections on March 26 for delegates to a new Council of the Commune. The results reflected a city divided. Only about half of the electorate turned out, in part because some supporters of the provisional government chose to boycott the vote, while others had already fled the city.

The newly elected council members held predictably conflicting views. Anarchists opposed to the very existence of government favoured a federation of local assemblies and municipal autonomy; socialists demanded that a strengthened central city government promptly implement various social and economic reforms; Jacobins, led by followers of Blanqui (who was still alive but had been placed under arrest by Thiers), wanted a crackdown on traitors and a total mobilization to prepare for civil war.

At one of the first meetings of the Commune council, the delegates solemnly agreed that it was undemocratic to call someone a "minister of war," so that person became, officially, "citizen delegate to the Ministry of War." The Commune gloried in such purely symbolic gestures: on April 7, National Guardsmen burned a guillotine at the Place Voltaire. New radical journals appeared in profusion—even as the Commune banned *Le Figaro* and other mainstream papers. Political clubs and local assemblies proliferated, each one claiming to be a direct expression of popular sovereignty. Meanwhile, service in the National Guard became compulsory for men between nineteen and forty years old.

If any one figure could be said to typify the sanguinary bravado of the Commune's most militant leaders, it would be Raoul Rigault, killed in the course of events, and almost instantly the subject of a short biography, *Raoul Rigault, Public Prosecutor*, published in 1871 under the rubric *Celebrities of the Commune*.

Born into a prosperous Parisian family in 1846, Rigault had been kicked out of both his home and an elite *lycée* by the time he was twenty-one. He became a free-floating *bon vivant* and troublemaker, well-known to the other habitués of bohemian Paris. Fancying himself a ruthless radical democrat in the style of the Enragés, he made a fetish of adopting the airs of a latter-day sans-culotte. He addressed everyone he met as *citoyen* or *citoyenne*. He joined the International Working Men's Association. A political brawler, he also had a Rabelaisian appetite for food, drink, and sex. He relished saying things like "God is the absurd," and sometimes ended drunken disputations with a dramatic flourish: "I am going to have you shot!"

On the morning of March 18, as the people of Paris were resisting the armed forces of Versailles, Rigault, characteristically, was in bed, sleeping off a late night of food and drink. Waking to the glad tidings of revolt, he raced off to the prefecture of police, where he had long planned to install himself, come the revolution. Enchanted by the idea of forming a secret society of insurrectionists, and accustomed to being tailed by the secret police of the Second Empire, Rigault had made a close study of their methods, in hopes of someday turning their techniques against them.

That afternoon, Rigault, acting on no authority but his own, issued an order to release all political prisoners. Ten days later, and after the new prefect had already issued arrest warrants for hundreds of people, the Commune formally appointed Rigault "civil delegate for general security." He promptly created eighty neighbourhood police offices and hired a large number of new agents to surveil and unmask traitors and spies. In the following days, Rigault and his friends filled Paris prisons with more than three thousand people accused of working for Versailles. At night, the prosecutor frequented the brothels and brasseries of the Left Bank. He became legendary for his outlandish tabs (one breakfast after a long night supposedly consisted of two fine Burgundies and *Chateaubriand aux truffes*).

Rigault's political enemies bristled at his conduct—but to no avail. "We are not dispensing justice," Rigault snapped at one critic. "We are making revolution." In hopes of securing the release of Blanqui from prison, he took hostage the archbishop of Paris. Unable to negotiate an exchange of prisoners, he had the archbishop shot instead. None of these acts were calculated to win the Commune new friends.

WITH LEADERS LIKE RIGAULT, it should come as no surprise that the Paris Commune ended in a bloodbath. The government's armed forces entered Paris with little resistance at the end of May 1871. The troops proceeded district by district, butchering anyone who stood in their way. When Rigault himself was apprehended, he shouted out, "Yes, I am Rigault! Vive la Commune!" An early American history of the Commune recounts what happened next: an "officer shot him with a pistol, and he was riddled with the bullets of the Versailles soldiery. The body was pounded and disfigured; one eye protruded; the head was a pulpy mass." By the time the battle had ended, thousands of Communards had been murdered in a massacre, and the heart of Paris was in flames—in a final act of defiant vandalism, the Communards had torched the Tuileries Palace and the Hôtel de Ville.

The Paris Commune may have been doomed from the start—but in defeat it became a paradoxical symbol of a better society still to come. The first and most influential of the writers to hymn its virtues was Karl Marx, in a report commissioned by the Working Men's International. Though his official assignment required that he acknowledge in some way the full range of political views held by members of the International, he did his best to marginalize both the anarchists as well as the part played by fanatics like Rigault.

Marx abhorred the votaries of conspiratorial insurrection— Blanqui, Bakunin, the whole lot. Their secret societies and obsessive scheming offended his core rationalism and his (Hegelian) hope that the sharp, open conflict produced by truly popular social movements would produce, in time, and in the crucible of civil wars, new men and new women, equipped to establish a new world of emancipated, and enlightened, equals.

He claimed to find fresh grounds for these hopes in the Commune's brief existence. It had "supplied the Republic with the basis of really democratic institutions" and—more than that—it was "essentially a working class government, the product of the struggle of the producing against the appropriating classes, the political form at last discovered under which to work out the economic emancipation of labour."

And so it went for the next half century on the revolutionary left. In a pamphlet first published in 1880, the exiled Russian anarchist Pyotr Kropotkin hailed the Commune as inaugurating "a new era in that long series of revolutions whereby the peoples are marching from slavery to freedom. Under the name 'Commune of Paris' a new idea was born, to become the starting point for future revolutions." Writing two generations later, in an article published the day before she was killed in an abortive insurrection in 1919, Rosa Luxemburg, the outspoken German Marxist champion of revolutionary democracy, put it this way: "The Chartist movement in Britain ended in defeat; the uprising of the Parisian proletariat in the June days of 1848 ended with a crushing defeat; and the Paris commune ended with a terrible defeat. The whole road of socialism—so far as revolutionary struggles are concerned—is paved with nothing but thunderous defeats. Yet, at the same time, history marches inexorably, step by step, toward final victory! Where would we be today *without* those 'defeats,' from which we draw historical experience, understanding, power and idealism?"

But there were problems with praising the Commune as (in Marx's words) "a glorious harbinger of a new society."

Such veneration was jarringly at odds with the realism that Marx and other tough-minded radical democrats championed in other contexts. A vaulting idealism might bolster hopes for a better world. But quixotic myth-mongering also encouraged zealots to use self-defeating tactics in quest of unworkable goals, and this would become a defining feature of many modern experiments in radical democracy. Kropotkin was a mild-mannered meliorist in his later years, and Rosa Luxemburg consistently refused to treat democratic principles as a pliable means rather than an end in itself; but Raoul Rigault, inspired by similarly sublime revolutionary ideals, had blithely pursued a destructive and utterly illiberal kind of "totalitarian democracy" that brooked no opposition.

No wonder some thoughtful observers recoiled in horror at the prospect of another democratic revolt like the Paris Commune of 1871.

And yet, ironically, it was, in part, a fear of the violence that radically democratic revolts might unleash that led gradually to a series of democratizing political reforms that spread throughout Europe in the years after the failure of the Paris Commune. In one country after another in Europe, the right to vote for political leaders was gradually extended to more male citizens, and property qualifications were loosened, though at a painfully slow pace. For example, in the United Kingdom, even after the Representation of the Peoples Act of 1884, nearly 40 percent of the male population lacked the franchise—it wasn't until 1918 that all men in England won the right to vote. In Belgium, universal manhood suffrage was granted in 1893; in Austria, in 1896; in Italy, in 1912; and in Russia, Poland, and Hungary only in 1917 or 1918.

In this context, Germany stood out for its relatively early adoption of universal manhood suffrage in 1871, the year Bismarck completed his unification project. Though the government simultaneously outlawed a variety of political groups, including the new country's two existing socialist parties, this was a watershed moment. And in the years that followed, even autocratic Germany cautiously opened up its political arena. The result was a new kind of political pluralism in Europe, premised on a tacit modus vivendi: democrats and autocrats, socialists and laissez-faire liberals, republicans and royalists would all compete for power peacefully, by contesting periodic popular elections to choose legislators and political leaders.

At the same time, a new kind of political institution, unknown to the ancient Greeks, took shape, producing what Hans Kelsen called "one of real democracy's most important elements: *the political party*, which brings like-minded individuals together in order to secure them actual influence in shaping public affairs."

III

THIS WAS AN AREA where the United States led the way, with Andrew Jackson and his successors turning the Democratic Party into a machine for the mass mobilization of voters. As the British scholar James Bryce put it (in the final, 1910 edition of his classic study, *The American*

Commonwealth): "The victories of the ballot box, no less than of the sword, must be won by the cohesion and disciplined docility of troops, and . . . these merits can only be secured by skilful organization and long-continued training."

Around the world, a variety of political groups of various persuasions began to emulate the American Democratic Party. In England, the first mass political party of this type was the National Liberal Federation of Joseph Chamberlain and Francis Schnadhorst, founded in 1877.

On the European continent, other new political parties—some of them avowedly conservative and deeply distrustful of democratic social movements—sprang up in response to the rapid growth of social democratic parties that were geared to producing a mass mobilization of voters sympathetic to the labouring classes. Indeed, recent research suggests that the participation of conservative parties in the electoral arena in this period paradoxically played a central role in *normalizing* representative regimes as they slowly evolved in countries like England and Germany. Throughout Europe, the rise of the party system contributed to a gradual process of democratization, involving the slow expansion of the franchise, the institutionalization of civil liberties, and the emergence of a central government accountable to voters, through either a parliament or a direct vote.

At the same time, social democrats were busy organizing new unions of workers in various industries and creating national federations of labour unions and international federations of labour parties and unions. The first International Working Men's Association had dissolved in acrimony in 1876, in part because of bitter disagreements between the anarchist Bakunin and Karl Marx. But more international congresses soon followed, and by 1891 a new, so-called Second International had appeared, organized around a biennial International Socialist Congress that met until the onset of the Great War in 1914.

It was within this self-consciously global context that German social democracy evolved. In order to resist the government's crackdown on socialist ideas and organizations, two German socialist groups, the

Social Democratic Labour Party, led by disciples of Karl Marx, and the General German Workers' Association, founded thirteen years earlier by Ferdinand Lassalle, in 1875 united to form the Socialist Workers Party, soon renamed the Social Democratic Party of Germany (or SPD, which still exists).

To start, the new party was most strongly influenced by the views of Lassalle, who had founded the Workers' Association in 1863. Seeing no contradiction between democratic and socialist goals, and trying to work within legal limits, Lassalle had hoped to expedite the creation of producer cooperatives through an expansion of suffrage to include previously disenfranchised workers. But Lassalle himself did not live to see the unification of Germany's two socialist parties—he had died in a duel a decade earlier.

Watching the merger from London, Marx was livid at Lassalle's posthumous influence on the so-called Gotha Program that the new, unified party had adopted in 1875. Privately heaping scorn on the platform, Marx scored its many political demands as naïve, containing "nothing beyond the old democratic litany familiar to all: universal suffrage, direct legislation, popular rights, a people's militia, etc."—a bizarre complaint, given the state's attempts to thwart socialist organizations and the lack in Germany in 1875 of direct legislation and popular rights, never mind a people's militia. At the same time, and in this fraught context, Marx reiterated his mature view that capitalism was in the midst of destroying itself, and that this would inevitably lead to "a political transition period in which the state can be nothing but *the revolutionary dictatorship of the proletariat.*"

Marx seemed unable, or unwilling, to appreciate the actual political context in Germany—or to understand that the Gotha Program was not a partisan broadside like the *Communist Manifesto* but rather a pragmatic platform meant to attract the broadest possible support for a party that hoped to win parliamentary elections. Nor did Engels help to clarify matters fifteen years later, when he decided to publish Marx's hitherto private notes on the Gotha Program, as well as republish *The Civil War in France* with a new introduction that concluded by endorsing the idea of a transitional dictatorship: "Gentlemen, do you want to know what this dictatorship looks like? Look at the Paris Commune. That was the Dictatorship of the Proletariat."

Having to contend with hallowed texts like these left the German Social Democratic Party in a bind. By 1891, when Engels endorsed the idea of (temporary) dictatorship, the German party had become avowedly "Marxist" and "revolutionary" in its orientation, a response in part to the government's efforts to suppress it. But at the same time, its power as an electoral party was rapidly growing: in the 1871 Reichstag election, 124,000 Germans voted for the two socialist parties. In 1877, the united party got 493,000; under repression, the total fell to 312,000 in 1881; but thereafter growth was steady: from 550,000 votes in 1884 to 763,000 in 1887, to 1,429,000 in 1891, and so on. By 1912, the Social Democrats were Germany's largest political party.

In order to attract members and mobilize popular support in election campaigns, the Social Democrats, like other political parties in this period, had found it helpful to create a structured organization, with party leaders whipping members into a disciplined parliamentary unit. But the German Social Democratic Party became renowned for the unrivalled efficiency of its operation. "A neatly structured hierarchy of professional politicians managed the party," as one historian has put it, "by a huge apparatus extending from the party executive at the top to the shop leaders and block leaders at the bottom." In effect, party leaders aspired to duplicate the command and control structure of the German army inside the wider social democratic movement.

This hierarchical organization, especially in a context where all orthodox Marxists paid lip service to a transitional "dictatorship," raised questions about the relationship between means and ends—and also about the relationship between the party's rhetoric and its real political form. Should a party that advocated democracy organize itself democratically? Did it matter if its rhetoric was revolutionary while its policies were reformist?

These discrepancies were a subject of Eduard Bernstein's 1899 *The Preconditions of Socialism and the Tasks of Social Democracy*. After reviewing the economic situation and the party's actual activities, Bernstein concluded that its brand of socialism was in fact evolutionary, not "revolutionary," and that its political structure was similarly pragmatic and well suited for campaigning to achieve parliamentary power. This was just as well, as capitalism was pretty clearly *not* going to self-destruct as Marx and Engels had forecast, but rather continue evolving in unpredictable ways.

Bernstein's heresy was swiftly reproved by various party grandees, most notably Rosa Luxemburg, who castigated Bernstein as an "opportunist" in her 1900 polemic, *Reform or Revolution*. Unlike Marx in 1875, Luxemburg refrained from sneering at "the old democratic litany." On the contrary, she emphatically agreed with Bernstein on the importance of the movement's democratic aims: "He who would strengthen democracy should want to strengthen and not weaken the socialist movement." But she just as strenuously rejected Bernstein's renunciation of the idea of a heroic, transformative revolutionary class struggle as a key precondition for social democracy: "He who renounces the struggle for socialism renounces both the labour movement and democracy."

These stirring sentiments were widely shared within the German Social Democratic Party. But it was far from obvious that the party itself, as it had developed by 1900, truly adhered *either* to a revolutionary strategy, *or* to democratic norms.

III

IN 1905, events in Russia abruptly transformed the debate over democracy and revolution within the German social democratic movement. The year had begun, dramatically enough, with a massacre in St. Petersburg, when police fired on a peaceful demonstration. The protesters' demands—a democratically elected constituent assembly, civil liberties for all citizens, an eight-hour working day—fell short of asking for the tsar to step down, but their implications, in the context of the country's rigid autocracy, were explosive.

In the months that followed, thousands of citizens in Russia's cities flocked to join a variety of political parties and newly formed associations, including a Union of Unions formed out of existing professional associations, and an All-Russia Peasants' Union. Actions taken included the circulation of petitions, peaceful demonstrations, labour strikes, peasant revolts, mutinies in the military, and armed insurrections in some cities and regions.

After months of inconclusive turmoil, the protesters in late summer began to converge on a common strategy—a general strike. It was, as one historian remarked, "a classic example of a momentous historical event that developed spontaneously."

It began when a group of printers called a strike in Moscow on September 20. Their shop was near the university, so students joined them. Police intervened, and barricades were built. The printers of Moscow formed a municipal council of worker delegates to coordinate strike activity. Protesters became defiant. The army shot ten of them. In response, printers in St. Petersburg staged a strike of their own. Meanwhile, a newly formed Central Bureau of the All-Russian Union of Railroad Employees and Workers called for a strike of all railway workers, to start on October 4. Within a week, service into Moscow ground to a halt, snarling transport throughout the empire.

The Russian socialist parties and most of the revolutionary activists had been on the sidelines so far, deeming the democratic programme of the strikers insufficiently radical, calling, as it did, for an amnesty for all strikers, a guarantee of political freedom, and the convocation of a legislative assembly elected on the basis of universal suffrage. Despite their indifference, the strike movement had by then developed momentum. First in St. Petersburg, and then in Moscow, it attracted not only industrial labourers and railroad workers but also telegraph operators, salesmen, the actors of the Imperial Theatres, municipal workers, even bank tellers. Students skipped classes. Doctors quit seeing patients. The Mariinsky Ballet stopped dancing.

"Neither gas nor electric lights work," a Moscow newspaper reported on October 16. "The movement of trams, either horse-drawn or electrical ones, has not resumed. The telegraph system, telephones, and post offices do not work. A majority of the stores are closed." Food was scarce, and water was only sporadically available. Law and order began to break down—and virtually every city in Russia was affected.

Observers had long wondered what might happen in such circumstances. In the run-up to the French Revolution, the French economist the Comte de Mirabeau had warned fellow aristocrats of his day against irritating "this people which produces everything and which to make itself formidable has only to become motionless." Like some other advocates of the democratic control of industry by workers (who in France were called "syndicalists"), the French philosopher Georges Sorel had enthusiastically endorsed the idea of a vast general strike—at least he championed the "myth" of such a confrontation, though he was characteristically lukewarm about the general strike that had actually occurred in Russia, considering it too timid and exclusively political in its demands.

Workers on the ground in Russia took a quite different view of developments in the autumn of 1905—and so, belatedly, did the various radical parties. In this case, one wing of the Russian Social Democratic Party, the Mensheviks, turned the moderate demand for democratic reforms into a call for "revolutionary self-government." At the height of the general strike, they sent a cadre of their organizers into factories, in hopes of persuading workers to elect radical deputies to a citywide assembly, one deputy for every five hundred workers. Within a few days, 562 deputies had been chosen, the majority of them metalworkers, though a number of textile workers participated, along with deputies from a variety of other industries.

On October 17, the new group met in the building of the Free Economic Society, elected a provisional executive committee, and formally named itself *Sovet rabocich deputatov* (Soviet of Workers' Deputies). "Soviet" is the Russian word for "council," and the new body was, in effect, a strike committee, meant to coordinate the activities of the movement in St. Petersburg.

The same day, coincidentally, the tsar, reluctantly, under pressure from his closest advisers, agreed to issue a public statement, the so-called October Manifesto. This vowed, among other things, "to grant the population the unshakeable foundations of civic freedom based on the principles of real personal inviolability, freedom of conscience, speech, assembly, and union." When the imperial decree was published on October 18, it was greeted with jubilation and widespread relief—but it was too little, too late.

Emboldened, the leaders of the Petersburg soviet on October 19 proclaimed freedom of the press, and also announced that workers would print only uncensored newspapers. They also announced (without a trace of irony) that official publications (which were subject to government censorship) would be banned and that newsstands that sold such papers would be destroyed.

No longer needed to coordinate a strike, the Petersburg soviet became a general assembly of the city's workers, who debated and passed resolutions on a variety of political issues. Nothing like it had existed before in Russia. Swept along by the passion of the deputies and the rhetoric of an increasingly militant executive committee led by a spell-binding young Menshevik orator, Leon Trotsky, the soviet prepared for an armed confrontation with the government.

In the words of another Menshevik, "We were certain in our hearts that defeat was inevitable. But we were all young and seized with revolutionary enthusiasm and to us it seemed better to perish in a struggle than to be paralyzed without even engaging in one. *The honour of the Revolution was at stake.*"

The air went out of this balloon on December 3, when the police arrested the leaders of the Petersburg soviet, as part of a broader clampdown on dissident activities throughout Russia. Street fighting erupted in Petersburg and then Moscow, but by mid-December, armed government reinforcements had arrived to restore order in both cities. By the time the uprisings were crushed, thousands of people had died, entire neighbourhoods had been reduced to rubble, whole villages laid waste—and almost every single socialist leader was either in jail or in exile.

III

THE PETERSBURG SOVIET may have been doomed from the start—but in defeat it joined the Paris Commune as an icon of "revolutionary self-government."

What had begun as an ad hoc response to a local challenge had become, by 1906, a new focus for the hopes of radical democrats and socialists around the world—and a fresh demonstration of the potentially transformative power of self-governing trade unions, controlled by ordinary workers.

As even Eduard Bernstein had acknowledged, unions had the potential to be uniquely democratizing forms of association, especially when they were in conflict with industries that were organized hierarchically. For some anarchists and syndicalists, both in Germany and France, militant union activism seemed to offer a way of life with its own *élan vital* and distinctive goal of forging a new form of industrial democracy. For such people, the idea of the general strike became one way of imagining a bold alternative to both pusillanimous parliamentary manoeuvring and to rigid trade union discipline.

In Russia, the two major wings of the Social Democratic Party scrambled to adjust. In November 1905, the Menshevik wing of the Russian Social Democratic Workers' Party held a conference to take stock and to decide how the governance of the party might be revised to dovetail more closely with the soviet aspiration to "revolutionary self-government." The Mensheviks (from the Russian word for minority), like their rivals, the Bolsheviks (from the Russian word for majority), both belonged to an outlawed party, forced to operate in secrecy. But buoyed by the apparent success of the Petersburg soviet, the Mensheviks passed a resolution at their conference that autumn, stating that "the Russian Social Democratic Workers Party must be organized according to the principle of democratic centralism." The resolution went on to specify that all party officials at all levels were to be chosen in open elections and hold office for a limited period, subject to recall. At the same time, the decisions of the party executive were to be binding on local party units, in this way reconciling democratic accountability with a clear locus of centralized authority.

A month later, the Bolsheviks followed suit, declaring, "The principle of democratic centralism is beyond dispute." This came as a surprise, since the Bolsheviks' leader, Lenin, had previously advocated a party structure that was closer to the conspiratorial secret societies favoured by Blanqui than to anything imagined by Karl Marx or the German Social Democrats.

In Germany, the political situation was complicated by a divergence between the official views of the party leaders and the views of the trade union members affiliated with it. The party leaders almost universally expressed their fealty to the revolutionary catechism of Karl Marx. The vast majority of union members wanted to improve their material well-being—not risk it in an uprising.

A trade-union congress held in Cologne in the spring of 1905 had rejected the general strike as a tactic and even proscribed any discussion of it. Yet a few months later, at a party congress held in Jena in the autumn of 1905, in the midst of the ferment in St. Petersburg, the party itself cautiously endorsed the use of a "mass work stoppage under certain circumstances." At the same time, the leadership took pains to dissociate the new policy explicitly from events in Russia, which were "so abnormal" that they should not serve as any kind of model for Germany.

Rosa Luxemburg emphatically disagreed. As she argued in her 1906 pamphlet, *The Mass Strike, the Political Party, and the Trade Unions*, a "spontaneous," self-organizing association of activists had achieved radical results in Russia with aggressively direct action and an unflinching willingness to countenance the use of violence, all without executing a plan handed down to them by party leaders. Describing the dynamics of what she called a "Mass Strike" (in order to distinguish it as sharply as possible from the kind of disciplined demonstrations favoured by moderate socialists, as well as the kind of "general strike" championed by anarcho-syndicalists and already disavowed by the German trade unions), she sought to justify it on impeccably Marxist grounds: in Russia, the Mass Strike had aroused, and helped to enlighten, workers in the most productive way possible, through confrontation and conflict.

Without encouraging self-governing workers to rise to the occasion in such historic moments, the Social Democratic Party and its affiliated trade unions were in danger of creating a bureaucratic structure that produced collective passivity, as workers became accustomed to following orders rather than seizing opportunities. Instead, social democrats, in Luxemburg's own words, should take heart from "the living picture of a genuine movement of the people, rising with elemental might out of the political situation and the extreme sharpening of class antagonisms, and unleashing itself in tempestuous mass struggles and mass strikes, political as well as economic."

Luxemburg's text had been commissioned by socialists in Hamburg, in hopes of influencing the resolutions of the next party congress, convened on September 23, 1906, in Mannheim.

Nothing of the sort occurred. On the contrary: bowing to unrelenting pressure from the trade union rank and file, the Mannheim congress tacitly revoked the party's previous support for the tactic of the Mass Strike.

Watching these events unfold, a young party member and German correspondent for the French syndicalist journal *Mouvement socialiste*, Robert Michels, reacted with bitter sarcasm. "The feeble embryo of the general strike has been killed off," Michels reported from Mannheim. "The remnants of Marxism have been debased, despised, degraded to a life of boorish laziness."

III

ROBERT MICHELS WAS perhaps the most acute observer of the European social democratic movements at the start of the twentieth century. For him, as for most of his allies and fellow travellers, whether reformists or revolutionaries, socialism was synonymous with democracy. Yet once Michels began to document the actual practices of the actually existing German Social Democratic Party, he felt that only one conclusion was possible: an institution ostensibly dedicated to the spread of democracy in all areas of social life was in fact controlled by a torpid bureaucracy run by a tiny elite, offering proof of what Michels, in a controversial series of scholarly monographs, and then a book, called "the iron law of oligarchy."

Michels was born in 1876 to a prosperous family imbued with a cosmopolitan reverence for other cultures, particularly the French. His career was international: he studied not only in Germany (in Berlin, Munich, Leipzig, and Halle, where he received a doctorate in history) but also in Paris. In Turin, Italy, he joined the Partito Socialista Italiano and became active in its syndicalist faction (he later wrote articles for the Italian syndicalist journal *Il Divenire Social*). Unable to get a teaching job in Germany because he was a socialist, he moved to Italy in 1907 and joined the faculty at the University of Turin. There he came into contact with Gaetano Mosca and Vilfredo Pareto, Italian scholars both renowned for their studies of elites, and their conclusion that a tiny minority of business and political leaders wield power regardless of a state's ostensibly democratic political practices.

At the same time, Michels had become friends with Max Weber, the era's greatest social scientist. As a result of their correspondence from 1906 to 1915, we have a priceless record of how two astute observers viewed the modern struggle for political and social equality, and the divergent ways they evaluated its prospects.

At the time they met, Weber had recently published "The Protestant Ethic and the 'Spirit' of Capitalism," his best-known essay. In this highly speculative work, Weber argued that the spread of religious asceticism was paradoxically associated with the rise, in the West, not just of the naked pursuit of wealth, especially in the United States, but also of a civilization that had become mechanical and "fossilized." Fearful of a future he nevertheless believed to be unavoidable, Weber was fascinated by the fierce democratic convictions of his young syndicalist friend, whose hopes for a revolutionary new form of self-government were so different from his own jaundiced views about the inevitable centrality of domination in human affairs. He encouraged

Michels to document the situation inside the German Social Democratic Party and helped him to get his essays published in the prestigious journal Weber coedited, *Archiv für Sozialwissenschaft und Sozialpolitik* (Archives of Social Science and Social Policy).

The German Social Democratic Party as described by Michels exemplified two trends that Weber had highlighted in his own work: the increasing power of bureaucracy and the tendency of leaders to dominate those they led. Both tendencies had already been documented a few years earlier in the case of the American Democratic and British Liberal parties by the French sociologist Moisey Y. Ostrogorski. About the general trends and basic facts, Michels and Weber scarcely disagreed; their argument was almost entirely over how to *evaluate* them.

Michels upheld a Rousseauian ideal of democracy and assumed that a just society should be a direct democracy insofar as possible. Even though he acknowledged that such a norm was an ideal, rather than achievable in practice, he insisted, as Rousseau had in the final pages of *Émile*, that adhering to the ideal was the only way a just soul could preserve its autonomy and ethical independence in a world full of unjust institutions.

Weber disagreed, and explained why in a remarkable letter he sent to Michels on August 4, 1908. "Such notions as 'will of the people' and 'genuine will of the people' have long since ceased to exist for me; they are *fictions*," he wrote, laying out two possible responses to acknowledging as much.

On the one hand, if someone like Michels nonetheless chooses to adhere stubbornly to such radical democratic ideals, then he must be prepared to embrace "a *revolutionary-ethic*" as uncompromising as those embodied by Christ and Tolstoy ("My kingdom is not of this world").

On the other hand, if someone like Michels instead concedes that his democratic ideals are unrealistic in a modern technological civilization, then he will have to acknowledge as well "the sociological conditions underlying *all* 'technologies,' be they economic, political, or whatever (all of which would find their *most highly developed expression* precisely in collectivist societies)." In that case, Weber continues,

> all talk of revolution is quite farcical. Any thought of abol-
> ishing the domination of man over man by any "socialist"
> social system whatsoever, or by any sophisticated
> form of "democracy" whatsoever, is a *Utopia*. Your
> own critique in this matter does not by any means go far
> enough. The moment anyone who wishes to live as a "modern
> individual," in the sense of having a newspaper every day and
> railways and electric trams, etc., as soon as he gives up the
> position of revolutionary enthusiasm *for its own sake*, that is,
> revolutionary enthusiasm without any goal, indeed
> revolutionary enthusiasm for which no goal is even *conceiv-*
> *able*, he necessarily *renounces* all those ideals which hover
> darkly before *your mind*.

Weber concludes on a note that is both condescending and wryly self-effacing, reassuring Michels that he is "a basically honourable fellow" who will eventually come around to an adult perspective on these matters, even if Weber's realism has "stamped me"—at least in the eyes of his correspondent—"as 'bourgeois.'"

In the years that followed, Michels incorporated some of Weber's critical comments as he completed his book on political parties and refined his notion of an "iron law of oligarchy" that applied to *all* forms of human association. When *Political Parties* was published in 1911, he dedicated the book to Weber.

But at no point did he, nor could he, abjure his democratic convictions. As Weber only partially understood, democracy was for Michels not a fiction but an inviolable matter of faith, precisely in Martin Luther's sense ("Here I stand, I can do no other").

Weber himself would subsequently rethink his own views on modern democracy, in part by analysing a feasible type of modern regime that he classified as a *"Führerdemokratie"* (leadership democracy), which he associated with a form of plebiscitary executive rule that had first appeared in the United States (Andrew Jackson is an early example). These were demagogues who could surmount the bureaucratic tendencies of the parties they led, and inspire large masses of people to believe that they were united in a common cause, even if, in fact, the relationship between leader and led was one of pure domination. In effect, Weber could see the advantage of handing effective political power in avowed democracies to shrewd demagogues, just as Athens had handed power to Pericles, who was able, according to Thucydides, to harness productively the otherwise dangerous passions of unruly and uninformed citizens.

The views of Michels evolved, too, in even more convoluted ways, in the years that followed the appearance of *Political Parties*. One of the ironies of the evolution of the German Social Democratic Party was the way the most radical adherents of revolutionary self-government found themselves isolated from the rank-and-file party members. The radical democrats of the SPD de facto constituted an elite, a kind of puritan political elect, not unlike the Jacobin vanguard that had seized power for itself in the Parisian insurrection of May 31, 1793, electing in this way to keep alive democratic ideals that were being resisted by feckless, ignorant masses: the pious peasantry in the French case; the obdurate union workers in Germany. Michels had experienced this painful paradox firsthand at the Mannheim party conference in 1906.

Later, living in Italy, he had witnessed the rise of Mussolini and his Fascist Party. And like many other anarcho-syndicalists (including his former French comrade in arms, Georges Sorel), he was now drawn to the Fascist experiment, perhaps seeing in it what Sorel had seen in the French syndicalists, that is, "a willing minority," a revolutionary community of latter-day saints, fervently devoted to an ideal of revolutionary self-government and "the myth of the general strike."

In his lectures in the 1920s on political sociology, Michels suggested that Weberian categories, such as "charismatic legitimacy," were an apt way to describe the highly emotional trust in a leader that

Mussolini, for example, inspired. By then, Michels himself had joined the Fascist Party, convinced that a charismatic leader like Il Duce could help counteract the bureaucratic inertia of normal politics, and in this way advance the struggle for political and social equality, by inspiring the otherwise docile masses of ordinary citizens to follow his muscular lead.

He may even have agreed with the Italian philosopher Giovanni Gentile, Mussolini's minister of public education, who declared "the Fascist State" to be "a people's state, and, as such, *the democratic State par excellence*. The relationship between the State and citizen (not this or that citizen, but all citizens) is accordingly so intimate that the State exists only as, and in so far as, the citizen causes it to exist. Its formation therefore is the formation of a consciousness of it in individuals, in the masses."

III

MORE THAN A HUNDRED YEARS after Condorcet had drafted the world's first democratic constitution, no nation in the world (with the possible exception of the United States, according to some observers) was any closer to realizing the democratic and radically egalitarian ideals that Condorcet had fought for. The French Revolution had ended in defeat, the Chartist movement had ended in defeat, and so had the Paris Commune and the Russian general strike of 1905.

If anything, by the time Michels delivered his Italian lectures on political sociology, the tide of modern politics seemed to be running in other directions. Russia had undergone a revolution in 1917—but in the course of it, the Bolsheviks had commandeered the urban soviets, in order to establish a "revolutionary dictatorship of the proletariat and peasantry."

These developments came as no surprise to Robert Michels. He had already chronicled the ebbing of democratic hopes in Germany, and he knew all too well the allure of an avowedly revolutionary vanguard. And yet, he insisted (in a sentiment he never renounced) that the spirit of democracy was, in an almost mystical way, unconquerable and unyielding:

> The democratic currents of history resemble successive waves.
> They break ever on the same shoal. They are ever renewed.
> This enduring spectacle is simultaneously encouraging and
> depressing. When democracies have gained a certain stage of
> development, they undergo a gradual transformation, adopting
> the aristocratic spirit, and in many cases also the aristocratic
> forms, against which at the outset they struggled so fiercely.
> Now new accusers arise to denounce the traitors; after an era
> of glorious combats and of inglorious power, they end by
> fusing with the old dominant class; whereupon once more they
> are in their turn attacked by fresh opponents who appeal to
> the name of democracy. It is probable that this cruel game will
> continue without end.

FIVE

A HALL OF MIRRORS

O N THE EVENING of April 2, 1917, the president of the United States, Woodrow Wilson, addressed a joint session of the House and Senate. In this momentous speech, one of the most carefully wrought and deeply pondered of his political career, Wilson urged Congress to authorize entry into Europe's Great War. He had not reached this resolution lightly. He abhorred the wages of war and had run for re-election in 1916 as an antiwar candidate. But the German navy's deployment of submarine torpedo boats to sink ships indiscriminately had forced him, reluctantly, he explained, to change his mind.

Still, far more than the safety of the shipping lanes was at stake, Wilson told Congress. "The world must be made safe for democracy," he declared. The United States "shall fight for the things we have always carried nearest to our hearts—for democracy, for the right of those who submit to authority to have a voice in their own governments, for the rights and liberties of small nations, for a universal dominion of right by such a concert of free peoples as shall bring peace and safety to all nations and make the world itself at last free."

In this pivotal speech, just what did Woodrow Wilson mean by "democracy"?

It is possible to answer this question with some precision because Wilson was an anomaly: a scholar of politics before he became a politician himself, he had written extensively on the subject of democracy, in academic books, in public lectures, and in extensive manuscripts published only posthumously. Not only that: Wilson was astonishingly consistent in the views he held about modern democracy.

Born into an extended family of Presbyterian ministers in 1856, Wilson grew up in the South but spent most of his adult life in the Northeast. A graduate of Princeton College, with a law degree from the University of Virginia, he abandoned his law practice in order to become a college teacher. In 1886, a year after publishing his first book, *Congressional Government*, he received a PhD in the new academic field of political science at Johns Hopkins. Four years later, he became a professor of politics at Princeton, eventually becoming the university's president. (Wilson was the first person with a PhD— and so far the last—to have been elected president of the United States.)

In 1885, shortly after finishing his first book, and while still a student at Johns Hopkins, Wilson produced a rough first draft of an ambitious new book project, which he titled "The Modern Democratic State." At Hopkins he had learned the scholarly approaches to law and politics then prevalent in England and Germany, where an evolutionary, "organic" outlook on social development was in vogue. "Democracy," wrote Wilson in his manuscript, "is, of course, wrongly conceived when treated as merely a body of doctrine. It is a stage of development . . . It is built up by slow habit. Its process is experience, its basis old wont, its meaning national organic oneness and effectual life. It comes, like manhood, as maturity to it is vouchsafed the maturity of freedom and self-control, and no other. It is conduct, and its only stable foundation is character."

Passages like this show the impact on Wilson of evolutionary social theorists, notably the British scholar Henry Sumner Maine. A historian, jurist, and early student of ethnography, Maine had advanced his most famous thesis in 1861 in *Ancient Law*, arguing that society makes steady progress toward a clear goal, and that this goal is a social order based on contract rather than kinship or status: "Starting, as from one terminus of history, in which all the relations of Persons are summed up in the relations of Family, we seem to have steadily moved toward a phase of social order in which all these relations arise from the free agreement of Individuals."

In these years, contradictory claims were being advanced by rival evolutionary social theorists: Karl Marx, for example, attacked Maine's account of progress, arguing that communism, not a market society based on contract, was the final goal of history.

But Maine posed a specific challenge for the young Woodrow Wilson. Like Max Weber a generation later, Henry Maine argued in his *Essays on Popular Government* that democracy was *not*, as so many of his Victorian contemporaries had begun to assume, *the* goal of modern social development. On the contrary, argued Maine, rule by an elite had historically achieved much better results—and would do so as well in modern market societies based on free agreements among individuals.

Maine's *Essays* appeared in late 1885, just as Wilson was setting pen to paper—and he received them as Maine had obviously intended them, as a provocation. Writing to a friend, Wilson explained that he was determined "to answer Sir Henry Maine's 'Popular Government,' by treating modern democratic tendencies from a much more truly historical point of view than he has taken." Though this specific work never appeared in Wilson's lifetime, most of its themes recur in various public lectures, and also in his magnum opus, *The State: Elements of Historical and Practical Politics*, published in 1889.

Wilson's "truly historical point of view" turns out to be astonishingly parochial. What took place in France in 1792—events that rightly preoccupy Maine—Wilson asserts have *nothing* to do with what had occurred in America up to Wilson's own day. "Democracy in Europe," he explains, "has acted always in rebellion, as a destructive force: it can scarcely be said to have, even yet, any period of organic development . . . Democracy in America, on the other hand . . . has had, almost from the first, a truly organic growth. There was nothing revolutionary in its movements"—as if the nation had never undergone a civil war. "It had not to overthrow other polities: it had only to organize itself. It had, not to create, but only to expand self-government"—a statement that applied, implicitly, only to America's white colonists of European ancestry (and not to their slaves, nor to the New World's indigenous peoples).

For Wilson, democracy was not merely a form of government—it was crucially a matter of customs, habits, and acquired instincts of moral responsibility, "that law written in our hearts which makes us conscious of our oneness as a single personality in the great company of nations." And while America's success as a democracy inhered in its specific "experiences as a Teutonic race," the implications were nonetheless universal, as the political experience of the United States laid bare "the general principles which lie at the foundation of all practicable government by the people" and which ought to inform "the present trend of all political development the world over towards democracy."

In Wilson's providential vision, democracy signified a new world, yet to be fully realized, created at first by autonomous, "Teutonic" individuals who were all able to think for themselves; and then similarly enlightened peoples who, following in their footsteps, became capable of self-government; finally forming a concert of democratic nations, each one established through a democratic process of self-determination.

In 1885, Wilson briskly summarized his conception of modern democracy in the form of three consecutive definitions, each one successively lowering the standards for judging a regime democratic.

Democracy "in its most modern sense, as used by practical thinkers of today," he wrote, means "a form of government which secures absolute equality of *status* before the law, and under which the decisive, final control of public affairs rests with the whole body of adult males." By this standard (as Wilson elsewhere acknowledges), the United States has *never* been a true democracy, since at no point in its history to date has final control of public affairs rested with the whole body of adult males, never mind the whole body of adult citizens.

"More briefly," Wilson continued, "it is government by universal popular discussion"—a definition that might appeal to contemporary deliberative democratic theorists, but, again, a standard by which the United States has yet to enjoy a true democracy.

"Most briefly," Wilson concluded, modern democracy "is government by popular opinion."

Here, at last, it seemed that Wilson had hit on a criterion by which the United States of his own and our day might actually count as a democracy. (Like Condorcet a hundred years earlier, Wilson was serenely optimistic about the enlightenment of the public and its opinions, expressing confidence that "practical political education is everywhere spreading and all nations which have not reached are nearing the adult age of their political development.")

If one sets to one side the white supremacist assumptions embedded in this manuscript, democracy as the highest form of political evolution sometimes sounds enticing in Wilson's telling. But he is disarmingly frank about its limits in practice.

For example, though the opinions held by (white) people are notionally sovereign in America, this "sovereignty is of a peculiar sort, unlike the sovereignty of a king, or of a small, easily concerting group of men. It is judicial, not creative. It passes judgment, or gives sanction; it does not direct. It furnishes standards, not policies . . . *The people can only accept the governing act of representatives.* They do not and cannot originate measures of policy; they acquiesce in policy which a few have originated . . . *They do not, in any adequate sense of the word, govern.*"

Wilson is as adamant on this point as the authors of the *Federalist*

Papers had been one hundred years earlier: America is *not* a pure democracy like the one that existed in fourth-century Athens. Nor does democracy in Wilson's view resemble at all the complex network of public assemblies imagined by Condorcet in his democratic draft constitution of 1793.

In fact, as Wilson concedes almost in passing (and apparently unaware that his remark supports, rather than refutes, the views of Henry Sumner Maine), a mature modern democracy must in practice *always* involve "the many led by the few: the minds of the few disciplined by persuading, and masses of men schooled and directed by being persuaded." In other words, Wilson's vision of perfected self-rule is closer to the "natural aristocracy" John Adams preferred than the plebeian democracy of Andrew Jackson.

According to Wilson, the American president ideally shall be the purest embodiment of popular sovereignty, his authority conveyed in eloquent public speeches, his paramount power confirmed by the periodic votes of "the whole body of adult males." Enlightened leaders in Congress, attuned, like the president, to public opinion, will ideally formulate policies that reflect the public's wishes. The proper execution of these policies will require the support of professional civil servants, trained like Wilson in the modern social sciences and with specialized knowledge about various topics (such as healthcare, the administration of justice, foreign affairs, etc.). Besides consenting to be ruled by their chosen representatives, the people in a modern democratic state will also submit to regulation by a distant army of administrators.

On the one hand, this is completely consistent with the form of democracy America had evolved, and even with the principle of popular sovereignty: a people can choose to elect representatives who ask civil servants to enforce the laws they have passed, just as they can elect a president who promises to expand the reach of government by creating new regulatory institutions. On the other hand, such an expansion of bureaucracy may subsequently come to be rejected by voters who regard it as an illicit usurpation of popular sovereignty by unelected experts.

(This is the main reason an American conservative, writing in 2017, could describe Woodrow Wilson as "America's worst and first fascist President.")

III

WOODROW WILSON ENTERED politics relatively late in his life, after serving as president of Princeton University for eight years (from 1902 to 1910). Elected as governor of New Jersey in 1910, he ran as a fresh face for the Democrats in the presidential campaign of 1912, in a four-way contest with the incumbent, William Howard Taft, running as a Republican; Theodore Roosevelt, running as a third-party candidate for the newly formed Progressive Party; and Eugene V. Debs, running as a Socialist. Because Taft and Roosevelt, formerly a Republican, split votes, Wilson won in a landslide, though with only a 42 percent plurality of the popular vote. This election occurred at the height of the progressive movement in America, with both Wilson and Roosevelt explicitly defending democracy as a regenerative force in American politics. In fact, Roosevelt went further than Wilson in his support for direct democracy in the western states, endorsing the initiative, referendum, and recall. These were all electoral devices that enabled voters to circumvent state legislatures by directly proposing laws, directly endorsing or rejecting laws, and directly dismissing elected officials before their term had expired—though Roosevelt cautioned that such remedies "should be used not to destroy representative government, but to correct it when ever it becomes misrepresentative." (Debs in turn went further still, calling for the creation of "an industrial and social democracy," paving the way for the people themselves to "take control of the people's industries.")

In his first term, Wilson took a broad view of his executive powers. He moved swiftly to build up the administrative capacity of the federal government, in part in an effort to limit the power of large corporations and to regulate the conditions under which workers had to labour in the new industrial economy. Wilson persuaded Congress to pass the Federal Reserve Act; the Federal Trade Commission Act; and the

Clayton Antitrust Act, expanding on the Sherman Antitrust Act of 1890. He championed the United States Revenue Act of 1913, which simultaneously lowered tariffs on international trade and reinstated a progressive income tax, in accord with the Sixteenth Amendment to the U.S. Constitution, which enables the federal government to tax income without having to raise the revenue on an equal per capita basis from each state. In keeping with his convictions about the superiority of the "Teutonic race," he oversaw a segregation of the federal workforce. He also supported beefing up federal policing and surveillance abilities, in order to be able to identify and imprison outside agitators, residents "born under other flags but welcomed under our generous naturalization laws to the full freedom and opportunity of America, who have poured the poison of disloyalty into the very arteries of our national life."

As the American scholar and New York senator Daniel Patrick Moynihan drily quipped of Wilson's federal policing initiatives, "And so the modern age began. Three new institutions had entered American life: Conspiracy, Loyalty, Secrecy. Each had antecedents, but now there was a difference. Each had become institutional; bureaucracies were established to attend to each. In time there would be a Federal Bureau of Investigation to keep track of conspiracy at home, a Central Intelligence Agency to keep tabs abroad, an espionage statute and loyalty boards to root out disloyalty or subversion. And all of this would be maintained, and the national security would be secured, through elaborate regimes of secrecy."

Yet while Wilson in these years was busy laying the foundation for what some (on both the left and right) now call a "deep" state, unaccountable because largely invisible to the American people, he was at the same time continuing to tout the virtues of democracy as a shared public ideal.

As a young scholar, Wilson had argued that a strong democratic leader should strive to reduce the perceived distance between himself and the people, by acting decisively and openly aiming to embody their general will. "The people," he speculated, will "feel a keen charm in the knowledge" that the democratic leader, though powerful, derives all of his power from the people. "They are conscious of being represented by him in respect to their greater and soberer aims. They gain in dignity as he gains in beneficent power. To follow him is to realize the greatest possible amount of real political life." Years later, in an address dedicating Abraham Lincoln's birthplace, he movingly spoke of how, in a democracy, "every door is open, in every hamlet and countryside, in city and wilderness alike, for the ruler to emerge when he will and claim his leadership in the free life . . . Here, no less, hides the mystery of democracy."

These sentiments seem apropos of Pericles, who was exemplary in his ability to inspire the ordinary citizens of Athens to do great things. But Wilson's words also recall Max Weber's suggestion that a *"Führerdemokratie"* would enable a charismatic leader to counteract the lethargy associated with the modern administrative state and inspire large masses of people to believe that they were united in a common cause— even if, in fact, the relationship between leader and led was one of pure domination.

Wilson was certainly self-conscious about how he ought to represent his nation's "greater and soberer aims." The war speech he delivered to Congress, and the American public, on April 2, 1917, is a fine example of an eloquent demagogue in full oratorical flight. While urging that Congress declare war on Germany, Wilson implicitly speaks for a nation, even as he offers himself, in his resoluteness and in the moral purity of his lofty democratic aims, as an exemplar, someone who perfectly embodies what *we*, the American people, want. "We shall fight for the things we have always carried nearest to our hearts," he avows, we shall fight for democracy, for human rights, for a world of peace and universal prosperity, and we shall do so knowing that "America is privileged to spend her blood and her might" for "the principles that gave her birth and happiness and the peace which she has treasured. God helping her, she can do no other."

The final, Protestant flourish is telling. In 1917, Woodrow Wilson committed America to a high-minded kind of new world order, consecrated in a leap of faith that he assumed would be widely shared, hence representative (and democratic) as well.

Yet democracy itself is "a process that has no endpoint, an argument that has no definite conclusion," the American political philosopher Michael Walzer observes. "No citizen can ever claim to have persuaded his fellows once and for all." In a democracy of the sort Wilson imagined, everything, especially how "we" interpret our deepest moral and political convictions, hinges, after all, on public opinion. Unlike Martin Luther, Woodrow Wilson was taking a stand on shifting sands.

III

IN 1917, America wasn't the only nation struggling to realize democratic ideals in fraught circumstances. It is easy to forget that Woodrow Wilson in his war speech to Congress *welcomed* news of a revolution in Russia. "Does not every American," he asked, "feel that assurance has been added to our hope for the future peace of the world by the wonderful and heartening things that have been happening within the last few weeks in Russia?" He answered his own rhetorical question with praise for Russia's political potential: "Russia was known by those who knew it best to have always in fact been democratic at heart, in all the vital habits of her thought, in all the intimate relationships of her people that spoke their natural instinct, their habitual attitude towards life."

Some Russian intellectuals were inclined to agree that a nation long ruled by a tsar was "democratic at heart," in some cases pointing to the mirs, self-governing communities of peasants that the tsarist regime had tried to stamp out, in still other cases pointing to the appearance in 1905 of the soviets in large cities like Moscow and St. Petersburg. And in a further irony, one of Woodrow Wilson's most cherished democratic principles—a right to national self-determination—had been endorsed two decades earlier by an International Socialist Congress meeting in London, and reaffirmed in 1916 by Lenin, the leader of the Bolsheviks, Russia's most ardent revolutionary party.

As had happened in 1905, Russia's democratic revolt began in the dead of winter, in the nation's capital and second-largest city, Petrograd (as St. Petersburg had been renamed in 1914). As before, the army was reeling from military defeats—in 1905 facing Japanese troops, in 1917 fighting in the Great War against German and Austro-Hungarian troops. Once again, the revolt began slowly with peaceful demonstrations—at first, over a lack of food in the stores—but then mushroomed, as workers joined in, and the police stood down. By Saturday, February 25, almost all of the city's factories had shut down and many shops had shuttered their doors. For the first time, political banners appeared: "Down with the Tsar!" "Down with the War!"

The next day, thousands of people started to stream toward Petrograd's snow-covered city centre. An eyewitness reported that "warnings not to assemble were disregarded," but that the crowd, to start, "was fairly good-humoured, cheering the soldiers and showing themselves ugly only toward the few visible police." A festive atmosphere prevailed, as workers, housewives, and children mingled in the streets. There were political activists in the crowd, too—but as one of them sheepishly admitted years later, "the revolution found us, the party members, fast asleep, just like the Foolish Virgins in the Gospel." (The most famous veterans of 1905 were in exile—Trotsky was in New York City, Lenin was in Zurich.)

As the throng converged on the Nevsky Prospekt shortly after 3:00 p.m., troops raised their rifles. One officer, unable to get his green recruits to fire, grabbed a rifle and fired at will into the crowd. The troops followed suit. Hundreds of demonstrators fell to the ground, and empty cartridge cases littered the blood-spattered snow. After the volleys, police cleared the street, while the crowd stood by, stunned but unflinching. Most showed no animosity toward the soldiers. They expressed sympathy instead: "We are sorry for you . . . You had to do your duty!"

That evening, mutinous troops joined workers in seizing the city's arsenal. As dawn broke on Monday, February 27, the tsarist armed forces dispersed in disarray, "disorderly groups of grey greatcoats, mingling and fraternizing openly with the working class crowd and casual passersby." Many people were now armed, and their ranks were reinforced by a growing number of disloyal soldiers, as well as inmates freed from the city's prisons. Among those released were the militant leaders of the Workers' Group of the Central War Industries Committee, who now joined a crowd marching toward the Tauride Palace, the graceful Palladian mansion built for Catherine the Great that, since 1906, had housed the state Duma, Russia's legislative assembly (created after the general strike of 1905, but without any real power under the tsar).

At 2:00 p.m., a number of local trade union and cooperative movement leaders joined with the members of the Workers' Group and the left-wing deputies to the Duma, to address a crowd of some twenty-five thousand people that had formed outside the palace. They proclaimed the creation of a Provisional Executive Committee of the Soviet of Workers' Deputies and announced the first plenary session of the soviet, hastily organized for that evening at 7:00. The soviet itself was to be a representative body, with delegates chosen by the workers of Petrograd; but that night, fewer than fifty delegates appeared, as there had been virtually no time to conduct elections.

The Executive Committee of the Petrograd soviet quickly emerged as a governing body in its own right, organizing shelter and supplies for now homeless military units. The next morning, in the first issue of *Izvestiia*, the official newspaper of the Petrograd soviet, and the only newspaper to appear that day, the leaders of the soviet issued an appeal to the city's residents: "In order to conclude successfully the struggle for democracy, the people must organize their power . . . Let us, all together, fight . . . for the annihilation of the old regime and the convocation of a constituent national assembly, to be elected by universal, impartial, direct and secret ballot."

That morning, many more enterprises held elections for deputies to the Petrograd soviet. At 1:00 p.m., the soviet held another plenary session, this one attended by about 120 official participants.

Meanwhile, street fighting continued throughout Petrograd, with an especially bloody skirmish occurring at the city's largest and most modern hotel, the Astoria, which had been requisitioned for use by Russian officers, their families, and officers of the allied armies. When a sniper on the roof opened fire on a crowd gathered out front, rebellious soldiers mustered three armoured cars with machine guns to rake the upper stories of the building with bullets while other armed forces stormed into the lobby, smashing mirrors and chandeliers. "The worst of the fighting took place in the vestibule," an eyewitness recalled, "and in a short time the big revolving doors were turning round in a pool of blood."

That evening, a member of the Petrograd Soviet Executive Committee, Nikolai Sukhanov, who was attached to the Menshevik wing of the Social Democratic Party, had dinner with Maxim Gorky, a renowned man of letters as well as a friend of Lenin. Gorky was appalled by what he'd witnessed. As Sukhanov recalled, he deplored "the chaos, the disorder, the excesses" and "forecast that the movement would probably collapse in ruin worthy of our Asiatic savagery."

Sukhanov sharply disagreed: "To me it seemed, on the contrary, self-evident that things were going brilliantly, that the development of the revolution couldn't have been better, that victory could now be considered secure, and that the excesses, the man-in-the-street's stupidity, vulgarity, and cowardice . . . —all this was only what the revolution could not in any circumstances avoid, without which nothing similar had *ever* happened anywhere."

III

WITHIN A WEEK, Tsar Nicholas II had abdicated and been placed under arrest, a new Provisional Government had been formed, and soviets had been established in Moscow, Kiev, and other cities throughout Russia.

The result was a desperate situation, in which two conflicting centres of political power coexisted. In theory, the nation's Provisional Government bore full responsibility for legislation and administering the Russian state. But in practice, the nation's soviets, led by the Executive Committee of the Petrograd soviet, now began to legislate and administer as well, independently of the leaders of the Duma.

The Provisional Government wanted to restore law and order and the authority of the Duma as quickly as possible. The social democratic intelligentsia in charge of the Petrograd soviet's Executive Committee, though they disagreed over tactics, and specifically the extent to which they should coordinate with the Provisional Government, all wanted to constitute a new republic of equals, with power democratically distributed in Russia's new network of soviets.

From the start, the Petrograd soviet's Executive Committee had issued various public demands, in effect turning itself into a "controlling organ of revolutionary democracy," attempting to dictate terms not just to the plenary assembly of the soviet but also to the nation, through the Duma, to the (limited) extent the formal government itself was able, in these circumstances, to exercise centralized authority over Russia as a whole.

As had happened in Paris more than one hundred years earlier, a small group of avowed democrats in this way seized control of a nation's nascent representative institutions. Most of the members of the Petrograd soviet Executive Committee were hardened conspirators, accustomed to operating in the shadows by the years of clandestine struggle against the tsarist regime. But the soviets themselves, like the Parisian sections in 1792, were the very picture of direct democracy in full bloom.

In Petrograd, the daily sessions of the soviet, which quickly grew to include six hundred delegates duly elected by the workers of Petrograd, soon came to resemble a chaotic village assembly without a fixed agenda. When regiments of soldiers in the city subsequently asked to join the soviet, the delegates resolved unanimously and without a formal vote to create a greatly expanded body, the Petrograd Soviet of Workers' and Soldiers' Deputies.

The soviet's voting procedures were ad hoc and arbitrary, so that a small regiment and a large factory might both be invited to elect a delegate, with the soldier representing perhaps twelve men and the worker representing two thousand. Of the three thousand delegates to the enlarged assembly, more than two-thirds were soldiers, even though workers outnumbered soldiers in Petrograd by three or four to one.

Anyone could address the group, and decisions were made by consensus. The deputies debated in front of a standing-room-only crowd of spectators, many of them bystanders and soldiers who didn't conceal their weapons—or their political views. In March 1917, this is what democracy looked like in the Petrograd soviet.

III

AT THE BEGINNING of April, Lenin, the acknowledged leader of the Bolsheviks, the most radical faction of the Russian Social Democratic Party, returned to Petrograd. "A man of astounding strength of will," as Gorky summed him up, "Lenin possessed in the highest degree the best qualities and properties of the revolutionary intelligentsia—self-discipline often amounting to self-torture and self-mutilation, in its most extreme form, amounting to a renunciation of art and to the logic of one of L. Andreyev's heroes: 'Other people are living hard lives, and therefore I must live a hard life.'" Untiring and indomitable, Lenin reasserted control of his party by laying out, with ruthless simplicity, a strategy to seize political power immediately.

In the previous months, while still in exile in Switzerland, Lenin had begun writing a book arguing that the Paris Commune of 1871 represented an ideal type of revolutionary regime, a "dictatorship of the proletariat" that was perfectly democratic—and also a suitable vehicle for a successful armed insurrection. By abolishing the distinctions among the legislative, executive, administrative, and judicial functions of a government, and establishing a single, unitary assembly of armed delegates subject to rotation and recall, a federation of municipal and rural councils like the Commune or the Russian soviets could solve several problems simultaneously. It could ensure that the sovereign will of the people prevailed over reactionary factions; it would subject all political officials to direct democratic control; and by empowering ordinary citizens in this way, it could thwart the threat of a counter-revolution engineered by the armed forces of the old regime.

However, to realize all these benefits in the Russian context, it was essential, Lenin argued, following Marx, to *"smash"* the "bureaucratic-military machine" of the old regime:

> The party of the proletariat cannot rest content with a bourgeois parliamentary democratic republic, which throughout the world preserves and strives to perpetuate the monarchist instruments for the oppression of the masses, namely, the police, the standing army, and the privileged bureaucracy.
>
> The party fights for a *more* democratic workers' and peasants' republic, in which the police and the standing army will be abolished and replaced by the universally armed people, by a people's militia; all officials will be not only elective, but also subject to recall at any time upon the demand of a majority of the electors; all officials, without exception, will be paid at a rate not exceeding the average wage of a competent worker; parliamentary representative institutions will be gradually replaced by Soviets of people's representatives (from various classes and professions, or from various localities), functioning as both legislative and executive bodies.

"All power to the soviets" became the slogan of the Bolsheviks—and by repeating it incessantly over the following months, Lenin helped his Bolsheviks build a majority among the executive committees of the various councils throughout Russia, including the all-important Petrograd soviet.

Because of their fluid voting procedures and frequent elections, the soviets were sensitive barometers of popular sentiment. But the assemblies were also susceptible, from the start, to control from above, by a handful of leaders in the executive committees. And once Lenin had entered the picture, as a historian of the soviets puts it, "the Russian soviet movement, which had begun as a democratic movement, became the trailblazer for Bolshevik dictatorship."

The transformation began with a putsch in Petrograd in late October 1917, and was clinched in 1922 by the creation, after a bloody civil war, of the Union of Soviet Socialist Republics—in theory, a proletarian and peasant democracy; in reality, a new state ruled by one party, the Bolsheviks, and, ultimately, by one man.

III

AMERICA'S ENTRY into the Great War, combined with the February Revolution in Russia, suddenly turned clashing democratic ideals into matters of global consequence. By then, "liberal" had belatedly entered the political lexicon of the United States and begun to be associated with the kind of strong modern state championed by Woodrow Wilson and intellectual allies like the journalist Walter Lippmann. Wilson had already articulated an expansive global vision of a new league of nations, committed to creating a world made safe for democracy.

This vision of democracy was explicitly internationalist—but so was its Russian rival. In one of his first official acts after the Bolsheviks had seized power in Petrograd, Lenin issued a "peace decree," calling upon "all the belligerent peoples and their governments to start immediate negotiations for a just, democratic peace," deploying a rhetoric (however disingenuous) that owed almost as much to Wilson as to Marx. Wilson responded in kind, on January 8, 1918, by issuing his Fourteen Points, outlining his hopes for peace and offering "to assist the people of Russia to attain their utmost hope of liberty," by helping Russia to join "the society of free nations under institutions of her own choosing."

That liberals as well as communists were committed in principle to an expansion of democracy suggested some common ground. Wilson and Lenin both seemed to uphold popular sovereignty as a political principle; both also affirmed a people's political right to self-determination. Yet the extent of active political participation in both the liberal and communist contexts was in practice carefully qualified. Wilson's administrative state transferred a great deal of power to the federal president and the unelected civil servants who reported to him, while Lenin's conception of "democratic centralism" concentrated power in the hands of a centralized government controlled by the elite of one party.

There was also some irony in the common embrace of self-determination as a global ideal. After all, the United States and the Soviet Union—like the United Kingdom and France—were de facto imperial powers, however much fealty they now professed to democratic norms. Indeed, almost all of their protectorates and colonies were effectively controlled by armed garrisons and governors who represented the interests of distant capitals and remote rulers.

These contradictions tempered the possibility that four years of carnage and bloody revolts might produce a new world order, but they didn't prevent Woodrow Wilson from attempting to do just that, by establishing a new League of Nations as part of the peace process in Paris after the United States and its allies had defeated Germany.

On June 28, 1919, Wilson, along with the leaders of England, France, Italy, Japan, and dozens of other nations, as well as representatives from the government of Germany, signed the treaty creating the new League and putting an end to the Great War at the Palace of Versailles, in the Hall of Mirrors. It was a pointed choice of venue. An architectural symbol of absolute sovereignty built during the reign of the Sun King, Louis XIV, the Hall of Mirrors was also the humiliating place where Bismarck had forced France to sign an armistice ending the Franco-Prussian War in 1871.

Two key principles lay behind the covenant of the League of Nations: nonviolent conflict resolution and the facilitation of a slow but steady evolution of all peoples toward self-determination. But in practice, the settlement also transferred formerly German colonies into other European hands even as it maintained the colonies of the United Kingdom and France, under the pretext that the nonwhite races needed more time to become fully mature peoples, fit for democratic institutions. The West had a civilizing mission, according to Wilson and his Western allies, and this mission was explicitly racial in its inflections. (When the Japanese mustered majority support at the Paris peace conference for a clause affirming the equality of races, Wilson chose to ignore it.)

For Wilson, the stress in a modern democracy was always on maturity, sobriety, and the peaceful harmonizing of interests. In this context, the focus of socialist militants on open class conflict was more than unwelcome: it represented a kind of blasphemy. America was a light unto the nations of the world, but its democratic promise was a matter of faith, and not an entirely new faith, at that, but one built on "organic" foundations, as the inheritance of a Protestant people of Aryan stock. The Versailles Peace Treaty in effect consecrated Wilson's soaring faith that democracy was a universal ideal. But for Woodrow Wilson, it was also "—at least for the foreseeable future—the white man's business."

Wilson's willingness to let racism set limits on his democratic convictions was ultimately self-defeating. The language of the League covenant triggered the hopes of subject peoples of all colours and faiths around the world. It encouraged an expectation of self-determination as a new and universal political right. And to the extent that nations like the United States, England, and France continued to flout their own avowed principles in practice, the expectation of self-determination guaranteed not peace and harmony but rather a world of conflict and unending civil war, as one subject nation after another, in the years that followed, fought for the right to join "the society of free nations under institutions of her own choosing."

III

IN THE YEARS before and after the Great War, a few social theorists, disregarding the scepticism of scholars like Henry Sumner Maine and Max Weber, continued to produce proposals for creating a more perfectly democratic society, one that could meet the challenges posed by the rise not just of hierarchical political parties but also of factory assembly lines. In 1912, the Dutch astronomer and labour activist Anton Pannekoek, inspired in part by the Russian soviets that had flourished in 1905, suggested that such local councils might represent a viable alternative to parliamentary party organizations. By then, a similar view of a more democratic approach to industrial organization had appeared in the United Kingdom, in the form of Guild Socialism, a movement that coalesced around the essentially romantic idea, first broached in the 1880s by the British textile designer, novelist, and Marxist agitator William Morris, that modern labour should look to medieval standards of craftsmanship in production, and also medieval forms of self-government in the workshop.

The most sophisticated of the Guild Socialist theorists was G.D.H. Cole, a precocious Oxford don and youthful agitator who had cut his teeth in leftist politics by attacking technocratic collectivists—most notably Sidney and Beatrice Webb, who had founded the Fabian Society in Britain in the 1880s as an evolutionary, policy-orientated socialist alternative to orthodox Marxism. In a series of books and pamphlets published between 1913 and 1921, Cole laid out his own alternative hopes for a future Guild Socialist society.

An adamant pluralist, he argued that a good society, even after the abolition of capitalism, would consist of many diverse and decentralized institutions, all claiming loyalty from assorted individuals. Since everyone in such a society had an interest simultaneously in more than one institution, a society could be truly democratic only if every person "should have as many distinct, and separately exercised, votes, as he has distinct social purposes," so that a coal miner, for example, might participate in a coal-mining guild; as an avid music lover, he might also join a Cultural Council; as a user of electricity and public transport, he might also participate in a Utilities Council; while as a citizen, he would have a direct say in a town Commune and could elect delegates to a regional Commune and also a National Commune (as Cole called what was left of a centralized state in his ideal society). Moreover, because the Guild Socialist participated in each of these arenas only as his interests dictated, his voice and votes would not be blind but must be informed by his sincere concern for the matters at hand.

Since the citizens of this ideal society would obviously be spending a great many evenings at one meeting or another, it represented Oscar Wilde's worst nightmare come true ("The trouble with socialism is that it takes too many evenings," he had reputedly quipped). In Cole's ideal society, it seemed as if everyone would be constantly debating and voting about everything. But Cole took it for granted that everyone naturally yearned for active involvement in public affairs, and that only a democratic society could give its members "that maximum opportunity for personal and social self-expression which is requisite to real freedom."

He additionally assumed that the greater the levels of participation in a democratic society, the wider and more enlightened the views of participants would become. "For democracy in industry and in every sphere of social life has for its supreme justification its power to call out in the mass of men the creative, scientific and artistic impulses which capitalism suppresses or perverts, and to enable the now stifled civic spirit to work wonders in the regeneration of the good things of life."

Still, Cole had to concede that not everyone would be eagerly rushing to an endless round of meetings. Anticipating the objection that this would vitiate the legitimacy of the guild scheme, Cole argued that if a "man is not interested enough to vote, and cannot be roused to interest enough to make him vote, on, say, a dozen distinct subjects, he waives his right to vote, and the result is no less democratic than if he voted blindly and without interest." This was a slightly peculiar conclusion, since Cole acknowledged that in an ideal democracy "many and keen voters are best of all"—but he also insisted that "few and keen voters are next best," and certainly preferable to a "vast and uninstructed electorate voting on a general and undefined issue," which is the sorry state of affairs "we call democracy to-day."

Cole's vision of a better future—along with his ardent support for workers' control—was appealing to some rank-and-file British trade unionists during the Great War. A few British unions even passed resolutions in support of Guild Socialist policies. When news of the Petrograd uprising of February 1917 reached London, Oxford, and Cambridge, it "had been welcomed with shouts of delight, by democrats, liberals, and socialists of every shade of opinion," one eyewitness recalled—and, for a moment, the Russian experiment with soviets seemed to confirm the value of the Guild Socialist model.

But the rapid appearance in Russia of a one-party state under Bolshevik control soon enough dampened the enthusiasm of British democrats for the soviet model. Even worse, the relative ease with which a few militants were able to take control of the Russian soviets suggested, among other things, that such decentralized, directly democratic councils were paradoxically vulnerable to domination by charismatic (and formally unaccountable) leaders.

The formation in 1920 of the Communist Party of Great Britain coincided with the disintegration of Guild Socialism as an intellectual and political movement. Some members of the movement, admiring the insurrectionist *élan* of the Bolsheviks, joined the Communist Party. Others, like Cole, abstained, recognizing that the putative "democratic centralism" of Lenin's party completely contradicted the kind of decentralized, pluralistic society of self-governing institutions that he imagined as the proper goal of a properly democratic form of socialism.

III

BUT PERHAPS TECHNOCRATS like the Webbs and Woodrow Wilson—and even Lenin, with his stress on the need for elite political leadership—were simply being realistic about the limits of what a "civic spirit" could accomplish. Was it really possible to create the kind of robust democracy that G.D.H. Cole imagined in a complex, modern industrial society—even one that, like Cole's guild utopia, was hypothetically no longer riven by class conflicts?

By taking this question seriously, and examining carefully some of the core assumptions that Cole shared with other proponents of more direct forms of modern self-government, Walter Lippmann produced perhaps the most challenging inquiry yet into the limits of modern democracy, *Public Opinion*, published in 1922. It was, to an unusual degree, the fruit of firsthand experience, refracted through a first-rate intelligence.

For almost a half century a prominent political commentator and confidant of American presidents from Woodrow Wilson to Lyndon Johnson, Lippmann had begun his political career as a twenty-year-old convert to socialism. Forming a Harvard chapter of the Intercollegiate Socialist Society in 1908, Lippmann joined a group of student agitators that included John Reed, subsequently the author of *Ten Days That Shook the World*, the first eyewitness account by an American of the Bolshevik seizure of power in Russia.

There was a viable Socialist Party in the United States in these years, led by Eugene V. Debs, with strong support in a number of the larger cities, both on the East Coast and in the Midwest, and there was also an independent union movement in America, the Industrial Workers of the World, a militant association of syndicalist unions, mainly covering labourers in the extractive industries, concentrated in the West.

At college, Lippmann was drawn not just to native socialist agitators, but even more strongly to the British intellectuals who in 1884 had formed the Fabian Society. Lippmann became a card-carrying Fabian, joining in 1909, and paying his £1 annual dues.

The next year, in his last semester at Harvard, Lippmann jumped at the chance to take a seminar with Graham Wallas, a founding member (along with the Webbs and George Bernard Shaw) of the Fabians. The son of an Anglican clergyman who had converted to the classicizing kind of democratic idealism fashionable in Oxford in the 1880s, Wallas arguably had the best mind of a very brilliant group, though he eventually broke with them, in part over the role democratic processes should play in a good society. As Wallas wrote to Shaw in 1903, "I know of no better way than democracy of securing that the 'end' of the State shall be the good of all and not the good of some."

In 1908, two years before he met Lippmann, Wallas had published *Human Nature in Politics*, "the first time that democracy had been discussed by a man amply acquainted with psychological research," as the British political theorist Harold Laski put it. "The political opinions of most men are the result," Wallas wrote, "not of reasoning tested by experience, but of unconscious and half-conscious inference fixed by habit." But despite acknowledging that the democratic movement of his own day "was inspired largely by a purely intellectual conception of human nature which is becoming every year more unreal to us," this lapsed Anglican never surrendered his faith in democracy, preferring instead to "increase the margin of safety in our democracy" by pressing for "moral and educational changes" that would improve the capacity of ordinary citizens to meet the challenges of helping to govern a complex modern society.

"Socialism stands or falls by its fruits in practice," Walter Lippmann wrote in 1910, shortly after his formative encounter with Graham Wallas. "If it can be shown that public enterprise, where tried under democratic conditions, fails to produce a beneficent effect on the health, happiness and general culture of a community, or that private enterprise is more beneficent, then the socialist case collapses."

Uncommonly open to the possibility that his own political convictions might in fact prove groundless, Lippmann went to work as a reporter, first for a Boston paper, then as a research assistant for the veteran muckraking journalist Lincoln Steffens, who was writing an exposé of financial corruption on Wall Street (*plus ça change*). Still active in the Intercollegiate Socialist Society, Lippmann also started writing for the American left-wing press, including the *International* and the *Masses*.

He was one of the leading young members of the American socialist movement at the most promising moment yet in its history: in 1910, Socialists were mayors of thirty-three American cities, and

Debs's national party continued to attract new members. For a few months in 1912, Lippmann served an abortive term as an aide to George Lunn, the newly elected Socialist mayor of Schenectady, New York. But the more Lippmann saw of socialism and democracy in practice, the more sceptical he became.

In an essay published in the *International*, he decried the "cult of democracy" for assuming "that the people have all the virtues and then pretend, when they don't exhibit them, that it is somebody else's fault." Like Woodrow Wilson, but in the context of the Socialist Party of Debs, Lippmann was concluding that managing the complexities of modern politics required realistic and tough-minded leadership, not just somehow organizing the spontaneous impulses of ordinary citizens.

In the years that followed, Lippmann published a pugnacious first book, *A Preface to Politics*, which was meant, in part, to popularize the ideas of his mentor Graham Wallas. He helped Herbert Croly launch *The New Republic* in 1914 as a new weekly American journal meant to "brighten the coinage of American opinion." He became fascinated with psychoanalysis and Sigmund Freud, and he sailed to England to meet more of his Fabian heroes face-to-face. While he was there, he got to see G.D.H. Cole and his young Guild Socialist friends disrupt a Fabian conference.

The Great War came. By then, Lippmann was widely admired as a writer and thinker, and in September 1917, he was asked to work on a secret project for President Woodrow Wilson, code-named "The Inquiry," meant to develop concrete terms for a postwar peace anchored by a new League of Nations. A memo Lippmann prepared became the basis for Wilson's Fourteen Points speech to Congress and, subsequently, the Versailles Peace Treaty.

Lippmann then spent several months in Paris writing propaganda leaflets to be dropped behind enemy lines. Unhappy about the direction negotiations were taking, he returned to *The New Republic* with a wealth of experience—and fresh doubts about the capacity not just of ordinary citizens but also of their elected leaders to meet the challenges of governing a complex society.

Despite his own intimate involvement in the early stages of the Versailles peace process, Lippmann joined with the other editors of *The New Republic* in denouncing the signed treaty as an abject capitulation to old-world imperialists, and merely "the prelude to quarrels in a deeply divided and hideously embittered Europe."

In a series of essays published in 1920 as a book, *Liberty and the News*, Lippmann highlighted the increasingly critical role played by the news media in modern societies, by disseminating reliable information to ordinary citizens. As a veteran reporter, presidential memo writer, and propagandist for the U.S. military, Lippmann knew from the inside what it was like to filter, select, and simplify complicated facts in a form that people could quickly absorb. He had become a critic of Wilson after the president turned to censorship and the suppression of civil liberties, in conjunction with what Lippmann regarded as crudely jingoistic propaganda. *Liberty and the News* had grown out of a lengthy analysis of *The New York Times*'s coverage of the Russian Revolution, which led Lippmann to conclude that "the news about Russia is a case of seeing not what was, but what men wished to see . . . The chief censor and the chief protagonist were hope and fear in the minds of reporters and editors."

This was a disheartening conclusion for anyone who believed, as Lippmann still did in 1920, that "the reliability of the news is the premise on which democracy proceeds." But reporters and editors were only human. As a consequence of the efforts of newsmen like Lippmann himself, who summarized and simplified the events of the day, "all news comes at second-hand." At the same time, utterly uninformed opinions were circulated as well, in the media and in face-to-face conversations. As a result, "all the testimony is uncertain, men cease to respond to truths, and respond simply to opinions. The environment in which they act is not the realities themselves, but the pseudo-environment of reports, rumors, and guesses."

Indeed, it was just as hard for America's elected representatives to grasp "the realities themselves," one reason Lippmann applauded the "establishment of more or less semi-official institutes of government research." (The American Bureau of Labor Statistics founded in 1884, the National Institute of Standards and Technology created in 1901, the reorganized Public Health Services expanded under Wilson in 1912, and the National Science Foundation launched in 1950 are all good examples of what Lippmann envisioned.)

But to imply that a bevy of objective facts, if faithfully relayed to the general public, or even to its elected representatives, would solve the problem of public opinion was profoundly misleading—and Lippmann knew it.

For the defects of public opinion were caused not just by biased newspapers, or blinkered reporters, or a lack of government-sponsored research institutes, or even by the growing number of secrets being kept by the American administrative state—the deepest problems were caused by the way people, *all* people, selected what they wanted to see and hear, filtering information through unavoidable "stereotypes," a word that Lippmann introduced into the lexicon of American social science. Building on the work of Graham Wallas, and also aware of Freud's findings, Lippmann in effect anticipated more recent research about "bounded rationality" (and the unavoidable cognitive errors that arise from what the psychologists Amos Tversky and Daniel Kahneman called "heuristics and biases").

In *Public Opinion*, published in 1922, Lippmann explored the implications of these limits to human rationality for what Woodrow Wilson had called "government by popular opinion." Unlike Robert Michels, who focused on the institutional limits of modern democracy, Lippmann analysed its *psychological* limits. In a complex environment, where only disconnected bits of information are available to the average citizen, it was almost impossible for the public's opinion on any matter of moment to be either cogent or coherent.

The book's epigraph is Plato's famous image, in the *Republic*, of inhabitants in a cave bewitched by shadows and unaware of the real world outside. What follows suggests that the great majority of modern men are inescapably prisoners of shadowy and unexamined assumptions, immersed in private lives involving the pursuit of various personal interests, with limited time, and even less attention to give to public affairs. This bleak account renders obsolete the dreams of Enlightenment democrats like Condorcet, who had hoped that citizens in the future would "approach a condition in which everyone will have the knowledge necessary to conduct himself in the ordinary affairs of life, according to the light of his own reason, to preserve his mind free from prejudice, to understand his rights and to exercise them in accordance with his conscience and his creed."

Lippmann concedes that in a simple, self-contained community it might be plausible to assume that one man was as competent as another to manage "simple and self-contained affairs"—he seems to have in mind New England towns with their annual town meetings. But the evolution of modern society turns that "democratic stereotype" into a dangerous cliché, insofar as men now "looked at a complicated civilization and saw an enclosed village." And insofar as modern American democracy under the direction of figures like Theodore Roosevelt and Woodrow Wilson had evolved into a centralized administrative state designed, in part, to regulate and curtail the semi-sovereign powers of modern corporations and banks, the facts of governance had grown ever more remote from the simple interactions of a few individuals in a small rural community.

At the same time, Lippmann, as a former Socialist, knew perfectly well that some democratic theorists hoped to meet the challenges of a modern industrial society by replacing the image of the idealized rural township with that of a self-governing workshop, and by acknowledging the complexity of social interests in a modern society by producing a correspondingly complex scheme of self-government.

The problem, he argues in a climactic chapter on the Guild Socialism of G.D.H. Cole, is that the Guild scheme rests on hopelessly unrealistic assumptions about the capacity of ordinary citizens immersed in work, or leisure pursuits, to transform "a self-centered opinion into a social judgment." Cole's theory "presupposes an unceasing, untiring round of civic duties, an enormous complication of the political interests that are already much too complicated."

Lippmann's conclusion is most bluntly stated in *The Phantom Public*, his sequel to the opinion book: "The individual man does not have opinions on all public affairs. He does not know how to direct public affairs. He does not know what is happening, why it is happening, what ought to happen. I cannot imagine how he could know, and there is not the least reason for thinking, as mystical democrats have thought, that the compounding of individual ignorances in masses of people can produce a continuous directing force in public affairs." As a result, the common interests, he concludes, "can be managed only by a specialized class"— informed commentators like Lippmann himself, and trained civil servants with an in-depth knowledge of the facts pertinent to formulating reasonable public policies.

III

IN A DISCERNING REVIEW of *Public Opinion* for *The New Republic*, the American philosopher John Dewey praised Lippmann for throwing "into clearer relief than any other writer the fundamental difficulty of democracy." He followed up with a book of his own, *The Public and Its Problems*, in 1927. In it, Dewey conceded the empirical accuracy of Lippmann's account. But he also reaffirmed his long-standing conviction, which he shared with Woodrow Wilson, that democracy was the rational goal of historical development, a natural result of evolution— and also a matter of shared faith.

Throughout his long life—born in 1859, he died in 1952—Dewey tried to inspire his readers with a can-do confidence in the possibility of scientific social reforms, animated by a serene faith in the value of a strong form of democracy. Knowledge, he argued, was an evolving product, the result of active experimentation in constantly changing historical circumstances. Rejecting authoritarian approaches to education, Dewey hoped to instill flexible habits and a sturdy sense of self-reliance in his students, helping them to become independent and active citizens. Applying similar principles to his own political commitments, he lent his support to the progressive voluntary associations of his day, from the American Civil Liberties Union to the National

Association for the Advancement of Colored People. In the pages of *The New Republic* and other liberal publications, he tirelessly expounded his faith in the value of unfettered inquiry and the institutions of democracy, with lasting effect on the ideals held by many American educators, and also on philosophers like the German critical theorist Jürgen Habermas, whose account of deliberative democracy owes a large debt to Dewey and his pragmatic allies.

Rarely has a political philosopher been so explicit about the religious motives behind an ostensibly scientific theory. "The next religious prophet who will have a permanent and real influence on men's lives," Dewey declared with disarming candour in 1893, "will be the man who succeeds in pointing out the religious meaning of democracy."

For Dewey, an egalitarian training in what he called "the method of intelligence," combined with intense engagement in a face-to-face community of similarly enlightened and self-governing friends, promised a kind of this-worldly redemption: the Kingdom of God, embodied in a perfect democracy.

By "democracy," Dewey did not mean simply a form of government. He rather meant to evoke a kind of church writ large, a communion of souls sharing the same faith in freedom and equality and fraternity, a congregation of individuals with unique talents, who had all been properly educated to think for themselves and empowered politically to rule themselves with dignity and intelligence. Democracy for Dewey was thus "a form of moral and spiritual association," a society, as he wrote in a youthful essay, while still an observant New England Congregationalist, in which "the distinction between the spiritual and secular has ceased, and as in Greek theory, and as in the Christian theory of the Kingdom of God, the church and the state, the divine and the human organization of society are one."

In 1893, at a time when Woodrow Wilson was treating the actually existing American state as the very apotheosis of democracy in practice, Dewey had declared that "democracy is still untried"—and in his understanding of democracy as a salvific form of life, that was certainly true. It was still true in 1927, when Dewey, in the conclusion to *The Public and Its Problems*, strikingly reaffirmed his political credo: "We lie, as Emerson said, in the lap of an immense intelligence. But that intelligence is dormant and its communications are broken, inarticulate and faint until it possesses the local community as its medium."

Of course, this was no refutation of Lippmann's empirical analysis of public opinion. This was Emerson and Whitman redux: democracy in America as a "state of vision," an elusive dream, a redemptive ideal, yet still worth struggling toward, even against the current of events.

III

IN THESE YEARS, Lippmann's work had also drawn the attention of Edward Bernays, a young man who fancied himself the father of modern public relations. Born in Vienna in 1892, Bernays had immigrated with his family to New York City the following year. A double nephew of Sigmund Freud (his mother was Freud's sister and his father's sister became Freud's wife), Bernays got his start as a publicist for the Ballets Russes and the Italian tenor Enrico Caruso. He designed an early media campaign to raise awareness of venereal disease and also served on America's Committee of Public Information, the Orwellian name for Woodrow Wilson's main propaganda operation during the Great War. He worked for the buccaneering book publisher Horace Liveright, who founded the Modern Library and also published top-tier American authors like T. S. Eliot. There Bernays trumpeted the publication of each new book, no matter how highbrow, like the opening of a Broadway show. He also arranged for Liveright to publish the first American edition of Freud's *Introductory Lectures on Psychoanalysis*.

Sensing an opportunity to promote public relations as a respectable profession after the impact made by Lippmann's *Public Opinion* in 1922, Bernays suggested to Liveright that he write a book called *Crystallizing Public Opinion*—the title itself was lifted from Lippmann's text.

Since Lippmann had in fact *criticized* the proliferation of corporate publicists and government press officers, lamenting their self-serving communication of highly selective information, Bernays had his work cut out for him. (To paraphrase Lippmann, those who hire a publicist control him—even worse, they ask him to blur the line between offering the public something it wants and helping to construct a public that will take whatever it gets.)

Bernays was brazen in his claims. Taking as his premise Lippmann's observations about the unexamined assumptions held by most people, he defended the conscious manipulation of information as one way to dissolve blind prejudices. "The average citizen," Bernays claims, "is the world's most efficient censor. His own mind is the greatest barrier between him and the facts." As a result, the "public relations counselor" (Bernays's preferred title for his line of work) is, counterintuitively and in contradiction to Lippmann's views, an agent of potential enlightenment. His propaganda represents "a purposeful, directed effort to overcome censorship—the censorship of the group mind and the herd reaction."

Competing lobbyists offer the public competing new sources of information, and in this way they help expand the horizons of each citizen. The public relations counsellor, knowing that "there is a different set of facts on every subject for each man," marshals coherent sets of "alternative facts," so to speak, and in this very way fulfils an invaluable, and impeccably liberal, public service:

> Society cannot wait to find absolute truth. It cannot weigh
> every issue carefully before making a judgment. The result
> is that the so-called truths by which society lives are born of
> compromise among conflicting desires and of interpretation by
> many minds. They are accepted and intolerantly maintained
> once they have been determined. In the struggle among ideas,
> the only test is the one which Justice Holmes of the Supreme
> Court pointed out—the power of thought to get itself accepted
> in the open competition of the market.

In his account of "the mirrors of the public mind," Bernays delighted in documenting the growing power of media, both new and old, to form public opinion. Lippmann, by contrast, despaired of the same trend: "under the impact of propaganda, not necessarily in the sinister meaning of the word alone, the old constants of our thinking have become variables." One potential casualty, Lippmann worried, was the very idea of truth. If consultants like Bernays had their way, public opinion would become a hall of mirrors.

At Versailles, the Hall of Mirrors was a symbol of absolute power, with the long corridor of mirrors reflecting a controlled landscape that, seen through the windows on the other side, seemed to stretch to infinity. What Bernays had called the "mirrors of the public mind" evoked not Versailles but a funhouse maze. As arranged by promoters and political publicists, these "mirrors" could produce disorientation and distorted reflections, with no reference at all to the world outside.

III

BY THE TIME Bernays began to publish his disingenuous justifications of propaganda as an enlivening contribution to the marketplace of ideas, new methods had been developed to sample political opinion, deploying statistical techniques far beyond the capacities of an imaginative huckster like Bernays.

Since the nineteenth century, American newspapers and magazines had published "straw polls" to get a sense of voters' preferences before an election. In the 1920s and 1930s, the most famous of these straw polls was organized by *The Literary Digest*, the largest-circulation newsmagazine of its era, which sent postcard ballots to millions of Americans who listed a telephone number or owned an automobile. At the height of its reach, in 1930, the *Digest* mailed more than twenty million ballots, and tabulated almost five million straw votes. (It was renowned for its straw polls not just on political campaigns but also on single issues, such as Prohibition.)

By then, trained statisticians had discovered that a self-selecting poll of millions was much less reliable than a far smaller but more rigorously selected random sample of a few hundred people. The first scientific use of house-to-house interviewing to ascertain attitudes in the United States occurred in 1916. By 1928, a bibliography listed nearly three thousand opinion surveys of Americans (though most of these fell short of the kinds of probability sampling refined by later survey researchers).

In 1936, the first statistical samples of the political preferences of American voters appeared in American newspapers and magazines. Three polls—conducted by Archibald Crossley (for the Hearst papers), Elmo Roper (for *Fortune* magazine), and George Gallup (for a syndicated column published by *The New York Times*, *The Washington Post*, and other newspapers)—tracked preferences in that year's presidential campaign between Democrat Franklin D. Roosevelt and Republican Alf Landon (Roosevelt won in a landslide).

The most famous of these polls was the one conducted by Gallup, who promoted his techniques by making a bold bet with the editors of *The Literary Digest*: Gallup wagered that his rigorous sample of a few thousand American voters would more accurately predict the outcome of the 1936 presidential election than the millions of postcard ballots processed by the *Digest*. By winning this bet, Gallup helped launch public opinion polling as an entirely new feature of modern democracies.

As Gallup saw things, he was taking "the pulse of democracy"—the title of his 1940 book on how polling could determine what "the common man is thinking." Even more, Gallup believed that he was *perfecting* democracy, and taking it to a new stage, by fulfilling the prophecy of the British scholar James Bryce that a new political era would dawn "if the will of the majority of citizens were to become ascertainable at all times, and without the need of its passing through a body of representatives, possibly even without the need of voting machinery at all."

To this day, professional students of public opinion take understandable pride (to quote a statement from the American Association for Public Opinion Research) that "to the extent that polls also are accurate in characterizing the attitudes, beliefs, and motivations of the electorate, we believe that pollsters, and the news media that use their poll findings, provide a great service to democracy by placing the opinions and preferences of the public in the forefront of the electoral process."

Still, it is worth remembering just how simplifying most survey questions are, and how small the samples are: at most a few thousand people out of tens of millions of eligible voters. When polling was still a novelty in the 1930s, the response rates—the percentage of people in a sample who participated in a survey—were quite high, often 90 percent; but in the decades since, response rates have plummeted, forcing researchers to contact ever more people, which costs ever more money, and also to devise statistically reliable ways to correct for differing rates of nonresponse.

As a result of such problems, the reliability of survey research remains highly variable, depending on the specific methods used by the researcher.

In any case, the impact of survey research on politics has not been quite as benign as Gallup had hoped. Although publicizing poll data may focus attention on public opinion, it also turns the data presented into part of a feedback loop that may in turn *influence* opinion (what professionals call the "bandwagon effect"). That is one reason why the publication of polls is outlawed in some European states in the days before an election occurs. The more refined such data, the greater its potential to manipulate decision making.

As one historian has summed up the situation, acidly but accurately, by the 1980s, corporations and governments "were increasingly listening to what people had on their minds—and increasingly listening (thanks to the new mass feedback technologies) whether people intended to tell them or not." Thanks to the Internet and the capacity it has created for companies like Google and Facebook to aggregate large amounts of information about the individual preferences and attitudes of millions of people, this is truer in the twenty-first century than ever before.

III

IT SHOULD NOT BE a surprise that the United States pioneered the application of market survey research to politics. The land of Whitman's democratic vistas was also a commercial republic of free individuals, who defined themselves by the things they possessed, the clothes they bought, the cultural goods they consumed—and these material preferences, as survey research revealed, could be roughly correlated with political preferences. Politics and capitalism could converge in ways unforeseen by Karl Marx.

In 1942, Joseph Schumpeter, an economist who had been born in Moravia and raised in Vienna before moving to the United States in 1932 to teach at Harvard University, accurately depicted the strange results of merging a democratic faith with marketing methods refined by behavioural scientists. "What we are confronted with in the analysis of political processes," he wrote, "is largely not a genuine but a manufactured will. And often this artifact is all that in reality corresponds to the *volonté générale* of the classical doctrine . . . The ways in which issues and the popular will on any issue are being manufactured is exactly analogous to the ways of commercial advertising." The analogy fails, Schumpeter conceded, in one crucial respect: "The picture of the prettiest girl that ever lived will in the long run prove powerless to maintain the sales of a bad cigarette. There is no equally effective safeguard in the case of political decisions."

These observations are the prelude to Schumpeter's famous "realist" redefinition of modern democracy, which was built in part on the previous findings of political sociologists like Moisey Ostrogorski and Robert Michels. Setting aside, as Max Weber had, all previous accounts of democracy as a form of government embodying the will of a people, Schumpeter advanced his own "view that the role of the people is to produce a government, or else an intermediate body which in turn will produce a national executive or government. And we define: the democratic method is that institutional arrangement for arriving at political decisions in which individuals acquire the power to decide by means of a competitive struggle for the people's vote." Democracy in modern societies like America, as it actually exists, involves voters selecting the least objectionable of the available candidates chosen by rival political parties to rule over them. In other words, democracy is *not* the rule of a people—instead, "democracy is the rule of the politician," someone skilled at winning elections whose power is chiefly balanced by his need to stand for re-election, and the requirement that he leave office peacefully, should he lose the vote.

Schumpeter was writing in the midst of World War II, which had led to the total mobilization of the civilian population in all combatant states. Worldwide, this unprecedented mobilization led to the unprecedented slaughter of sixty million souls, the majority of them civilians, and six million of them Jews. In the United States, it entailed a dramatic increase in the powers of the administrative state and of the state's armed forces; it also triggered a concomitant rise in the perceived need to keep key political deliberations and decisions concealed from the public.

Under the circumstances, it is no wonder that Schumpeter himself was pessimistic about future political prospects, fearing that a "socialist democracy may eventually turn out to be more of a sham than capitalist democracy ever was."

III

AND YET, as World War II unfolded, just as had happened during the Great War that preceded it, there was a paradoxical resurgence of democratic idealism, inspired by Allied claims that their victory would help forge a world "made safe for democracy," just as Woodrow Wilson had promised two generations earlier. In 1941, shortly before America's entry into the war, the British prime minister Winston Churchill and American president Franklin Roosevelt had issued a press release, the so-called Atlantic Charter, solemnly vowing to restore self-government in all countries that had been occupied during the war, and reaffirming the democratic right of all peoples to choose their own form of government.

After savouring the defeat of Hitler and Mussolini, and learning of the horrors of the Nazi genocide of Jews, many hoped that the peoples of the world would never again resort to violence on this industrial scale. After some hesitation, and with compromising caveats similar to those that undermined the League of Nations covenant—above all, a continuing effort to protect the imperial and racial prerogatives of the great powers—the victors agreed to create a new international organization, the United Nations. This time, communists as well as social democrats participated in planning the new international body, alongside liberals and conservatives from the representative democracies of Great Britain, France, and the United States. One result was the active involvement of a broad range of divergent intellectual and political interlocutors in drafting one of the body's most prominent founding documents, the Universal Declaration of Human Rights adopted in 1948.

It is easy to minimize the import of a normative political document arrived at after long deliberation and issued with no means of enforcing the norms it proclaimed. Yet the language of the Declaration helped to inspire later human rights movements. And Article 21 of the Declaration explicitly affirms that

(1) Everyone has the right to take part in the government of his country, directly or through freely chosen representatives.

(2) Everyone has the right of equal access to public service in his country.

(3) The will of the people shall be the basis of the authority of government; this will shall be expressed in periodic and genuine elections which shall be by universal and equal suffrage and shall be held by secret vote or by equivalent free voting procedures.

To the extent that nations like the United States and the Soviet Union thus committed themselves to democratic principles, and yet continued to flout these principles in practice, the expectation of popular sovereignty gave a warrant to recurrent protest movements and revolts, demanding the right of everyone to take part more fully in the government of his or her country.

III

HERE IS A KEY IRONY of the modern world. To this day, democracy as a form of government in most actually existing regimes is more or less a sham, even according to the criteria laid out in the Universal Declaration of Human Rights, and just as Schumpeter said.

And yet, this "sham" also represents an epochal transformation: in the early twenty-first century, very few regimes, unlike most of those that existed in the early eighteenth century, can rule over a subject population with impunity. On the contrary: the rulers of every contemporary regime that professes democratic values, however feebly realized, must periodically face the mundane threat posed by ordinary citizens, however uninformed, periodically queuing at a polling station, to exercise their right to vote, and so to transfer power, if they choose, to an entirely new set of political leaders.

This is, as the Cambridge historian John Dunn puts it in the dyspeptic but accurate conclusion to his 2005 history of democracy, "a world in which faith, deference, and even loyalty have largely passed away, and the keenest of personal admiration seldom lasts for long"— a wan description of what the modern democratic spirit has wrought.

Yet this is also a world where the ideal of democracy is more universally honoured than ever before in human history, and sometimes taken quite seriously, for better or worse.

For example, in the decades since the ratification of the Universal Declaration of Human Rights in 1948, the world has seen most American presidents and diplomats try to follow in Woodrow Wilson's footsteps by promoting liberal democratic expectations around the world, sometimes at gunpoint.

It has seen the election of demagogues who can appeal to the visceral impulses of ordinary citizens, and the emergence of political parties that are vehemently hostile to remote elites—even as these elites in most places retain their grip on power, as a few superrich individuals and families just keep getting richer and ever more insulated from the accidents of fate that define everyday life for the remaining 99 percent of the globe's population.

Under these circumstances, it's perhaps not surprising that our world has also witnessed, in virtually every single country, both poor and developed, socialist or communist, autocratic or liberal, a fitful, sometimes futile series of popular uprisings and protests, when crowds of ordinary people unite to demand a fairer share of the common wealth—and to claim for themselves a larger share in more truly democratic institutions, come what may.

CODA:

WHO ARE WE?

O N JANUARY 21, 2017, tens of thousands of protesters inched up Fifth
Avenue in Manhattan. It was a sunny Saturday afternoon, and the mood
was festive, as men, women, children, grandparents, black, white, brown, all
moved toward Trump Tower, a gilded skyscraper near Central Park, and the
home of Donald J. Trump, the forty-fifth president of the United States,
who had assumed office the day before.

The street was a river of "pussyhats," pink hats with cat ears. They
were an allusion to a video recording made public in the final weeks
of the presidential campaign the previous autumn, revealing that
Trump, at the height of his celebrity as the host of the reality-television
show *The Apprentice*, had bragged to a fellow TV host about forcing

himself on women: "When you're a star," Trump had said, "you can do it. They let you do anything," adding, "Grab 'em by the pussy. You can do anything."

Despite such revelations of boorish behaviour, and despite losing the popular vote to Hillary Clinton, Mr. Trump had won a clear victory in the Electoral College—the peculiarly American institution created in the Constitution as a compromise between electing the president by a vote in Congress, or electing the president by direct popular vote (in most states, the winner of the popular vote in that state wins all of that state's electors, who in turn cast votes in the Electoral College).

Trump's rallies had attracted large crowds of impassioned people. A cartoon of self-reliant cockiness, the candidate adored being the centre of attention and, like a louche comedian, merrily defying the norms of civil discourse. He took pleasure in demeaning people publicly and in making the many targets of his scorn seem small, insignificant, and worthy only of contempt. He made fabricated claims with impunity, in part because he mocked credentialed experts, and in part because he asserted that most traditional sources of news were flogging fake stories, while he alone was levelling with people. The billionaire who bragged about bribing politicians was ready to blow the whistle on a shadowy world of political fixers: "Nobody knows the system better than me, which is why I alone can fix it."

The anti-Trump protest in Manhattan, though inspired by the Women's March on Washington being held the same day, had quickly exceeded the ability of the original organizers to control it. Fifth Avenue crackled with energy, almost giddiness, as participants took turns brandishing their handmade posters to the cheers of participants: "Fuck the Electoral College." "I can't believe we're still protesting this." "Pussy Power." "Equality Includes Every '1.'" "Our voices together can't be silenced."

Every few minutes, a chant would rise and fall:

"We are the popular vote!"

"Not my president!"

I joined in the shouting, joyful at the crowd surrounding me—more than four hundred thousand people in all, according to the mayor's office, making it one of the largest public demonstrations in New York City's history. (The largest was perhaps the anti-nuclear march in Central Park held on June 12, 1982, which attracted more than one million people.)

"What does democracy look like?" someone shouted every few minutes. And every few minutes, the crowd roared back:

"This is what democracy looks like!"

III

OUR CALL-AND-RESPONSE implied that *we* were the real democrats—not *them*.

But that was a facile assumption. The same claim—"This is what democracy looks like"—could just as well apply to the complex electoral process that had produced a Trump presidency. And it certainly applied to the broader political movement he inspired, which invited angry white voters to decide for themselves, "Who was sovereign? The people, or money?"

Hence the pathos of the Manhattan anti-Trump protest: for who, after all, were *we*?

I had felt proud of Trump's predecessor, Barack Obama. It wasn't because I agreed with all of his policies—I didn't—but in part, it was because he had made history as our first black president, and I longed for America to become an ever more inclusive country. It was also because Obama was a trained professional, a lawyer, a professor, an intellectual, and a writer. And not only that, he lived near the University of Chicago campus, where I had attended the lab school that John Dewey had founded. In other words, Obama was closer than any other president in my lifetime to being a member of *my* tribe.

The election of Trump shocked me. I was in Norway at the time, where I was to deliver a talk on the function of cultural criticism in a democratic society. As soon as the results were clear, and still shaken by the implications, I sent a somewhat overwrought email the next morning to my three sons:

The sun is shining in Norway as another day begins in Europe, the site of the world's most recent auto-da-fé. And I am reminded of the epigraph, by William Morris, which I included at the front of the book I dedicated to my three sons, *"Democracy Is in the Streets"*: "Men fight and lose the battle, and the thing that they fought for comes about in spite of their defeat, and when it comes it turns out not to be what they meant, and other men have to fight for what they meant under another name." Dearly beloved, I am sorry that I and my generation of compatriots have failed you, and your children, as our country reaps the whirlwind. It is you, and they, who will have to make it right, if right it can be made. But you know, and you care, about what is right, and in that I find some measure of comfort in this dark time.

"That's not who we are," Obama liked to say as president, in an effort, I assume, to appeal to our better angels. He wanted to gesture toward the idea that America is a nation of immigrants and a model of liberal democratic values, like tolerance, civil rights for minorities, and civil liberties for all. All these things seemed to me good, and deeply in the American grain.

Trump, in stark contrast, highlighted other aspects of democracy in America: the appeal of a demagogue who mirrors the simplest impulses of the meanest among us; a certain racially inflected nativism; an animus against trained experts who can be intimidating and bureaucrats who can be bossy; and a fascination with celebrities who, to an exaggerated degree, seem to enjoy some version of the so-called American Dream.

By 2016, we Americans were more polarized than ever. And the nation's complex form of indirect electoral democracy always had the potential to thwart majorities, in addition to producing results that would inevitably leave large groups of people in a bitterly divided country feeling like strangers in their own land.

Obama's election had obviously made a large number of Americans feel that way in 2008 and 2012. Now it was my turn.

III

"IN THE UNITED STATES," the American political scholar Samuel P. Huntington remarked, what seems like a broad "ideological consensus"—for example, over the values of democracy and self-reliant individualism, and the providential arc of an American history that bends toward justice—"is the source of political conflict." In America, he observed, "polarization occurs over moral issues rather than economic ones." The land suffers "moral convulsions" because the pursuit of widely shared ideals—including democracy itself—inevitably leads to the recurrent recognition that these ideals are both understood differently by different groups of citizens and, often, being honoured in the breach: "The image of the triumphant realization of the American promise or ideal was an exercise in patriotic unreality at best and hypocrisy at worst. The history of American politics is the repetition of new beginnings and flawed outcomes, promise and disillusion, reform and reaction."

These now seem to me sensible observations—but Huntington's work, when I first read it, angered me. I bristled at his hostility to the New Left and his scepticism about the value of participatory democracy. I can see from my tattered and marked-up copy of his contribution to the 1975 study *The Crisis of Democracy* that I was primed as a young professor of politics, just starting to teach at the University of Texas in Austin, to be outraged by his barbed quips, for example: "What the Marxists mistakenly attribute to capitalist economics"— constant conflict—"is, in fact, a product of democratic politics."

Huntington's thesis was deceptively simple: the very "vigor" of democracy in the United States in the 1960s had contributed to "a democratic distemper," involving an unstable combination of growing popular demands for more government services, on the one hand, and a growing popular distrust of governmental authority, on the other. What ailed the country was an excess of democracy. America needed a new "balance," in which citizens would remember that in many situations "expertise, seniority, experience, and special talents may override the claims of democracy as a way of constituting authority."

Perhaps, Huntington implied, John Adams had been right to warn, almost two hundred years ago (roughly the lifespan of the Athenian democracy), that "there never was a democracy yet that did not commit suicide."

Such worries, which seemed absurd to me as a young man, seemed eerily apt as I was writing this book—and discovering that my own views had grown closer to Huntington's than I imagined possible.

III

A QUINTESSENTIAL PRODUCT of America's liberal aspirations and meritocratic institutions in the relatively prosperous and progressive milieu he was raised within, Samuel Huntington came of age during the height of what some, during and after World War II, began boastfully to call "the American Century." He descended from old Yankee stock, his forebears having arrived in 1633, not long after the *Mayflower* had brought the first Puritan refugees to New England. He grew up among wordsmiths: his mother was a writer, his father was an editor, and his maternal grandfather had been a publisher who championed the progressive views of Theodore Roosevelt and Woodrow Wilson.

A prodigy, the young Huntington tested into New York's elite Stuyvesant High School, left early to attend Yale College, and graduated early again, at the age of eighteen; in 1950, after a stint in the army, he became a full-time teacher at Harvard. He was twenty-three years old.

Modest in demeanour and mild-mannered by temperament, he belonged to the uppermost stratum of American scholarly and intellectual life, joining the small number of bright young men (in those days it was only men) clustered in Cambridge, New Haven, New York, Princeton, Chicago, and Palo Alto, on call to offer policy advice or join the administration of the U.S. government. He was just the kind of learned expert that Woodrow Wilson, and Walter Lippmann after him, had hoped would help steer American society on a steady course toward the realization of its guiding liberal democratic principles.

But he was fated to live in interesting times.

By 1947, a global cold war had begun after both Winston Churchill and Harry Truman warned that the world was now divided into two rival camps by an "iron curtain," imposed on Europe by Joseph Stalin, premier of the Soviet Union and also, more importantly, general secretary of the Central Committee of the Communist Party of the Soviet Union (dictators for life must wear many hats).

As a result of this epochal showdown, liberal representative democracies on the western side of a militarized zone confronted soviet-style "democratic centralist" regimes on the eastern side.

Each of these self-styled "superpowers" claimed to be more authentically democratic—more representative of the wishes of their sovereign people—than the other.

Of course, these claims were breathtakingly misleading. The leaders of the rival nations had assiduously perfected strong central states defined not by transparency and broad popular political participation but rather by "hierarchy, coercion, secrecy and deception" (in Huntington's words, describing the American side of this Faustian pact). Even more alarming, their existential struggle, however muted for public consumption, made sensitive observers worry about the fate of the earth. An arms race consumed the rival peoples' resources. Both sides stockpiled a growing number of ever more sophisticated nuclear weapons. Both sides manoeuvred for advantage, in part through proxy wars that engulfed distant lands in death and destruction, and in part through hair-raising episodes of "nuclear brinksmanship." The most memorable example of the latter came during the Cuban missile crisis of 1962, when, as declassified documents show, Soviet and American leaders came dangerously close to irradiating a large portion of the Northern Hemisphere.

Meanwhile, a series of newly independent nations appeared,

claiming their right to self-determination, starting with the partitioning of British India into the new nations of the Republic of India and the Dominion of Pakistan in 1947. The Republic of Korea and the Democratic People's Republic of Korea followed in 1948, the former located in the southern part of the Korean peninsula, the latter in the north. The Lao People's Democratic Republic was declared after Laos obtained its freedom from France in 1949. The Netherlands granted independence to Indonesia the same year. The United Kingdom of Libya was formed in 1950. The following year the United States established a formal association with the Commonwealth of Puerto Rico that stopped short of offering the former protectorate full rights of self-determination.

And so it went through the 1950s, with perhaps the most bitter proxy war and struggle for independence erupting in Vietnam. This was a thirty-year war that started in 1946 with a revolt against the nation's French colonial masters, and then evolved after 1954, when the French withdrew, into a civil war, with the United States supporting an autocratic "Republic of Vietnam" against a communist "Democratic Republic of Vietnam" in a losing battle that ended only in 1975, with the fall of Saigon.

Samuel Huntington devoted a lifetime to understanding these epochal developments, and to analysing the institutions, national identities, and political ideals that lay behind them. A lifelong supporter of America's Democratic Party—he wrote speeches for its candidate Adlai Stevenson in his losing 1956 presidential campaign against the Republican World War II hero Dwight D. Eisenhower—he became obsessed with how best to maintain political order in a world where political conflict was chronic, and potentially catastrophic. An Episcopalian, he admired the midcentury Protestant theologian Reinhold Niebuhr, who thought wicked men could not survive without strong institutional restraints—Niebuhr famously declared that "man's capacity for justice makes democracy possible; but man's inclination to injustice makes democracy necessary." (It is worth noting that Niebuhr's 1944 maxim makes no sense unless "democracy" means the kind of representative regime directing a strong central state that President Franklin D. Roosevelt presided over in America's war against Hitler's Germany and the Empire of Japan.)

After the war, Huntington's curiosity was piqued by President Harry Truman's firing of General Douglas MacArthur for insubordination at the height of the Korean War. What, he wondered, should be the proper relation of *The Soldier and the State*, to borrow the title of his first book, published in 1957. His central thesis was that only a professionally trained officer corps, given autonomous command of a large standing army, could assure both national security and civilian control, offering as one model the nineteenth-century German army, which was composed of "average men succeeding by superior education, organization and experience." He praised West Point as "a bit of Sparta in the midst of Babylon"—and that zinger was enough to convince his Harvard colleagues to deny him tenure that year, on the grounds that he was infatuated with Prussian-style militarism. (He would return to Harvard after only five years in the wilderness, teaching at Columbia.)

In 1968, several years after completing a comparative study of the United States and the Soviet Union with his friend Zbigniew Brzezinski, Huntington published his next significant book, *Political Order in Changing Societies*, analysing the global scene. In this context, Huntington admonished American policymakers to temper their characteristic "hopeful air of unreality" when it came to foreign affairs. He warned that it was counterproductive for American policymakers to assume that newly independent peoples, freed from the domination of their Westernizing masters, would rush to embrace the liberal democratic institutions that most postwar theorists of "modernization," like Woodrow Wilson before them, had naïvely assumed were the logical goal of global historical development.

By then, Huntington had joined the administration of President Lyndon Johnson. At the president's behest, he chaired the Vietnam subcommittee of the Southeast Asia Development Advisory Group from 1966 to 1969—its very existence suggested the global reach of

American power in this period. In an infamous essay published in 1968 in *Foreign Affairs*, Huntington publicly expressed optimism that the Orwellian American policy of "forced-draft urbanization"— dragooning South Vietnamese peasants into relocating to adjacent urban areas with a garrison—might succeed in shoring up resistance to communist forces. Yet as declassified documents subsequently revealed, Huntington behind closed doors was arguing the opposite, trying to convince Johnson and his vice president, Hubert Humphrey, that the administration's military strategy in Vietnam was doomed to failure.

His public comments turned Huntington into a villain in the eyes of antiwar protesters like myself, and our judgement was mainly moral: his apparent support for the Vietnam War was not merely misguided, or ill-judged, it was *wicked*. But in retrospect Huntington is perhaps better seen not as the embodiment of pure evil, as some of us too hastily concluded, but rather as something subtler, and perhaps more insidious: the ideal type of the modern-day liberal technocrat—the tough-minded expert insider who is willing to speak truth to power but who is loyal to a fault and therefore speaks truth only in secret, while behaving obsequiously in public.

When Hubert Humphrey, in his losing campaign to become president in 1968, belatedly delivered a speech announcing that if elected president he would pursue a political, not a purely military, solution to the war in Vietnam, it was Huntington who wrote it. But it was too little, too late. Humphrey lost, Richard Nixon became president, and Huntington left Washington with dirty hands and a signal failure to play a winning inside game.

Reviled by outspoken student radicals, Huntington became the target of personal attacks after his return to Harvard. His young son awoke one day to find "War Criminal Lives Here" painted on the front door of his family's Cambridge home. Harvard's Center for International Affairs, where Huntington worked, was firebombed. In the eyes of critics like Noam Chomsky, he was one of the "new mandarins of American power."

Yet Huntington, despite the violence in the air, was imperturbable;

if anything, he seemed to relish the attention. He grew ever more fearless in his willingness to broach provocative ideas in print, expressing the conservative core of his liberal democratic views with aphoristic force: "Men may have order without liberty, but they cannot have liberty without order. Authority has to exist before it can be limited." He frankly feared anarchy more than he feared domination: "'Who governs?' is obviously one of the most important questions to ask concerning any political system," he remarked. "Even more important, however, may be the question, 'Does anybody govern?'" (For the many peoples around the world in the last century who have had to endure massacres and famines in failed states, these are not academic questions.)

Although Huntington briefly worked for Brzezinski when his old friend became national security adviser for the Democratic president Jimmy Carter in the late 1970s, he mainly focused his energies on teaching undergraduates at Harvard—and on episodically commenting in books and articles on the main currents of history as he perceived them.

When the Soviet Union unexpectedly collapsed in 1989, and a renewed democratic spirit afterward led to mainly peaceful transitions to liberal democratic regimes in Poland, Czechoslovakia, and Hungary, Huntington saw no cause to celebrate. Where his student Francis Fukuyama perceived the apparent triumph of liberal democracy as the logical climax of world history, Huntington discerned the ascendance of new centres of political power in China and the Islamic world, both representing mature civilizations of great antiquity—and both offering religious and authoritarian alternatives to Western liberal ideals of human rights and representative democracy. "A multicultural world is unavoidable because global empire is impossible," Huntington concluded. "In a multicivilizational world, the constructive course is to renounce universalism, accept diversity, and seek commonalities."

Huntington's position was nuanced—but his book's title characteristically was not. As a result, *The Clash of Civilizations* provoked furious opposition when it was first published as an essay in *Foreign Affairs* in 1993, and then as a book in 1996.

Several years later, after the destruction of New York's Twin Towers on September 11, 2001, had inaugurated what, as I write, seems to be an unending and unwinnable American "War on Terrorism," I found myself debating Huntington's thesis at a three-day conference billed as Jihad, McWorld, Modernity: Public Intellectuals Debate "The Clash of Civilizations." The keynote speaker, the political theorist Benjamin Barber, a well-known advocate of "strong democracy," tore into our topic with gusto. Professor Huntington was a "hyperbolic commentator" whose views were "redolent of 18th-century imperialism," Barber thundered, before going on to blame American popular culture for offending Muslims by beaming vulgar music videos around the world instead of promoting the poetry of Walt Whitman. The title of Huntington's book had become a sound bite, and Barber, like most of us that weekend, missed Huntington's point entirely.

A similar fate awaited Huntington's final book, *Who Are We?* published in 2004, about "the challenges to America's National Identity," as the subtitle put it. This time Huntington analysed what he took to be the long-term implications of demographic and cultural trends on America's sense of national identity. Once again, critics were infuriated, this time by the matter-of-fact way Huntington described the influx of undocumented immigrants and the rapid growth of the country's Spanish-speaking population as dangerously weakening the traditional hold of white, Anglo-Saxon, Protestant men on the levers of political power.

"One very plausible reaction" to such an erosion of power, he warned with chilling accuracy,

> would be the emergence of exclusivist sociopolitical
> movements composed largely but not only of white males,
> protesting and attempting to stop or reverse these changes
> and what they believe, accurately or not, to be the diminution
> of their social and economic status, their loss of jobs to

immigrants and foreign countries, the perversion of their culture, the displacement of their language, and the erosion or even evaporation of the historical identity of their country. Such movements would be both racially and culturally inspired and could be anti-Hispanic, anti-black, and anti-immigration. They would be the heir to the many comparable exclusivist racial and antiforeign movements that helped define American identity in the past—social movements, political groups, intellectual currents, dissidents of various sorts who share these characteristics in many ways but still have enough in common to be brought together under the label "white nativism."

Huntington highlighted four main components of American identity in this final work. The first and most important, he suggested, was racial, as America for more than two centuries had defined itself in terms of white supremacy, "which involved the enslavement, subordination, and segregation of blacks, the massacre of Indians, and the exclusion of Asians." Ethnicity as a criterion of American identity had been subsequently mobilized by Anglophile elites after 1924 to marginalize immigrants from Southern and Eastern Europe, most of them Catholic or Jewish. A third and ever more salient factor in the dominant shared culture became a deep sense of religiosity ("In God We Trust"), primarily associated with Anglo-Protestant forms of Christian worship.

The final key aspect of American identity, according to Huntington, was "an ideology (the 'American Creed') articulated in the Declaration of Independence," and a handful of other documents that had enunciated shared political principles.

As Huntington well knew, America's democratic ideology was egalitarian and inclusive in principle. But he had previously shown that it also generated chronic conflict, as liberalizing reforms produced, in turn, furious political resistance (as had happened, for example, with the civil rights movement of the 1960s, which was followed by a striking resurgence of racially inflected conservative political movements in the decades that followed).

Hence the pointed question Huntington posed in his final book: "Can a people remain a people if all that holds them together is a set of political principles?" He answered, "Perhaps. But the historical evidence is not encouraging as was underlined by the collapse of the other contemporary superpower whose identity was solely defined by its ideology."

If the Soviet version of democratic idealism had proved impotent under duress and collapsed, to be replaced by a renascent, religiously inflected form of Russian nationalism, why should Americans assume that *their* version of democratic idealism would prove any more resilient, if put to the test by white nativism?

For Samuel P. Huntington at the end of his life, this is what American democracy looked like: a fragile ideology, with cloudy prospects.

III

"THIS IS WHAT democracy looks like!"—for some of us protesting Trump in New York on January 21, 2017, this was a familiar chant. We'd heard it before, earlier in the decade, during the Occupy Wall Street movement. That movement had been inspired, in part, by the staggering growth of inequality in the United States and around the world, as a result of the partial dismantling of social insurance policies that, earlier in the twentieth century, had been the chief egalitarian achievement of labour, liberal, and social democratic political parties worldwide.

Occupy Wall Street was inspired as well by the wave of democratic uprisings that had begun in January 2011 in Tunisia, Egypt, Libya, and Syria, among other Arab countries, before spreading to Russia, Spain, and Greece. Samuel Huntington had identified "three waves" of global democratization: the first occurring in the United States and Europe from 1776 to 1945; the second occurring around the world as a result of decolonization after World War II; and the third occurring after the collapse of the Soviet Union in 1989, and sweeping through Eastern Europe,

Latin America, and Asia. Since then, other scholars have suggested a "fourth wave," this one including much of sub-Saharan Africa and the Arab World, and cresting in 2011.

The Occupy movement was prompted, in part, by the impressive speed with which Arab activists had harnessed social media to mobilize large masses of protesters, as if to prove (as one Internet guru boasted) "the power of organizing without organization"—an anarchist's dream come true. At the same time, Occupy was modelled more closely on the direct-democratic public assemblies of protesters favoured that year by the Indignados—the Outraged—a Spanish anti-austerity movement that occupied Puerta del Sol square in Madrid in May 2011.

Hoping to produce a similar upwelling of democratic discontent in America, a group of self-selected activists, about sixty in all, met on the afternoon of August 2, 2011, at Bowling Green, a park in downtown Manhattan with the famous bronze statue of a charging bull, installed in 1989 as a tribute to the financial power of nearby Wall Street.

The people had gathered by the bull in response to a call for a general assembly that would organize an occupation of Wall Street. The idea, which originated with *Adbusters*, an anti-advertising Canadian print magazine (run, naturally, by veterans of the advertising industry), was popularized on social media by the hacker collective Anonymous, whose followers fetishized the wearing of Guy Fawkes masks from the graphic novel and film *V for Vendetta*. In the event, only a few dozen seasoned activists showed up, from a variety of political backgrounds. Some were students, others were union organizers. There were socialists, but a surprising number were libertarians committed to "leaderless resistance" and also allied with Ron Paul, who had been a maverick Republican candidate for president in 2008.

But still more were partisans of direct-democratic public assemblies, who in some cases considered themselves anarchists. Expecting an open assembly, the radical democrats and anarchists had found instead a few people with megaphones and prefab placards, trying to rally participants for a conventional march that would make conventional demands. In response, the radical democrats, led by an anthropology professor and avowed anarchist named David Graeber, retreated to a corner of the park to discuss alternative steps.

Sitting in a circle, they debated how they might better organize a Wall Street occupation. They agreed that they would take seriously the online call to create a general assembly—and proposed implementing one of the most radical forms of direct democracy conceivable: a daily meeting, open to all, where virtually all decisions would be made without voting, by consensus, and formally subject to veto by a single "block," if anyone felt a proposed decision violated an ethical principle.

It all seemed hopelessly idealistic. But the direct democrats prevailed. And against all odds, the movement they helped to launch briefly changed the political conversation in America. Occupy Wall Street compelled the media to pay fresh attention to voices on the left. It focused fresh attention on the dramatic rise in economic inequality in the United States and around the world. And despite a deliberate lack of explicit demands, it "reignited hope in the possibility of a free society," in part by exemplifying, in the words of one participant, a new world that was "participatory and democratic to the core."

In this way, Occupy Wall Street resurrected a recurring feature of the international left since the 1960s: an overriding commitment to participatory democracy, understood as the making of decisions in a face-to-face community of friends and not through elected representatives.

I myself had once advocated a similar form of democracy, as an activist in Students for a Democratic Society in the late 1960s, inspired by the vision of "participatory democracy" on offer in the organization's founding manifesto, "The Port Huron Statement." But my own experiments in radical democracy quickly fell apart, as my friends and I tired of the endless meetings and suppressed disagreements that the quest for consensus entailed. As I wrote in my 1987 book, *"Democracy Is in the Streets": From Port Huron to the Siege of Chicago*, perhaps the most important result of the SDS experience was to demonstrate "the incompatibility of rule by consensus with accountable, responsible government in a large organization—or even in a small group of people with divergent interests and a limited patience for endless meetings."

In fact, the young people who drafted "The Port Huron Statement" in 1962 had never meant to propose rule-by-consensus as a working definition of participatory democracy—this was an understanding that evolved later in the decade and was fiercely contested at the time, notably by pragmatic veterans of the Port Huron conference. Yet even this modest lesson about the limits of rule-by-consensus has proved hard to learn, perhaps because, as I also wrote, "for anyone who joined in the search for a democracy of individual participation—and certainly for anyone who remembers the happiness and holds to the hopes that the quest itself aroused—the sense of what politics can mean will never be quite the same again."

The result, for many subsequent groups on the global left, has been an unstable political idealism, an amalgam of direct action and direct democracy, with many of the virtues of a utopian and romantic revolt—passion, moral conviction, a shared joy in the joining of battle—but also some of the vices: above all, an obsession with directly democratic processes and an addiction to creating ever more intense situations of felt personal liberation, regardless of the wider political ramifications.

Avowedly anti-authoritarian, nonhierarchical, and leaderless, Occupy assemblies cropped up in cities across the United States. Most of them adhered to rule-by-consensus as an end in itself and as the best way to show that direct democracy really is workable. The assemblies were a free association of self-selected participants. In principle, anyone might join and participate, just as anyone might exit at any time. The assemblies thus enshrined, in a radical form, the principle that "every person is free to do as they wish."

While the freedom of the individual was in principle inviolable in the assemblies, another goal was to forge, through consensus, a new form of *collective* freedom. Naturally, the assemblies could not hope to realize this goal without some help. Since leaders were not formally acknowledged, help took the form of so-called facilitators, individuals trained to foster what one guide to the process called "Collective Thinking":

> When faced with a decision, the normal response of two people with differing opinions tends to be confrontational. They each defend their opinions with the aim of convincing their opponent, until their opinion has won or, at most, a compromise has been reached. The aim of Collective Thinking, on the other hand, is to construct. That is to say, two people with differing ideas work together to build something new. The onus is therefore not on my idea or yours; rather it is the notion that two ideas together will produce something new, something that neither of us had envisaged beforehand. This focus requires of us that we actively listen.

If a single person blocks consensus, the group must listen even more carefully and seek to find common ground in a way that might win over the individual with objections; "Prejudice and ideology must be left at home." Another goal was to forge a "new subjectivity," expressed in a new form of political speech.

The joy of collectively creating a new political space was palpable in the earliest firsthand accounts of those who occupied Zuccotti Park on September 17: "If you want to see what real democracy, run horizontally, with full participation, looks like, you should be here," wrote one Occupier the next day. Here was a real, and striking, alternative to simply pulling levers to choose between candidates selected in advance by others, and often selected precisely in order to defend the interests of an oligarchic elite. "There is an energy and an amazing consensus process working with 50+ people in general assembly several times a day," wrote another participant a few days later, marvelling at how the group was successfully "making decisions about how to run the occupation—from when to do marches, to how to communicate, to ideas about food, art, entertainment, and all kinds of issues that anyone can bring up."

The first surge of enthusiasm gradually waned. As time passed and the Occupiers dug in, the general assembly in New York became bogged down in logistical details. A great deal of time and energy was devoted to making sure the Occupiers had sleeping bags and food and were able to clear garbage from the site. Meetings often lasted for hours. To keep the assembly moving, the facilitators became ever more forceful in setting an agenda and limiting the scope of debate. Sometimes the group resorted to a form of "modified consensus," which instead of unanimity required a supermajority of at least two-thirds. Even then, anyone had a right to veto a proposal if he or she felt it violated some fundamental principle that might cause him or her to quit the group.

Effective decision making on many matters, both logistical and political, simultaneously devolved to a number of decentralized "working groups" that met separately and fell under the effective control of various individuals who assumed de facto power within the movement. (As one of the leaderless group's leaders confided, "Consensus only works if working groups or collectives don't feel they need to seek constant approval from the larger group, if initiative arises from below.") The groups working on direct action and confrontations with the police naturally put a premium on solidarity and discretion, not an open airing of doubts and disagreements.

This process of political experimentation slowly ground to a halt, as small groups of neo-anarchists, most notably in New York City, inspired by the militancy of Occupy Oakland, kept searching for confrontational "experiences of visionary inspiration"—at the time, it seemed as if the painstaking task of creating a sustainable movement had proved too painful, and boringly pragmatic, for many followers who had been inspired by Occupy Wall Street in its early months. Even worse, the police departments in cities like New York proved adept—thanks in part to the vulnerability of social media to government surveillance—at infiltrating various groups working on direct action, and arresting activists before they could act.

In the early hours of November 15, 2011, the New York Police Department had little trouble clearing Zuccotti Park of its tents and occupants. Although protesters were allowed back into the park without camping equipment, the downtown occupation had lost precious momentum.

Over the winter, activists tried to regroup and to plan another big citywide protest. But a planned May Day blockade of New York City's bridges and tunnels failed to materialize—and after a brief, last hurrah in September 2012, New York City's experiment in rule-by-consensus was effectively finished—the latest in a long line of failures on the international left to elaborate new forms of horizontal self-governance that can transcend the consensus model and solve some of the manifold problems of democracy in a complex modern society.

III

THE FIRST and perhaps most obvious problem is scale. It is one thing to create a participatory community of five hundred or a thousand—or even a democracy of forty thousand direct participants, as the Athenians did in the fifth and fourth centuries B.C. It is quite another thing to imagine direct, participatory interaction in large and complex societies on the scale of the United States. Perhaps one can envision a federation of nested assemblies, along the lines proposed by Condorcet in 1793 or G.D.H. Cole in his Guild Socialist essays, but any serious effort to implement such a structure will require a delegation of authority and the selection of representatives—in short, the creation of an *indirect* democracy, and at some distance from most participants.

Even more challenging is the fact that many of the protesters' concerns—for example, systemic debt, structural unemployment, the unfettered power of finance capital, global warming—involve dilemmas that can be addressed best by new forms of global and transnational regulation and governance, not by local assemblies.

Equally insidious are the paradoxical results that occur in a polarizing protest movement that simultaneously demands consensus in its organs of self-government. As a result of the willingness of moderates within such a movement to compromise, the consensus view that prevails is generally the most radical alternative on offer (as had happened before in SDS in the late 1960s—yet another illustration of what Cass Sunstein has called "the law of group polarization").

Some of these problems could be papered over briefly. Occupy proved that a handful of networked activists can exploit social media to muster a large, ostensibly leaderless protest movement. But when the tear gas and crowds have dispersed from the city squares, those left behind will have to face the fact that "organizing without organizations" is a fantasy—not a winning long-term political strategy.

In any case, the very conditions of the Occupy general assembly's existence—it was, after all, a free association of self-selected participants—meant that these experiments in participatory democracy never had to confront seriously the toughest challenge to social democratic ideals in a complex and large modern society. That challenge is coping with participants with incommensurable beliefs and convictions, including radically different views on whether or not social justice requires less income inequality, never mind the abolition of capitalism.

One glance at the world we actually live in should suffice to remind us of the many other things people do *not* share: notably moral values and religious faith, but also a passion for political participation. As Hannah Arendt remarked—and this is in fact a crucial point—one of "the most important negative liberties we have enjoyed since the end of the ancient world" is "freedom from politics, which was unknown to Rome or Athens and which is politically the most relevant part of our Christian heritage."

The larger a group, the more ineradicable such diversity will be, unless the group is willing to resort to coercion, in an effort to force unity and guarantee political participation (as has happened routinely in a great many avowedly democratic and socialist organizations and states over the years).

In other words, I seriously doubt that experiments in rule-by-consensus, like those I experienced in the 1960s, or the Occupy movement in 2011, will *ever* generate the kinds of alternative institutions that are needed to meet the challenges of our current situation.

III

INSTEAD OF SINGLE-MINDEDLY PURSUING a new form of "collective thinking" through endless meetings meant to forge consensus—a quixotic and self-destructive goal that led astray the sans-culottes in 1793, the soviets in 1905 and 1917, and the New Left of the 1960s— we would do better to explore new ways to foster a tolerant ethos that accepts, and can acknowledge, that there are many incompatible forms of life and forms of politics, not always directly democratic or participatory, in which humans can flourish. This, in part, is what I understand by the aspiration to create a liberal democracy.

III

IN 2017, CONDOLEEZZA RICE, the secretary of state under George W. Bush and a professed champion of liberal democracy, published a book with a title that seemed eerily irrelevant in the early months of Donald J. Trump's presidency—*Democracy: Stories from the Long Road to Freedom*. The daughter of an African American educator, she had grown up in Alabama at a time when that state was still segregated. After college, she did graduate work in political science, becoming an expert in Soviet politics and international relations. In 1981, she joined the faculty of Stanford University, subsequently serving in the National Security Council under President George H. W. Bush, where she had her first real experience in government as part of the foreign policy team that oversaw the start of democratic transitions in Eastern and Central European countries after the fall of the Berlin Wall in 1989, and the collapse of the Soviet Union in 1991.

She was, in other words, like Samuel Huntington before her, just the kind of liberal technocrat that the direct democrats in Occupy Wall Street regarded as complicit in ongoing American war crimes.

The cover of Rice's book features a famous black-and-white photograph of Martin Luther King, Jr., at the head of a march from Selma to

Montgomery, Alabama, in 1965—a high point of the American civil rights movement, which Rice covers in the first chapter of her book. Subsequent chapters focus on Russia and the rise of democracy in Poland, recounting how the United States under George H. W. Bush tried to foster a "new world order," based on the peaceful global spread of liberal democracy and capitalism. Drawing on her own experience in the 2000s, Rice also details the more daunting democratic challenges faced in Kenya, Colombia, Iraq, and Egypt in that decade.

Rice apparently harbours few of the qualms about modern democracy's universal appeal that haunted Huntington's thinking. On the contrary, she is unabashed in her conviction that the United States is exceptional in the universal obligation it bears to support the democratic aspirations of all peoples—in some cases, such as Iraq, through the use of armed force.

Rice's own career as national security adviser and secretary of state to George W. Bush highlights the ease with which a principled goal—for example, the reconstruction, under American supervision, of Iraq in 2005 as a "democratic, federal, representative republic"—may also trigger depraved conduct (such as torturing Iraqi prisoners in Abu Ghraib, a crime acknowledged but played down in Rice's terse account). One is reminded of the murderous consequences of other modern efforts to institute democratic ideals. But I also found myself struck by the contrast with Trump, who seemed in 2017 to stand for nothing at all, apart from reaping the rewards of office and representing the collective egoism of America.

Rice offers only an implicit definition of liberal democracy, by referring to the 1948 Universal Declaration of Human Rights: its components must include the right to life, liberty, and security of person; freedom of thought, conscience, and religion; freedom of opinion and expression; freedom of peaceful assembly and association; and the right to take part in government, directly or through freely chosen representatives. And with this implicit definition in mind—and in a context of arguing for the universal relevance of American liberal democratic values—she reaches an optimistic conclusion: "If democracy is broadly understood to mean the right to speak your mind, to be free from the arbitrary power of the state, and to insist that those who would govern you must ask for your consent, then democracy—the only form of government that guarantees these freedoms—has never been more widely accepted as right."

III

OTHER SOCIAL SCIENTISTS are more sceptical. Some have even decried a "democratic recession," others, a "democratic disconnect." But of course everything hinges on precisely how we decide to define modern democracy, and especially liberal democracy, and chart its vicissitudes over time.

In 1970, Robert Dahl, his generation's greatest American scholar of democracy as a form of government, proposed that a political regime must meet eight institutional requirements to be considered a democracy: (1) almost all adult citizens have the right to vote; (2) almost all adult citizens are eligible to hold office; (3) political leaders have the right to compete for votes; (4) elections are free and fair; (5) all citizens may form and join political parties and other kinds of political associations; (6) all citizens can freely express their political opinions; (7) diverse sources of information about politics and public policies exist and are legally protected; and (8) government policies depend on votes, or other expressions of public opinion.

This is a fairly minimal definition of democracy—yet it's not clear that the United States in the 2010s met even these basic requirements. For example, the political scientists Christopher Achen and Larry Bartels in 2016 marshalled a great deal of empirical evidence to show that in the United States elections demonstrably do *not* produce a responsive government. Instead, individuals sort themselves into segmented groups, choose political parties based on tribal attachments, and then adjust their views of public affairs, and even their perception of reality, to match these attachments; as a result, elections generally turn on voters holding views that are "thin, disorganized, and ideologically incoherent," leaving the country "badly governed by incompetent and untrustworthy politicians beholden to special interests," rather than to the voters they ostensibly represent.

At the same time, voter suppression (via the circulation of negative propaganda, among other tools) is a standard tactic in modern American elections, and many states make it difficult, not easy, to cast a vote. And while it is true *de jure* that all adult citizens in America are eligible to hold public office, de facto only a minority of more or less affluent citizens can afford to run for political offices. There is also a convincing body of empirical research—by Martin Gilens and Benjamin Page, as well as Bartels—suggesting that in America, at least, poorer citizens have almost zero impact on public policy.

In recent years, several organizations devoted to liberal values have tried to define modern democracy more rigorously, in order to produce annual statistics indicating whether it is in retreat—or expanding. For many years, the best-known such index was that produced by Freedom House, an American government-funded nonprofit organization dedicated (in its own words) "to the expansion of freedom and democracy around the world." Ever since the late 1970s, it has graded countries on a scale from 1 to 7, measuring ten indicators of political freedom and fifteen indicators of civil liberties, and then sorting 195 countries into three categories: free, partly free, not free. Its annual report for 2018, titled "Democracy in Crisis," found that a total of seventy-one countries had suffered net declines in political rights and civil liberties, compared with only thirty-five that registered gains: "This marked the 12th consecutive year of decline in global freedom."

Since 2006, *The Economist*, through its Intelligence Unit, has compiled a more fine-grained Democracy Index, and since 2010 the index has been compiled annually. In addition to the political and civil liberties measured by Freedom House, *The Economist* measures the functioning of government, to determine if democratically reached decisions are implemented; the democratic health of the political culture, with apathy and quiescent citizens seen as inconsistent with democracy; and the extent of active, freely chosen participation of citizens in public life, not only through voting but also by joining political parties and taking part in public debates and protests. Based on a scoring of these various indicators, each country is then classified as one of four types of regime: a full democracy; a flawed democracy; an authoritarian regime; or a "hybrid regime," combining authoritarian and democratic features. In its 2017 Democracy Index, *The Economist* concluded that 49.3 percent of the world's population resides in some sort of democracy, though only 4.5 percent live in a "full democracy." The report also finds that in 2017

the average global score fell from 5.52 in 2016 to 5.48 (on a scale of 0 to 10). Some 89 countries experienced a decline in their total score compared with 2016, more than three times as many as the countries that recorded an improvement (27), the worst performance since 2010–11 in the aftermath of the global economic and financial crisis. The other 51 countries stagnated, as their scores remained unchanged compared with 2016.

It is noteworthy that *The Economist*, like Freedom House, does *not* measure levels of social and economic well-being. However, the United Nations does cover these areas in its Human Development Index (which measures good health, access to knowledge, human rights, human security, standard of living, absence of discrimination, dignity, and the extent of political self-determination). Social democrats have long argued that there are social and economic preconditions for fully developing the individual and the collective capacities for self-government—the UN Human Development Index is meant to track progress in fostering these capacities.

Though all three of these indexes are rough instruments (and some scholars dispute their results), their measures, despite some discrepancies in their findings, produce roughly similar conclusions. These conclusions have now been confirmed by a fourth, much more comprehensive new annual report, first issued in 2017 by a joint Swedish-American research venture, the V-Dem Institute. The institute compiled an uncommonly large and detailed data set that covers 177 countries, a staggering 117 years, and more than 350 indicators, as well as 52 indexes measuring various aspects of democracy.

The V-Dem report, interpreting its data within a much longer time frame than the other surveys, concludes that "the average levels of democracy in the world are still close to their highest ever recorded level even if a slight (statistically insignificant) decline may be detectable over the last few years."

The countries with the most freedoms, and the most fully realized democracies, are in general also prosperous, with developed market economies. They also generally score highest on the UN Human Development Index, led by the Scandinavian countries (Norway, Sweden, Iceland, Finland, Denmark), followed by Canada, Australia, and various Northern European countries (Netherlands, Germany, Luxembourg, Switzerland, Ireland). High-ranking Asian nations include Japan and South Korea. Of the Latin American nations, Uruguay ranks high, along with Chile. Africa lags behind the rest of the world. China ranks much higher on the Human Development Index than on the freedom or democracy indexes.

And the United States, which ranks "very high" on human development, and is considered "free" by Freedom House, in 2016 was ranked twenty-first in *The Economist* index, tied with Italy, making it a "flawed democracy" for the first time in the history of the index.

The chief reason for this demotion was not the election of Donald Trump. It was the extremely low level of popular trust in government, elected officials, and political parties in the United States. Indeed, Trump tapped into this popular disaffection with politics and won office in part by mobilizing normally quiescent citizens, arguably *increasing*, not diminishing popular political participation, at least in the course of his campaign to win office.

In other words, the rise of Trump, like the ensuing popular resistance to the legitimacy of his presidency, is, I think, best understood not as a protest against democracy per se but rather as a protest against the *limits* of modern democracy. The British referendum on leaving the

European Union in 2016 similarly mobilized large numbers of previously apathetic citizens to vote. Both elections expressed a desire, however inchoate and potentially self-defeating, for *more* democracy, for a larger voice for ordinary people—not unlike the New Left I was part of in the 1960s, which idealized participatory democracy.

Around the world, several other contemporary popular (or "populist") movements have appeared that are narrowly nationalistic, or sharply opposed to current global trade policies. In some countries, strongmen preside over regimes that have a written constitution, hold elections, and have a superficially open public sphere; a few of these regimes (for example, in 2017, Hungary, Venezuela, and China) are proudly, and explicitly, *illiberal*—but that, in itself, does not make any of them undemocratic.

III

AS A CITIZEN, even of a "flawed democracy," I was free in January 2017 to protest a political leader whose character and public policies I found repugnant. But I was also expected to acknowledge, and peacefully coexist with, compatriots who preferred Trump's policies and personal style. That is a part of what it means to be a citizen in a liberal democracy.

And as I contemplate what democracy has become in modern times, I find myself feeling uncertain about its future

(1) as a name for various actually existing forms of government;

(2) as an ideology, an ideal manipulated by a ruling elite in the material interests of a few, not the many;

(3) as a moral vision, of free institutions as a better solution to the problems of human coexistence than the authoritarian alternatives.

On the one hand, I am painfully aware of the challenges to democracy as an actually existing form of government—the challenges are manifold, and perhaps intractable, as I have tried to suggest in this short history.

On the other hand, because of a democratic faith that was instilled in me from birth, I find it impossible to renounce altogether certain moral and political principles. And even though the line between my considered ideals and what someone else might see as an internalized ideology is blurry, I find as a result that I harbour hopes that form part of who I take myself to be, and therefore inform my own picture of "who we are."

My experience with participatory democracy has taught me the limits of any regime of consensus, which risks silencing disagreements over political alternatives that are important to debate openly. Our ability to reason and exercise sound political judgement is more limited than Condorcet supposed—rendering "the wisdom of crowds" a shaky assumption. But I also believe that modern institutions can do more to appeal to, and engage, people's capacities for reflection and collective deliberation. As the American philosopher David M. Estlund observes, "We sometimes expect too little" from our liberal democracies "precisely because" we prematurely give up on an "aspirational theory," a "normative standard that forces the question of whether more can realistically be expected."

Modern commercial societies, when laxly regulated, are monstrous engines of inequality. But under a democratic form of government with a justly regulated economy—the aspiration of all social democrats and many liberal democrats as well—citizens would not only have equal civil and political rights; they would also know that those who are lucky enough to be born with greater natural talents are not going to get rich at the expense of those less fortunate: in such a society, as John Rawls put it, "men agree to share one another's fate."

The American experience itself proves that a liberal democracy, if one seriously tries to achieve this goal, can be egalitarian and inclusive, and welcoming to immigrants and outsiders regardless of their origin or religious faith. The American experience also proves that sentiments of solidarity can coexist with the kinds of self-reliance and self-determination prized by democratic individualists like Emerson and Whitman.

Still, it will always take effort to realize a society in which citizens are generally tolerant, certainly in America, where the struggle already has involved a bloody civil war over race-based slavery. It is hard to balance the natural yearning for a bounded community—the foundation for feeling part of a "we"—with the open horizons and pluralism of values inevitably produced by global networks of exchange (of ideas, of people, of goods). Practical wisdom may be found in men and women of all sorts—and as the British philosopher A. D. Lindsay put it, "a modern democratic state is only possible if it can combine appreciation of skill, knowledge, and expertness with a reverence for the common humanity of everyday people." But so-called common sense is rare, particularly in people who are experts in some narrowly defined field of knowledge.

And these are just some of the reasons that it is hard to meet the manifold challenges to realizing democratic ideals in large and complex modern societies.

III

IN THE VIEW of Václav Havel, the Czech dissident who helped guide his nation through its deliberately nonviolent transition to free institutions after the destruction of the Berlin Wall in 1989, the very difficulties facing modern liberal democracies will episodically lead to a temptation: people will conclude that political life, viewed realistically, "is chiefly the manipulation of power and public opinion, and that morality has no place in it."

This literally de-moralized view of politics would mean, according to Havel, losing "the idea that the world might actually be changed by the force of truth, the power of a truthful word, the strength of a free spirit, conscience and responsibility—with no guns, no lust for power, no political wheeling and dealing." If we abandon a virtue like truthfulness, we put at risk a public sphere created, in part, by acknowledging a shared reality, and a handful of core, common values, over and above the "hall of mirrors" constructed by competing political parties and the rival worldviews they propagate.

At the time Havel wrote his essay, in 1991, in a series of "Summer Meditations," he was overseeing his nation's reformation as the first freely elected president of post-communist Czechoslovakia. "I am convinced," Havel remarked, "that we will never build a democratic state based on rule of law if we do not at the same time build a state that is—regardless of how unscientific this may sound to the ears of a political scientist—humane, moral, intellectual and spiritual, and cultural. The best laws and best-conceived democratic mechanisms will not in themselves guarantee legality or freedom or human rights—anything, in short, for which they were intended—if they are not underpinned by certain human and social values." And here Havel is insistent: "I feel that the dormant goodwill in people needs to be stirred. People need to hear that it makes sense to behave decently or to help others, to place common interests above their own, to respect the elementary rules of human coexistence."

This is one man's modern liberal democratic faith, plainly stated, without complacency or false confidence.

Democracy as a modern form of government may have first crystallized, as I believe, in the draft constitution Condorcet presented to the French Convention in 1793. But nothing like that consistently democratic document has ever been implemented anywhere. In part, this failure has occurred because Condorcet's constitution presupposes a shared commitment to forging a society of equals, and the trend toward ever greater levels of social and economic inequality in many advanced industrial countries today, as documented by the French economist Thomas Piketty in *Capital in the Twenty-First Century*, if left unchallenged, effectively nullifies such hopes.

But the original revolutionary democratic project was also perverted when, in the hands of fanatics like Babeuf, Rigault, and Lenin, its partisans resorted to brute force and tried to level every single political opponent and institutional obstacle in its path. Václav Havel embraced a democratic revolution that was "self-limiting," precisely because he had experienced, and abhorred, the historical alternative: "Censorship, the terror, and concentration camps are consequences of the same historical phenomenon that produced the collapsing centralized economy we inherited from communism. In fact, they are two dimensions of the same error that began with this ideological illusion, this pseudo-scientific utopia, this loss of a sense of the enigma of life."

The right of a people to form free institutions through political self-determination, enunciated by both Woodrow Wilson and Vladimir Lenin at the dawn of the twentieth century, was undermined when peoples were placed under the tutelage of self-appointed external elites and efforts were made by evangelical democrats to export soviet socialist and liberal regimes at gunpoint. It was also recurrently scarred by insurrections and civil wars that in many cases produced not the new men and new women that Marx (and Frantz Fanon after him) hoped would emerge from the crucible of violence but a hardened ruling class, sometimes more ruthless and cynical than the tyrants it replaced.

Even in circumstances that are far less fraught, Condorcet's key premise of an enlightened public opinion is more threatened than ever by official regulations keeping secret many aspects of executive decision making, and the increasingly sophisticated command and control of information by behavioural scientists and attention merchants, who are able to use behavioural data tracking and other new technologies on the Internet to aim messages with unprecedented precision at responsive audiences. Through online platforms like Facebook, Google, and Twitter, contemporary political propagandists, both foreign and domestic, compete to mould the beliefs of ordinary citizens, most of whom lack equal access to either reliable information or political power in the imperfectly free institutions that actually exist in modern societies. Disinformation is easier than ever to disseminate to understandably suspicious, even paranoid, citizens over global communication networks. Along with the spread of government secrecy, these ever more sophisticated means of propagating lies and creating confusion form a standing threat to any modern democracy.

III

STILL, THE IDEAL SURVIVES.

And democracy, once it is treated by large numbers of ordinary people as a transcendental norm, and functions as a shared faith, is open to being born again, as witness the so-called colour revolutions in the Philippines in 1986, Georgia in 2003, Ukraine in 2004, and Iran in 2009; the nonviolent, self-limiting revolutions in Poland and Czechoslovakia in 1989; the abortive umbrella revolution in Hong Kong in 2014; and the various popular protests in urban squares, from Tiananmen in Peking in 1989, to Tahrir in Cairo in 2011, to Maidan in Kiev in 2014.

Of course, the short-term results are often discouraging, and the goals pursued are sometimes illiberal, even catastrophic. Democratic revolts, like democratic elections, can produce perverse outcomes.

But because a longing for redemptive social change is ingrained in democratic ideals and liberal principles that are now deeply held and widely shared globally, I believe that it is not unreasonable to uphold, however sceptically, and knowing that these words represent a riddle, not a recipe, Abraham Lincoln's characteristically American hope, especially in the darkest of times: "that government of the people, by the people, for the people shall not perish from the earth."

NOTES

PRELUDE: WHAT IS DEMOCRACY?

4 *"If we take the number of people"*: Roberto Stefan Foa and Yascha Mounk, "The Democratic Disconnect," *Journal of Democracy* 27, no. 3 (July 2016): 16. Cf. Arne Næss, Jens A. Christophersen, and Kjell Kvalø, *Democracy, Ideology and Objectivity* (Oslo: Oslo University Press, 1956).

4 *"sovereign democracy"*: Ivan Krastev, "'Sovereign Democracy,' Russian-style," *OpenDemocracy* (November 16, 2006), a gloss on Nikita Garadya, ed., *Sovereignty* (Moscow, 2006; in Russian).

4 *"Democratic People's Republic"*: See the text of the 2016 revised constitution, at https://nkleadershipwatch.wordpress.com/2016/09/04/dprk-constitution-text-released-following-2016-amdendments.

10 *the heart and soul of modern democracy*: Cf. Kloppenberg, *Toward Democracy*, and Levitsky and Ziblatt, *How Democracies Die*. Like many other proponents of

liberal democracy, these authors of two important recent studies tend to focus not on revolts but rather on the salience to modern democracy of an "ethic of responsibility" and of "tolerance" and "forbearance" as political norms.

12 *"The history of philosophy"*: Quentin Skinner, *Liberty before Liberalism* (New York: Cambridge University Press, 1998), 116–117.

12 *They have suggested instead*: See, for example, the contributors to Benjamin Isakhan and Stephen Stockwell, eds., *The Secret History of Democracy* (New York: Palgrave Macmillan, 2011).

13 *"their impact on history, on later societies"*: Finley, *Democracy Ancient and Modern*, 14.

13 *a friend*: The novelist Rick Moody, email of July 30, 2017, sent after a public reading of a portion of this book: "I think in the common discourse of the papers and the middle schools, etc., there is still this propagandistic idea that we are conducting a democracy, which seems very nearly laughable. But what I also liked about the implications of what you read is the opposite thought, too, that neither do we have NOTHING to do with a democracy. It's just not as simple as all that."

14 description of nineteenth-century origins of "liberalism": See Rosenblatt, *The Lost History of Liberalism*. Cf. Duncan Bell, "What Is Liberalism?," *Political Theory* 42, no. 6 (2014): 682–715.

14 *In the United States, liberalism was introduced*: See Walter Lippmann, "Liberalism in America," *The New Republic* (December 31, 1919), 150.

15 *collective freedom to wield their power*: A point memorably made by Benjamin Constant in "The Liberty of the Ancients Compared with That of the Moderns," speech delivered at the Athénée Royal in Paris, 1819.

15 *"It was not religious liberty they sought"*: Edmund S. Morgan, *Inventing the People: The Rise of Popular Sovereignty in England and America* (New York: W. W. Norton, 1988), 98.

15 *"What! Freedom can only be maintained"*: Rousseau, *Contrat social*, 3:xiv.

15 *"Even with the limitless expansion of state power"*: Hans Kelsen, *The Essence and Value of Democracy*, trans. Brian Graf (Lanham, MD: Rowman & Littlefield, 2013), 32.

16 *"illiberal state"*: Viktor Orbán, speech at the 25th Balvanyos Free Summer University and Youth Camp, July 26, 2015, http://budapestbeacon.com/public-policy/full-text-of-viktor-orbans-speech-at-baile-tusnad-tusnadfurdo-of-26-july-2014/10592.

16 *"Few leaders and movements in the West"*: William Galston, "The Populist Moment," *Journal of Democracy* 28, no. 2 (April 2017): 30.

16 *Such worries are nothing new*: Crozier, Huntington, and Watanuki, *The Crisis of Democracy*.

1. A CLOSED COMMUNITY OF SELF-GOVERNING CITIZENS

19 *When American political scientists speak of democracy*: For these and other criteria of a modern democracy, see Larry Diamond, "What Is Democracy?," lecture delivered at Hilla University for Humanistic Studies, January 21, 2004, https://web .stanford.edu/~ldiamond/iraq/WhaIsDemocracy012004.htm.

20 *"insolence, anarchy, wastefulness, and shamelessness"*: Plato, *Republic*, 560e.

21 *"subservience to the rulers of the day"*: Demosthenes, "Against Timocrates," *Orations*, 24 §171. Cynthia Farrar, *The Origins of Democratic Thinking* (New York: Cambridge University Press, 1988), makes a heroic effort to deduce democratic theories from the modest evidence we have for philosophers like Protagoras and Democritus, while Josiah Ober deftly analyses the rhetoric deployed by democratic orators in *Mass and Elite in Democratic Athens*.

21 *"like frogs around a pond"*: Plato, *Phaedo*, 109b.

21 *the exact number of total residents, including slaves*: "no more than a tenth of the whole population": Hansen, *The Athenian Democracy in the Age of Demosthenes*, 94.

22 *Insofar as ordinary citizens (the demos) had a role to play*: Dean Hammer, "Plebiscitary Politics in Archaic Greece," *Historia: Zeitschrift für Alte Geschichte* 54, no. 2 (2005): 107–131.

22 *He was legendary for enhancing the power*: Herodotus, *The Histories*, 1.29.

22 *A period of relative stability began*: Ibid., 1.59.

23 *Shortly afterward, Cleisthenes personally intervened with the Pythia*: Ibid., 5.63.

23 *"process of steady expansion of political equality"*: Kurt Raaflaub, "Equalities and Inequalities in Athenian Democracy," in *Dēmokratia*, ed. Josiah Ober and Charles Hedrick (Princeton: Princeton University Press, 1996), 143–148.

24 *The result in Athens . . . was also a "revolution"*: Josiah Ober, "The Athenian Revolution of 508/7 B.C.: Violence, Authority, and the Origins of Democracy," in Ober, *The Athenian Revolution: Essays on Ancient Greek Democracy and Political Theory* (Princeton: Princeton University Press, 1996), esp. pp. 46–50. For the argument against Ober's interpretation, see Kurt A. Raaflaub, "Power in the Hands of the People: Foundations of Athenian Democracy," in Ian Morris and Kurt A. Raaflaub, eds., *Democracy 2500? Questions and Challenges* (Dubuque, IA: Kendall/Hunt, 1998), 41–42.

24 *"Although Athens had been a great city before"*: Herodotus, *The Histories*, 5.66.

25 *At the time, the Athenian citizenry consisted of free-born males*: Martin Ostwald, *From Popular Sovereignty to the Sovereignty of Law: Law, Society, and Politics in Fifth-Century Athens* (Berkeley: University of California Press, 1986), 24.

25 *An amphitheatre was built for the Assembly*: Pierre Lévêque and Pierre Vidal-Naquet, *Cleisthenes the Athenian*, trans. David Ames Curtis (Atlantic Highlands, NJ: Humanities Press, 1996), 13, 16 figure 4.

25 *"one of the first things that most forcibly struck outside observers"*: Cartledge, *Democracy*, 68.

26 *As it evolved in Athens, a central role*: Following the account in John J. Winkler, "The Ephebes' Song: *Tragoidia* and *Polis*," *Representations* 11 (Summer 1985): 26–62. Cf. A. W. Pickard-Cambridge, *Dramatic Festivals of Athens*, 2nd ed. (London: Oxford University Press, 1968), 59–67.

27 *To anyone accustomed to the importance of periodic elections*: For the history and use of this device from ancient Athens to modern societies, see Hubertus Buchstein, *Demokratie und Lotterie* (New York: Campus Verlag, 2009).

27 *That is why Aristotle regarded elections*: Aristotle, *Politics*, IV. 9, 1294b8.

28 *By the end of the century, there were perhaps several hundred*: Cartledge, *Democracy*, 146–147.

28 *The polis in Athens began to eclipse in ethical significance*: Raaflaub, "Power in the Hands of the People," 49.

29 *The significance of this exclusivity was incalculable*: Cf. Thucydides, *The Peloponnesian War*, 2.41.1: "As a city we are the school of Hellas; while I doubt if the world can produce a man, who where he has only himself to depend upon, is equal to so many emergencies, and graced by so happy a versatility as the Athenian."

29 *Aristotle, a careful analyst of the structure of Greek city-states*: Aristotle, *Politics*, 1291b14–30.

29 *Still, it is a bit misleading to call such eloquent leaders of the Assembly "politicians"*: See Mogens Herman Hansen, "The Athenian 'Politicians,' 403–322 B.C.," in Hansen, *The Athenian Ecclesia II*, 3–4.

30 *"Our constitution," says Pericles*: Thucydides, *The Peloponnesian War*, 2.37.1. I am using the translation of Donald Kagan in *Pericles of Athens and the Birth of Democracy* (New York: Free Press, 1991), 143, who also makes the connection with Lincoln's Gettysburg Address.

31 *By the time he delivered his funeral oration*: Plutarch, "Pericles," 39.

31 *"The rest of their array moved out and on"*: Aeschylus, *The Persians*, 399–405, the 1908 verse translation by Edmund Doidge Anderson Morshead.

32 *"No one, moreover, if he has it in him to do some good"*: Thucydides, *The Peloponnesian War*, 2.37.1.

32 *As soon as he was eligible*: Kagan, *Pericles of Athens*, 38.

33 *Ephialtes represented a new kind of Athenian leader*: Christian Meier, *Athens: A Portrait of the City in Its Golden Age*, trans. Robert and Rita Kimber (New York: Metropolitan Books, 1998), 291.

34 *"Remember, too, that if your country has the greatest name"*: Thucydides, *The Peloponnesian War*, 2.64.3.

34 *"sixty triremes annually"*: Plutarch, "Pericles," 11.

35 *He also introduced a fund*: Vincent Azoulay, *Pericles of Athens*, trans. Janet Lloyd (Princeton: Princeton University Press, 2014), 73.

35 *"to redistribute wealth to the people on a scale never before seen in history"*: Ibid., 80.

35 *"the growth of the power of Athens"*: Thucydides, *The Peloponnesian War*, 1.23.6.

35 *"in assemblies, courts, theatres, army camps"*: Plato, *Republic*, 492bc.

36 *The place where the Assembly convened*: Cartledge, *Democracy*, 69.

36 *Large crowds packed into confined public spaces*: The short-lived experiment with general assemblies in Occupy Wall Street in New York in the autumn of 2011 is a good example; real deliberation occurred only offstage, in various smaller working groups, as I explain in my coda. For the Swiss comparison, see Hansen, *The Athenian Ecclesia*, 207–226.

36 *"There were no theoretical limits to the power of the state"*: Finley, *Democracy Ancient and Modern*, 116.

36 *"The Athenian community during the Periclean time"*: Alfred E. Zimmern, *The Greek Commonwealth* (Oxford: Clarendon Press, 1911), 367n.

36 *So wrote the British scholar*: Mark Mazower, *No Enchanted Palace: The End of Empire and the Ideological Origins of the United Nations* (Princeton: Princeton University Press, 2009), 66–103.

37 *the prevailing tradition in the West*: see Jennifer Tolbert Roberts, *Athens on Trial: The Antidemocratic Tradition in Western Thought*.

37 *"Throughout the world the aristocracy are opposed to democracy"*: "The Constitution of the Athenians," §5, in J. M. Moore, ed. and trans., *Aristotle and Xenophon on Democracy and Oligarchy* (Berkeley: University of California Press, 1975), 38.

37 *By empowering an impoverished multitude in this manner*: The Cambridge classicist Paul Cartledge, basing his work in part on the authority of Aristotle's suggestion in his *Politics* that democracy in its most radical (Athenian) form was rule by the poor, makes a surprisingly strong argument for seeing ancient Athens as a "dictatorship of the proletariat" in his excellent *Democracy*.

38 *"he was the first to shout when addressing the people"*: "First to shout": *The Constitution of Athens*, 28.3. For the rest, I am paraphrasing the portrait painted by George Grote, *A History of Greece* (London, 1870), 6:27.

38 *"the most violent man at Athens"*: Thucydides, *The Peloponnesian War*, 3.36.6.

38 *As Thucydides himself emphasized*: The revisionist views on this matter of M. I. Finley, above all in *Democracy Ancient and Modern*, have become widely shared (for example, by Josiah Ober and Paul Cartledge).

39 *"led the multitude rather than being led by it"*: Thucydides, *The Peloponnesian War*, 2.65.8–9.

40 *As tensions flared in Athens, Socrates tried to stay above the fray*: Freely paraphrasing Xenophon, *Memoirs*, I, 2, 36.

40 homonomia, *literally, same-mindedness*: See Ober, *Mass and Elite in Democratic Athens*, 297.

41 *"Do you know anyone who is less a slave?"*: Xenophon, *Apology*, 18.

41 *But in the eyes of his philosophical followers*: See Cartledge, *Democracy*, 175–180, for the most trenchant short defence of the democratic legitimacy of the trial of Socrates.

41 *"no knowledge of true being"*: I am using a nineteenth-century summary of Book VI of Plato's *Republic* by Benjamin Jowett: see *The Dialogues of Plato*, trans. Jowett (Oxford, 1871), 2:59.

41 *In this parable, Socrates asks his audience*: see Plato, *Republic*, VI, 488a–489a. I am using the translation of G.M.A. Grube, revised by C.D.C. Reeve, in John M. Cooper, ed., *Plato: Complete Works* (Indianapolis: Hackett, 1997), 1,111.

42 *"The problem was that democracy pandered"*: Runciman, *The Confidence Trap*, 7.

43 *"acknowledged folly"*: Thucydides, *The Peloponnesian War*, 6.89.6.

43 *"It was no light matter to deprive the Athenian people"*: Ibid., 8.68.4.

43 *"a remarkably efficient State"*: A.H.M. Jones, *Athenian Democracy* (Oxford: Blackwell, 1957), 99. This is a collection of the classical historian's pioneering monographs from the 1950s, which paved the way for the subsequent work of Finley, Hansen, Ober, and Cartledge.

44 *"polis was supposed to multiply the occasions to win 'immortal fame'"*: Hannah Arendt, *The Human Condition* (Chicago: University of Chicago Press, 1958), 197.

44 *"a deed deserving fame would not be forgotten"*: Ibid.

44 *"the Greeks, in distinction from all later developments"*: Ibid., 194.

46 *A pig was slaughtered and dragged around the Pnyx*: For this and other details about how the Assembly functioned in the third quarter of the fourth century, see Hansen, *The Athenian Democracy in the Age of Demosthenes*, 125–160.

46 *"Who of those above fifty years of age wishes to address the assembly?"*: Aeschines, *Against Timarchus*, 1.23, 3–4.

46 *Apollo . . . advised leaving the land in question fallow*: Cartledge, *Democracy*, 133.

46 *any citizen, if he chose, could charge under oath*: See Hansen, *The Athenian Democracy in the Age of Demosthenes*, 205–210. Some uncertainty surrounds how this institution operated; for more details, see Hansen, *"Graphe Paranomon against Psephismata Not Yet Passed by the Ekklesia,"* in *The Athenian Ecclesia II*, 271–281.

46 *"the Herald having read prayers"*: Demosthenes, "Against Timocrates," *Orations*, 24 §§20–21.

47 *Roughly once a month, the Assembly, according to a fixed agenda, voted*: For more details on the duties of the Council, see Aristotle, *Constitution of Athens*, esp. §§42–52; Cartledge, *Democracy*, 110–114.

47 *"Never before or since in world history"*: Hansen, *The Athenian Ecclesia II*, 265.

48 *"participatory democracy with a vengeance"*: Cartledge, *Democracy*, 111.

48 *"an inevitable cost of the democratic decision-making mode"*: Ibid., 159.

48 *"spirit of feverish litigation"*: Jacob Burckhardt, *The Greeks and Greek Civilization*, ed. Oswyn Murray, trans. Sheila Stern (New York: St. Martin's Press, 1998), 229.

49 *"the constitutional trend in political actuality"*: Cartledge, *Democracy*, 244.

49 *"calamitous verbal collapse"*: Ibid., 265.

49 *"there has been established through out the world"*: Quoted ibid., 273.

50 *"the safest general characterization"*: Alfred North Whitehead, *Process and Reality*, ed. David Ray Griffin and Donald W. Sherburne (New York: Free Press, 1978), 39.

50 *Faced with the scepticism of critics like Plato*: For the link between Mill and Grote, see Kyriakos N. Demetriou, "The Spirit of Athens: George Grote and John Stuart Mill on Classical Republicanism," in Demetriou and Antis Loizides, eds., *John Stuart Mill: A British Socrates* (New York: Palgrave Macmillan, 2013), 176–206.

51 *In sharp distinction to the Romans*: Cartledge, *Democracy*, 148–149.

51 *administrative tasks under the democracy*: See Paulin Ismard, *Democracy's Slaves*, trans. Jane Marie Todd (Cambridge, MA: Harvard University Press, 2017); cf. Cartledge, *Democracy*, 139.

51 *"does not sit at his post"*: Ronald Stroud, "An Athenian Law on Silver Coinage," *Hesperia* 43, no. 2 (April–June 1974): 157–188.

52 *It wasn't as obsessed with cultivating the martial virtues*: The links between war making and state making were acutely noted by my colleague the sociologist Charles Tilly, perhaps most memorably in his paper "War Making and State Making as Organized Crime," in Peter B. Evans, Dietrich Rueschemeyer, and Theda Skocpol, eds., *Bringing the State Back In* (New York: Cambridge University Press, 1985), 169–191.

2. A REVOLUTIONARY ASSERTION OF POPULAR SOVEREIGNTY

53 *They represented a cross section of ordinary Parisians*: From a census of civilian casualties taken after August 10, quoted in Christopher Hibbert, *The Days of the French Revolution* (New York: William Morrow, 1980), 156. Cf. a census of the occupations of leading figures in one Parisian section in 1789–1790, in Rose, *The Making of the Sans-Culottes*, 65.

54 *"there was no other perpetrator of August 10"*: Jules Michelet, *Histoire de la Révolution Française* (Paris, 1849), IV: 6n.

54 *"No insurrection has ever been more openly prepared"*: Albert Mathiez, *Le dix Août* (Paris: Hachette, 1934), p. 84.

55 *In many neighbourhoods, Parisians who had assembled*: See Rose, *The Making of the Sans-Culottes*.

56 *"The great become small, the rich become poor"*: Rousseau, *Émile*, Book III, in Rousseau, *Œuvres complètes*, ed. Bernard Gagnebin and Marcel Raymond (Paris: Gallimard, 1959–1995), 4:468.

56 *"Nobody has proposed a more just idea of the people"*: *Œuvres de Maximilien Robespierre*, ed. Société des études Robespierristes, 11 vols. (Paris: Presses Universitaires de France, 1910–1967), 8:90. The quote is from Rousseau, *Social Contract*, bk. 2, chap. 6.

56 *"democratic or popular"*: *Révolutions de Paris* 18 (November 8, 1789): 2.

57 *"the Immortal Rousseau"*: Quoted in Haim Burstin, *Une révolution à l'œuvre: Le Faubourg Saint-Marcel, 1789–1794* (Paris: Champ Vallon, 2005), 391.

57 *For example, at the Gobelins section*: Ibid., 404–405.

57–58 *"Swift now, therefore"*: Thomas Carlyle, *The French Revolution: A History* (London, 1837), bk. 2, chap. 6.

58 *"When the people place themselves in a state of insurrection"*: Quoted in Hibbert, *Days of the French Revolution*, 154.

58 *an "assembly of delegates"*: From declarations made on August 10, 1792, in the Archives Nationales, quoted in Morris Slavin, *The Making of an Insurrection* (Cambridge, MA: Harvard University Press, 1986), 189n14.

58 *"an indefeasible right, an inalienable right"*: Remarks made in an assembly of the *Cité* section, November 3, 1792, quoted in Soboul, *The Sans-Culottes*, 95.

58 *"propelled by an impulse so violent"*: Charles-Alexis Alexandre, from the section of Gobelins, quoted in Burstin, *Une révolution à l'œuvre*, 403.

58 *For the first time since ancient Athens*: Cf. François Furet, *Interpreting the French Revolution*, trans. Elborg Forster (New York: Cambridge University Press, 1981), 24.

59 *"the licence and lawlessness"*: Polybius, *The Histories*, bk. VI, §4, 6–9. Cf. Cicero, *De Re Publica*, I, xxviii.

59 *"like a well-trimmed boat"*: Polybius, *The Histories*, bk. VI, §10, 6–11.

60 *"The best armies are those of armed peoples"*: Niccolò Machiavelli to Francesco Vettori, August 23, 1513, in Machiavelli, *The Chief Works, and Others*, trans. Allan Gilbert (Durham, NC: Duke University Press, 1965), 3:925.

60 *"Machiavellian democracy"*: John P. McCormick, *Machiavellian Democracy* (New York: Cambridge University Press, 2011).

60 *"spirit of extreme equality"*: Niccolò Machiavelli, *History of Florence*, bk. 4, chap. 1. Montesquieu, *Spirit of the Laws*, bk. 8, chap. 2.

60 *It was in order to avoid such confusion that James Madison*: *Federalist*, no. 10. On the widespread conflation of republic and democracy in this era, see Akhil Reed Amar, *America's Constitution: A Biography* (New York: Random House, 2005), 276–281.

60 *In the context of conventional republican theories*: Rousseau's views were not, how-

ever, unprecedented; he was following an insight first broached, though not consistently elaborated, by Thomas Hobbes in his 1642 treatise *De Cive* (translated from the Latin into English in 1651 by Hobbes as *The Citizen: Philosophicall Rudiments Concerning Government and Society*). See Tuck, *The Sleeping Sovereign.*

62 *"aristo-democracy"*: See James Miller, *Rousseau: Dreamer of Democracy* (New Haven: Yale University Press, 1984), 13–17; and the much more detailed account of Conovan politics, and Rousseau's relation with various Conovan activists, in Rosenblatt, *Rousseau and Geneva.*

62 *In one famous passage, he remarks that a democracy*: Rousseau, *On the Social Contract; or, Principles of Political Right*, bk. 3, chap. 4, in *Œuvres complètes*, 3:406.

62 *"the peculiar advantage of a democratic government"*: Ibid., bk. 3, chap. 17, in *Œuvres complètes*, 3:433–434. Cf. Hobbes, *De Cive*, 7:5.

62 *"If one seeks what precisely comprises the greatest good of all"*: Rousseau, *Social Contract*, bk. 2, chap. 11, in *Œuvres complètes*, 3:391.

62 *Although in a genuine community the general will*: This is a condensed account of the longer analysis and interpretation offered in my *Rousseau*, esp. pp. 61–65.

63 *"which its members call State when it is passive"*: Rousseau, *Social Contract*, bk. 1, chap. 6, in *Œuvres complètes*, 3:361–362.

63 "destructive *of society and* of all government": Quoted in Miller, *Rousseau*, 82.

63 *"The democratic constitution"*: Rousseau, *Letters Written from the Mountain*, in *Œuvres complètes*, 3:837–838.

64 *"virtue and freedom find refuge"*: Mme Roland is quoted in Jacques Godechot, *The Taking of the Bastille, July 14th, 1789*, trans. Jean Stewart (New York: Scribner, 1970), 31.

64 *"sovereignty lies with the people"*: Quoted ibid.

66 *"as many perhaps as one adult French male"*: Patrice Higgonet, *Goodness Beyond Virtue: Jacobins During the French Revolution* (Cambridge, MA: Harvard University Press, 1998), 14.

66 *Like the Parisian sectional assemblies*: See Rose, *The Making of the Sans-Culottes.*

66 *"so long as a revolution is not complete"*: Condorcet, *Chronique de Paris*, February 21, 1792, 38, quoted in Keith Michael Baker, *Condorcet: From Natural Philosophy to Social Mathematics* (Chicago: University of Chicago Press, 1975), 310.

67 *"public opinion grows more enlightened"*: *Chronique de Paris*, June 16, 1792, quoted in Baker, *Condorcet*, 311.

68 *The Legislative Assembly decreed that all citizens*: Decree on pikes, August 1, 1792, *Archives parlementaires de 1787 a 1860 . . . Première série (1787 à 1799)*, 2nd ed. (Paris, 1879–1914), 47:365–366.

68 *"an exemplary and unforgettable act of vengeance"*: From the Brunswick Manifesto (English translation: https://history.hanover.edu/texts/bruns.html).

69 *"the truth of the thunderous anathema"*: Rousseau, *Social Contract*, bk. 3, chap. 15, in *Œuvres complètes*, 3:431.

69 *"the primary assemblies have the power to evaluate"*: Robespierre, *Œuvres*, 8:410–420.

69 *"The country is in danger"*: Morris Slavin, *The French Revolution in Miniature: Section Droits-de-l'Homme, 1789–1795* (Princeton: Princeton University Press, 1984), 109.

70 *Although the neighbourhood contained 2,000 active citizens*: Ibid., 111.

71 *"Secret Directory of the Insurrection"*: Ibid., 112.

71 *They were pursued by soldiers and sans-culottes*: See the accounts in Michelet, *Histoire de la Révolution Française*, vol. 4, chap. 1, 35–39; and Hibbert, *The Days of the French Revolution*, 160–162.

71 *"I remained . . . until four o'clock"*: M. Cléry, *Journal de ce qui s'est passé à la Tour du Temple, pendant la captivité de Louis XVI, Roi de France* (Paris, 1798), 4. This memoir, a bestseller in its day, was written by Jean Baptiste Cléry, valet de chambre to the king.

72 *"bloodshed was not the unfortunate by-product of revolution"*: Simon Schama, *Citizens* (New York: Knopf, 1989), 615.

72 *previous scholars have been wrong to imply*: In her rich and suggestive *On Revolution*, Hannah Arendt praises the sans-culottes for their political institutions while blaming their violence on their various social demands—an arbitrary and quite unhistorical distinction that cannot withstand serious scrutiny.

72 *"the uneasy coincidence of democracy and fanaticism"*: Ruth Scurr, *Fatal Purity: Robespierre and the French Revolution* (New York: Metropolitan Books, 2006), 6.

73 *"The solemn manner in which"*: Robespierre, "Sur les événements du 10 août 1792," *Le Défenseur de la Constitution*, no. 12; Robespierre, *Œuvres*, 4: 352–353.

74 *"even major political issues could only rarely"*: Rose, *The Making of the Sans-Culottes*, 93.

75 *rationalize the drafting of laws*: See Baker, *Condorcet*, p. 243. Baker was one of the first modern historians to stress Condorcet's tacit preoccupation with offering his own novel answers to questions Rousseau had explored in the *Social Contract*.

75 *unique among the revolutionary leaders*: Alexandre Koyré, "Condorcet," *Journal of the History of Ideas* 9, no. 2 (April 1948): 131. The most vivid short essay on Condorcet in English remains the chapter on him in Frank Manuel, *The Prophets of Paris* (Cambridge, MA: Harvard University Press, 1962), 55–102.

75 *"godfather of modern probability theory"*: Ian Hacking, *The Taming of Chance* (New York: Cambridge University Press, 1990), 42; *"mathématique sociale"* ap-

pears in Condorcet's posthumously published *Outlines of an Historical view of the progress of the human mind*, written while he was in hiding in 1793.

76 *"religious scrupulosity"*: John Morley, "Condorcet," in *Critical Miscellanies* (London, 1858), 2:255.

76 *"In politics a total rejection of any idea"*: M. Arago, *Biographie de Marie-Jean-Antoine-Nicolas Caritat de Condorcet*, read to the Academy of Sciences, December 28, 1841 (Paris, 1849), vi.

76 *a "volcano covered with snow"*. Ibid., cvii.

76 *"Men who, like the French, love true liberty"*: Condorcet, *On the English Revolution of 1688, and That of the French, August 10, 1792* (London, 1792), 7, 11, 18.

77 *"the common reason"*: See the discussion in Lucien Jaume, *Le discours Jacobin et la démocratie* (Paris: Fayard, 1989), 305–323.

77 *"Take away from these . . . wills the pluses and minuses"*: Rousseau, *Social Contract*, bk. 2, chap. 3, in *Œuvres complètes*, 3:371.

78 *According to Condorcet's mathematical argument*: See Hélène Landemore, *Democratic Reason: Politics, Intelligence, and the Rule of the Many* (Princeton: Princeton University Press, 2013), 70–75.

78 *"the wisdom of crowds"*: James Surowiecki, *The Wisdom of Crowds* (New York: Doubleday, 2004).

79 *"I saw people pass by, arm in arm"*: Louis-Sébestien Mercier, *Paris pendant la Révolution (1789–1798), ou, Le Nouveau Paris* (Paris, 1862), bk. 3, chap. 82.

79 *"To form a constitution for a territory"*: An Authentic Copy of the New Plan of the French Constitution, as Presented to the National Convention, by the Committee of Constitution, to Which Is Prefixed the Speech of M. Condorcet, on Friday, February 15, 1793, (M. Breard, President,) Delivered in the Name of the Committee of Constitution (London, 1793), i. By now many of the important speeches by the key leaders of the French Revolution were being quickly translated into English and widely distributed in both England and the United States. There is a good analysis of the draft in Jaume, *Le discours Jacobin et la démocratie*, 312–323.

79 *Because Condorcet was hoarse that day*: Elisabeth Badinter and Robert Badinter, *Condorcet, 1743–1794: Un intellectual en politique* (Paris: Fayard, 1988), 540.

80 *"private societies"*: Speech of M. Condorcet . . . , vi.

80 *"No man should be deprived of any means"*: Ibid., vii.

80 *Elsewhere Condorcet had also made it plain*: Condorcet, *The Nature and Purpose of Public Education*, the first of five journal articles published in 1791 on the educational views behind his plan for public education, which he presented to the National Assembly in 1792, in Baker, *Condorcet: Selected Writings*, 105–142.

80 *"it would be equally dangerous"*: Speech of M. Condorcet . . . , xiii.

80 *"primary assemblies"*: Ibid., xi–xii.

80 *"the constitution to reform, at a determined epoch"*: Ibid., xlvi.

80 *In later years, Thomas Jefferson*: Thomas Jefferson to Samuel Kercheval, July 12, 1816, Thomas Jefferson, *Writings* (New York: Library of America, 1984), 1395–1403. A long letter (admired by Hannah Arendt) in which Jefferson proposes periodic constitutional conventions, and also a system of wards, strikingly similar to the primary assemblies of Condorcet.

81 *"contrary to that equality between the parts"*: Speech of M. Condorcet . . . , xi.

81 *"is no new institution"*: Ibid., xxx.

81 *"a constitution expressly adopted by the citizens"*: Ibid., xlviii.

81 *But inside the Convention*: Badinter and Badinter, *Condorcet*, 540–541.

82 *"Everything the sectional assemblies do so well"*: Marat, "Idée de la nouvelle Constitution, Observations rapides sur ce fatras girondin," *Journal de la République Française, par Marat, L'Ami du Peuple* 126, February 26, 1793.

82 *"The power of ideas can inflame"*: Dan Edelstein, *The Terror of Natural Right* (Chicago: University of Chicago Press, 2009), 171.

83 *"sovereignty of the people, with equality"*: Speech of M. Condorcet . . . , i.

83 *Meanwhile, the Parisian sans-culottes*: The standard source remains Soboul, *The Sans-Culottes*.

83 *"written from the heart"*: Louis-Antoine Saint-Just, *Œuvres complètes*, ed. Michèle Duval (Paris: Gérard Lebovici, 1984), 423.

83 *"to give to every government the force necessary"*: Robespierre, *Œuvres*, 9:495–496, 498–502.

84 *"Under the eyes of so great a number of witnesses"*: Ibid., 9:503.

84 *By then, the people would either*: Condorcet, *Discours prononcé à la Convention, sur la convocation d'une nouvelle Convention nationale*, in *Œuvres Complètes*, 12:583–597.

86 *"The people, Rousseau says, are sovereign"*: Benjamin Constant, *Principes de politique applicable à tous les gouvernements—et particulièrement à constitution actuelle de la France* (Paris, 1815), chap. 1; in English, *Political Writings*, trans. and ed. Biancamaria Fontana (New York: Cambridge University Press, 1988), 179.

86 *In the context of the American Revolution*: See Alexander Hamilton to Gouverneur Morris, May 19, 1777, https://founders.archives.gov/documents/Hamilton /01-01-02-0162.

87 *"Simple Democracy was society governing itself"*: Thomas Paine, *Rights of Man*, pt. 2, chap. 3.

87 *"A democracy is not a state where the people"*: Robespierre, "Report on the Principles of Public Morality," speech to the Convention, February 5, 1794, *Œuvres*, 10:352–353.

88 *By slowly but surely alienating*: See Albert Soboul, "Robespierre and the Popular Movement of 1793–4," *Past and Present* 5 (1954): 54–70.

89 *Before this pioneering venture in "total war"*: David A. Bell, *The First Total War: Napoleon's Europe and the Birth of Warfare as We Know It* (Boston: Houghton Mifflin, 2007), 156.

3. A COMMERCIAL REPUBLIC OF FREE INDIVIDUALS

91 *"America's most distinguishing characteristic"*: Wiebe, *Self-Rule*, p. 1.

92 *"All power is derived from the people"*: Benjamin Rush, "Address to the People of the United States," delivered at the American Museum, Philadelphia, February 1787, in Colleen Sheehan and Gary McDowell, eds., *Friends of the Constitution: Writings of the "Other" Federalists, 1787–1788* (Indianapolis: Liberty Fund, 1998).

92 *"moral and political depravity"*: Jefferson to Thomas Cooper, September 10, 1814, https://founders.archives.gov/documents/Jefferson/03-07-02-0471.

92 *"I tremble for my country"*: Jefferson, *Notes on the State of Virginia* (London, 1787), Query XVIII, "Manners: The particular customs and manners that may happen to be received in that state?"

92 *"played out in counterpoint to chattel slavery"*: Judith N. Shklar, *American Citizenship: The Quest for Inclusion* (Cambridge, MA: Harvard University Press, 1991), 1.

93 *a vision eloquently expressed by Thomas Paine*: See Joyce Appleby, *Capitalism and a New Social Order: The Republican Vision of the 1790s* (New York: New York University Press, 1984).

93 *The first issue included a profile of Voltaire*: John Keane, *Tom Paine: A Political Life* (Boston: Little, Brown, 1995), 92–95.

94 *By the end of the year*: See Bernard Bailyn, *The Ideological Origins of the American Revolution* (Cambridge, MA: Harvard University Press, 1967).

95 *"Virginians may have had a special appreciation"*: Edmund S. Morgan, *American Slavery, American Freedom* (New York: W. W. Norton, 1975), 376.

95 *"art of democratic writing"*: Danielle Allen, *Our Declaration: A Reading of the Declaration of Independence in Defense of Equality* (New York: Liveright, 2014), 83–104.

95 *"meant to set up a standard maxim"*: Abraham Lincoln, "Speech on the Dred Scott Decision," June 26, 1857, http://www.virginia.edu/woodson/courses/aas -hius366a/lincoln.html.

95 *The idea of "consent"*: For more on the genealogy of this concept, see my essay, "Consent," *Political Concepts: A Critical Lexicon* 3, no. 5 (Autumn 2016), www.politicalconcepts.org/consent-james-miller.

96 *In English, the word "individual"*: See the entries for "individual" and "indi-

vidualism" in the *Oxford English Dictionary;* cf. Steven Lukes, *Individualism* (London: Basil Blackwell, 1973).

96 *"Our plan is commerce"*: Thomas Paine, *Common Sense*, in Thomas Paine, *Collected Writings* (New York: Library of America, 1995), 24.

96 *"It is a pacific system"*: Thomas Paine, *Rights of Man*, part 2, ibid., 508–509.

96 *"Society is in every state a blessing"*: Paine, *Common Sense*, 6.

97 *Paine in time acknowledged the tension: Agrarian Justice* (1787), ibid., 400–408.

97 *"was in the minds of the people"*: John Adams to Thomas Jefferson, August 25, 1815, https://founders.archives.gov/documents/Jefferson/03-08-02-0560.

98 *"representative democracy, where the right of election"*: Alexander Hamilton to Gouverneur Morris, May 19, 1777.

98 *"the rich and the well-born"*: Quoted in Max Farrand, ed., *The Records of the Federal Convention of 1787* (New Haven: Yale University Press, 1911), 1:299.

98 *"the Government which this Bodie Politick"*: Government of Rhode Island—March 16–19, 1641, http://avalon.law.yale.edu/17th_century/ri02.asp.

98 *In 1717, the word "democracy"*: John Wise, *A Vindication of the Government of New-England Churches* (Boston, 1717), 57, 61.

98 *"would still grope for terms"*: Michael Zuckerman, *Peaceable Kingdoms: New England Towns in the Eighteenth Century* (New York: Knopf, 1970), 46.

98 *In the case of the Pennsylvania constitution*: See Wood, *The Creation of the American Republic*, 226–237; for the constitution's influence on Brissot and Condorcet, see Foner, *Tom Paine and Revolutionary America*, 235–236.

99 *Many of them began to confuse republicanism*: See Willi Paul Adams, *The First American Constitutions: Republican Ideology and the Making of the State Constitutions in the Revolutionary Era*, expanded ed. (Lanham, MD: Rowman & Littlefield, 2001), 103–110.

99 *Only a small percentage of Americans*: Alexander Keyssar, *The Right to Vote: The Contested History of Democracy in the United States* (New York: Basic Books, 2000), 2.

99 *"which have ever been spectacles"*: James Madison, *Federalist*, no. 10.

100 *"a democracy is a volcano"*: Fisher Ames, speaking at the Massachusetts Convention, January 1788, in *The Debate on the Constitution* (New York: Library of America, 1993), part 1, 892.

100 *"In giving a definition of the simple kinds"*: James Wilson, "Remarks in Pennsylvania Convention," in Kermit L. Hall and Mark David Hall, eds., *Collected Works of James Wilson* (Indianapolis: Liberty Fund, 2007), 1:235.

101 *"sent them through the city in triumph"*: Thomas Jefferson to John Jay, July 19, 1789, scans of some manuscript pages available at www.archives.gov/exhibits/eyewitness/html.php?section=1.

101 *"the earth belongs to each of these generations"*: Thomas Jefferson to James Madison, September 6, 1789, in Jefferson, *Writings*, 960.

101 *When Jacques-Louis David presented his portrait of Marat*: See *National Gazette*, December 19, 1792 (for *Père Duchesne*); *General Advertiser*, February 10, 1794 (for David and Marat); *Columbian Gazetter*, September 5 and 9, 1793 (for the Jacobin Constitution); *General Advertiser*, March 10–14, 1794, and May 2 and 3, 1794 (for Robespierre speeches). Also see Howard Mumford Jones, *America and French Culture, 1750–1848* (Chapel Hill: University of North Carolina Press, 1927), 534–35n.; Alfred F. Young, *The Democratic Republicans of New York: The Origins, 1763–1797* (Chapel Hill: University of North Carolina Press, 1967), 350; Charles Downer Hazen, *Contemporary American Opinion of the French Revolution* (Baltimore, 1897), 248. A more extensive version of this section appears in James Miller, "Modern Democracy from France to America," *Salmagundi* 84 (Autumn 1989): 177–202.

102 *"breathe the air of liberty"*: Hazen, *Contemporary American Opinion of the French Revolution*, 166–169.

102 *"all the old spirit of 1776 is rekindling"*: Jefferson to James Monroe, May 5, 1793, quoted in Eugene Perry Link, *Democratic-Republican Societies, 1790–1800* (New York: Columbia University Press, 1942), 46.

102 *"What an age of WONDERS and REVOLUTIONS!!"*: "Turn-Coat" (from the *Virginia Gazette*), *National Gazette*, August 3, 1793.

103 *"democratic" society*: Link, *Democratic-Republican Societies*, 16.

103 *"not only to discuss the proceedings of Government"*: Quoted in Stanley Elkins and Eric McKitrick, *The Age of Federalism: The Early American Republic, 1788–1900* (New York: Oxford University Press, 1993), 457.

103 *To make plain their own patriotism*: Young, *The Democratic Republicans of New York*, 411.

104 *"the different members of the government"*: *Newark Gazette*, December 31, 1794, quoted in Link, *Democratic-Republican Societies*, 106.

104 *"The government is responsible to the sovereign people"*: Declaration of the *New York Democratic Society*, quoted in Young, *The Democratic Republicans of New York*, 426–427.

104 *"Self-interest, the great moving principle"*: An American Sans Culottes, "To the Freemen of America," *General Advertiser*, April 3, 1794.

104 *"We have too long been amused and misled by names"*: Anon., "For the *National Gazette*," *National Gazette*, December 12, 1792.

104 *"I am, sir, a true Democrat"*: *General Advertiser*, May 27, 1794.

104 *"I pronounce them all Democrats"*: Quoted in Young, *The Democratic Republicans of New York*, 416.

105 *"self-created"*: George Washington, Sixth Annual Message to Congress, November 19, 1794, University of Virginia, *Washington Papers*, Presidential Series [1788–1797].

105 *Washington suspected radical democrats*: Thomas P. Slaughter, *The Whiskey Rebellion* (New York: Oxford University Press, 1986), 165.

106 *"The American people came to believe"*: Walter Lippmann, *Public Opinion* (New York: Harcourt, 1922), 179.

106 *This political culture was nourished*: An important point made by Gary Gerstle, *Liberty and Coercion: The Paradox of American Government from the Founding to the Present* (Princeton: Princeton University Press, 2015).

107 *"every thing to which a man may attach a value"*: James Madison, "Private Property," *National Gazette*, March 29, 1792, in *The Papers of James Madison*, vol. 14, ed. Robert A. Rutland (Charlottesville: University of Virginia Press, 1983), 266.

107 *"In America, . . . [every man] will with pleasure"*: Anon., "Extract," *National Gazette*, May 1, 1793.

107 *because the franchise was broadened*: I am paraphrasing Robert H. Wiebe, *Who We Are: A History of Popular Nationalism* (Princeton: Princeton University Press, 2002), 68–69, who is summarizing an argument he makes more extensively in his 1995 book *Self-Rule*.

108 *"all the presidents had been statesmen"*: James Bryce, *The American Commonwealth* (Indianapolis: Liberty Fund, 1995), 1:74.

108 *"It will not be too strong to say"*: Alexander Hamilton, *Federalist*, no. 68.

108 *"at the head of the Democracy"*: New York journalist and editor William Leggett, quoted in Sean Wilentz, *Andrew Jackson* (New York: Times Books, 2005), 6.

108 *"the democracy of numbers"*: Jurist James Kent, quoted ibid.

109 *his most indomitable political passion was hatred*: Here and elsewhere I am relying on the facts marshalled in Wilentz, *Andrew Jackson*, 9.

109 *"the planter, the farmer, the mechanic, and the laborer"*: Jackson, Farewell Address as President, March 4, 1837, http://www.presidency.ucsb.edu/ws/index.php?pid=67087.

110 *"democracy is the oxygen or vital air"*: Vividly defending his father's Federalist convictions two generations later, John Quincy Adams, *The Social Compact, Exemplified in the Constitution of the Commonwealth of Massachusetts, with Remarks on the Theories of Divine Right of Hobbes and Filmer, and the Counter Theories of Sidney, Locke, Montesquieu and Rousseau* (Providence, RI, 1842), 31–32.

111 *overall number of eligible voters*: Robert V. Remini, *Andrew Jackson*, vol. 2, *The Course of American Freedom, 1822–1832* (New York: Harper, 1981), 147–148.

111 *"mighty democratic uprising"*: Frederick A. Ogg, *The Reign of Andrew Jackson* (New Haven: Yale University Press, 1919), p. 114; "soaring turnouts": Wiebe, *Self-Rule*, 180–181.

111 *"the self made man had a right to his success"*: Frederick Jackson Turner, "The West and American Ideals," *The Washington Historical Quarterly* 5, no. 4 (October 1914): 251.

112 *"Jacksonian democracy flourished"*: Ibid.

113 *Early that morning, Tocqueville and Beaumont*: See George Wilson Pierson, *Tocqueville and Beaumont in America* (New York: Oxford University Press, 1938), pp. 179ff., for these and other details about Tocqueville's Fourth of July in Albany.

114 *"Child of the skies"*: Quoted ibid., 182n.

114 *"A profound silence reigned in the meeting"*: Quoted ibid., 183.

115 *"more like a true religion"*: Runciman, *The Confidence Trap*, 5.

115 *"Christianity that can best be described"*: Alexis de Tocqueville, *Democracy in America*, trans. Arthur Goldhammer, 2 vols. (New York: Library of America, 2004), 1:332.

115 *"Thus, even as the law allows the American people"*: Ibid., 1:338.

115 *"can be seen to be more equal"*: Ibid., 1:59.

115 *"Democracy does not give the people"*: Ibid., 1:280–281.

116 *"the dogma of popular sovereignty"*: Ibid., 1:64.

117–20 The most recent scholarly work on Dorr and his rebellion is Erik J. Chaput, *The People's Martyr: Thomas Wilson Dorr and His 1842 Rhode Island Rebellion* (Lawrence: University of Kansas Press, 2013); see also Wilentz, *The Rise of American Democracy*, 539–545.

118 *"As I would not be a slave"*: Abraham Lincoln, "Definition of Democracy" [August 1, 1858?], in Roy P. Basler, ed., *The Collected Works of Abraham Lincoln* (New Brunswick, NJ: Rutgers University Press, 1953–1955), 2:532. Some historians wonder if Lincoln really wrote these words on the scrap of paper that contains them.

118 *"magazine beneath the fabric of civil society"*: Quoted in Christian G. Fritz, *American Sovereigns: The People and America's Constitutional Tradition Before the Civil War* (New York: Cambridge University Press, 2008), 263.

119 *"Even the most conservative estimates"*: Ibid., 246.

119 *"alter and amend their system"*: Jackson to Francis Blair, May 23, 1842, quoted in Chaput, *The People's Martyr*, 64.

119 *On a visit to the city*: Ibid., 133.

119 *A small-d democrat with a weakness for pageantry*: Ibid., 135.

120 *"Thomas Wilson Dorr Governor of the State of Rhode Island"*: Ibid., 136.

120 *The powder flashed*: Ibid., 139.

121 *"these barriers were expressions of the nation's reluctance"*: Keyssar, *The Right to Vote*, p. 67. Other historians are less nuanced, cf. Daniel Walker Howe in *What Hath God Wrought: The Transformation of America, 1815–1848* (New York: Oxford University Press, 2007), 489–490.

121 *Many states also maintained residency requirements*: This information comes from the invaluable tables compiled by Keyssar, *The Right to Vote*, pp. 337–402.

122 *"The imagined demon of the black rapist"*: David Blight, from the typescript of his biography of Douglass, *Frederick Douglass: Prophet of Freedom* (New York: Simon & Schuster, 2018).

123 *an extraordinary increase in America's prison population*: Jean Chung, communications manager at the Sentencing Project, *Felony Disenfranchisement: A Primer* (updated January 2017), http://sentencingproject.org/wp-content/uploads/2015/08/Felony-Disenfranchisement-Primer.pdf, figure B, p. 3.

123 *"Its advantages far outweigh the normative"*: Arend Lijphart, "Unequal Participation: Democracy's Unresolved Dilemma," *The American Political Science Review* 91, no. 1 (March 1997): 1–14.

124 *"I see an innumerable multitude of men"*: Tocqueville, *Democracy in America*, 2:816–821.

124 *a distinctively clamorous style of public culture*: See Eric Lott, *Love and Theft* (New York: Oxford University Press, 1993), esp. 63–88.

125 *In midcentury America, it was popular novels and public lectures*: This has been argued at length by Michael Rogin and Greil Marcus, among other students of American politics and popular culture.

125 *"the universal diffusion of knowledge"*: Robert D. Richardson, Jr., *Emerson: The Mind on Fire* (Berkeley: University of California Press, 1995), 418–419.

125 *"the herd of independent minds"*: See Irving Howe, *Socialism and America* (San Diego: Harcourt, 1985), 134–135. Cf. Harold Rosenberg, "The Herd of Independent Minds: Has the Avant-Garde Its Own Mass Culture?," *Commentary*, September 1, 1948, www.commentarymagazine.com/articles/the-herd-of-independent-mindshas-the-avant-garde-its-own-mass-culture.

125 *"I do not wish to expiate but to live"*: Ralph Waldo Emerson, "Self-Reliance," in Emerson, *Essays and Lectures* (New York: Library of America, 1983), 263, 262.

126 *"a new degree of culture"*: Emerson, "Circles," ibid., 408.

126 *"Some fetish of a government"*: Emerson, "The American Scholar," ibid., 64.

126 *"make the gallows as glorious as the cross"*: See James Elliot Cabot, *A Memoir of Ralph Waldo Emerson* (Boston, 1888), 2:597.

126 *When the self-reliant Emersonian*: Cf. Henry David Thoreau, *Collected Essays and Poems* (New York: Library of America, 2001), 396–421.

126 *"it is read equally in the parlor and the kitchen"*: Quoted in Richardson, *Emerson*, 508.

127 *his story was dramatized throughout America in minstrel shows*: The staging of Uncle Tom is examined at length in Lott, *Love and Theft*, 211–233, and Linda Williams, *Playing the Race Card* (Princeton: Princeton University Press, 2001), 45–95.

127 *"blackface was their bohemianism"*: Williams, *Playing the Race Card*, 68.

128 *"We lived and moved at that time"*: Henry James, *A Small Boy and Others* (New York: Scribner, 1913), 167–168.

129 *"Whoever degrades another degrades me"*: Walt Whitman, *Leaves of Grass* (Brooklyn, 1855), 29.

129 *"In all people I see myself"*: Ibid., 26.

129 *"The people! Like our huge earth itself"*: Walt Whitman, *Democratic Vistas* (New York, 1870), 18.

129 *"We had the strangest procession here"*: Letter quoted in Ed Folsom, "Textual Note," in Walt Whitman, *Democratic Vistas: The Original Edition in Facsimile* (Iowa City: University of Iowa Press, 2010), xxix.

130 *"I will not gloss over the appalling dangers"*: Whitman, *Democratic Vistas*, 4.

130 *"perfect individualism"*: Ibid., 16.

4. A STRUGGLE FOR POLITICAL AND SOCIAL EQUALITY

133 *The delegates were escorting a petition*: Malcolm Chase, *Chartism: A New History* (Manchester, UK: Manchester University Press, 2007), 73. David J. Moss, *Thomas Attwood: The Biography of a Radical* (Montreal: McGill-Queen's University Press, 1990), 284.

134 *Each demand had been ratified*: See the early accounts in William Lovett, *The Life and Struggles of William Lovett in his pursuit of Bread, Knowledge and Freedom* (London, 1876), 201–205. R. G. Gammage, *History of the Chartist Movement 1837–1854* (Newcastle-on-Tyne, 1894 [1854]), 105–130.

134 *The delegates included shoemakers*: See list of delegates posted on Chartist Ancestors website, www.chartists.net/conferences_and_conventions/first-convention-1839.

134 *"Reasoning from effect to cause"*: Gammage, *History of the Chartist Movement*, 9.

135 *"No man is too poor to unite with us"*: Quoted in Jennifer Bennett, "The London Democratic Association 1837–41: A Study in London Radicalism," in James Epstein and Dorothy Thompson, eds., *The Chartist Experience: Studies in Working-Class Radicalism and Culture, 1830–60* (London: Macmillan, 1982), 90.

135 *"a new social order into society"*: Bronterre O'Brien, "To the Reader," in *Buonarroti's History of Babeuf's Conspiracy for Equality* (London, 1836), xv.

135 *"the enjoyment of an equal share"*: "Analysis of the Doctrine of Babeuf," a text posted throughout Paris in April 1796, and reprinted as Piece No. VIII, ibid., 318.

135 *"schoolmaster of Chartism"*: Feargus O'Connor, quoted in Dorothy Thompson, *The Chartists: Popular Politics in the Industrial Revolution* (New York: Pantheon, 1984), 101.

136 *When fully unfurled, the petition was three miles long*: Chase, *Chartism*, 73.

136 *"We perform the duties of freemen"*: Text of the first Chartist Petition, Chartist Ancestors website, www.chartists.net/petitions/first-chartist-petition-1839.

136 *"It appeared to have the circumference"*: *The Examiner*, June 16, 1839.

136 *"loud laughter"*: Gammage, *History of the Chartist Movement*, 138.

136 *"that it might please their honourable House"*: Hansard, HC Deb 14 June 1839 vol. 48 cc222–7.

137 *For many Chartists, temperance*: Ulterior measures ratified in 1839, Chartist Ancestors website, www.chartists.net/conferences_and_conventions/first -convention-1839.

138 *The prominent Whig and future Liberal Party leader*: Gammage, *History of the Chartist Movement*, 141.

138 *"I owe the British Government no allegiance"*: *The Northern Star* (August 3, 1839): 7.

139 *Between January 1839 and June 1840*: Eileen Yeo, "Some Practices and Problems of Chartist Democracy," in Epstein and Thompson, *The Chartist Experience*, 361.

140 *a banquet held on September 22, 1845*: A. R. Schoyen, *The Chartist Challenge: A Portrait of George Julian Harney* (London: Heinemann, 1958), 135.

140 *Like Blanqui, Schapper fancied secret societies*: The British utopian socialist John Goodwyn Barmby, who knew of Babeuf and was familiar with other early French proponents of communism as well, claimed credit for popularizing the English word in these years. In 1841, he founded the London Communist Propaganda Society, which he later turned into a church.

140 *"governments elected by, and responsible to, the entire people"*: *The Northern Star* (September 26, 1846): 7.

141 *"a still barely moving yet faintly stirring"*: Gareth Stedman Jones, "The Redemptive Power of Violence? Carlyle, Marx and Dickens," *History Workshop Journal* 65, no. 1 (2008): 1–22.

142 *"democracy is the solved riddle"*: Karl Marx, *Critique of Hegel's "Philosophy of Right,"* in *Marx/Engels Collected Works* [hereafter *M/ECW*], 50 vols. (Moscow, 1975–2004; in English), 3:29.

142 *"egoistic, independent individuals"*: Karl Marx, "On the Jewish Question," ibid., 3:168.

142 *"In order to bring true democracy to life"*: Joseph A. Schumpeter, *Capitalism, Socialism, and Democracy* (New York: Harper, 1950), 236.

142 *the coming violent conflict*: Karl Marx and Friedrich Engels, *The Communist Manifesto*, chap. 1, "Bourgeois and Proletariats."

142 *"Robespierre saw in great poverty"*: Karl Marx, "Critical Notes on 'The King of Prussia and Social Reform,'" in *M/ECW*, 3:199.

143 *"where the proper aim and spirit"*: Ibid., 3:205.

143 *As his friend and frequent collaborator*: Friedrich Engels, *Anti-Dühring*, part 3, chap. 2, in *M/ECW*, 25:268. (In this English translation, the famous phrase "withering away" withers away, even though it remains in the index: "The state is not abolished. *It dies out.*")

144 *"achieved the result of structuring"*: Marcel Gauchet, "Tocqueville, America, and Us: On the Genesis of Democratic Societies," trans. Jacob Hamburger, *The Tocqueville Review* 37, no. 2 (2016): 180, 184.

144 *"the democratic tendency of our times"*: Mazzini, "Thoughts Upon Democracy in Europe," in *Life and Writings of Joseph Mazzini* (London, 1891), 6:98.

145 *"The law of God has not two weights"*: Ibid., 6:100–101.

146 *"Rome of the People"*: Bolton King, *Mazzini* (New York: Dutton, 1902), 127.

146 *inseparable from explicitly* national *movements*: See Pierre Manent, "Populist Demagogy and the Fanaticism of the Center," *American Affairs* 1, no. 2 (May 20, 2017), https://americanaffairsjournal.org/2017/05/populist-demagogy-and-the-fanaticism-of-the-center.

146 *Mazzini also hoped that a democratic revolt*: The standard biography in English is Denis Mack Smith, *Mazzini* (New Haven: Yale University Press, 1994).

147 *"to have more love, more feeling for the beautiful"*: Mazzini, "Thoughts Upon Democracy in Europe," 109.

148 *"the mere liberty of all"*: Ibid., 115.

150 *"Women were the first to act"*: Prosper-Olivier Lissagaray, *History of the Paris Commune of 1871*, chap. 3, "The 18th of March." First published in French in Paris in 1876 and translated into English by Eleanor Marx (one of Karl Marx's daughters) in 1886.

151 *Barricades of cobblestones sprang up*: See John Merriman, *Massacre: The Life and Death of the Paris Commune* (New York: Basic Books, 2014), 30. Despite his sympathy for the Communards, Merriman presents a vivid and trustworthy account. See also Frank Jellinek, *The Paris Commune of 1871* (London: Gollancz, 1937), a more orthodox Marxist chronicle.

151 *"One returns from such exaltations"*: Louis Barron, *Sous le drapeau rouge* (Paris, 1889), 112.

152 *Only about half of the electorate turned out*: Merriman, *Massacre*, 38.

152 *"citizen delegate to the Ministry of War"*: Ibid., 42.

152 *The Commune gloried in such purely symbolic gestures*: Ibid., 52.

152 *If any one figure could be said to typify*: Jules Forni, *Raoul Rigault, Procureur de la Commune* (Paris, 1871).

153 *"I am going to have you shot!"*: Merriman, *Massacre*, xxii–xxv. Details about Rigault come from Forni's biography and Merriman's book.

153 *"We are not dispensing justice"*: Merriman, *Massacre*, 60.

154 *"officer shot him with a pistol"*: George B. Benham, *The Proletarian Revolt: A History of the Paris Commune of 1871* (San Francisco, 1898), 152. A work written from a frankly Marxist perspective and featuring an epigraph on the title page from Rigault: "War is immoral, yet we fight."

154 *"supplied the Republic with the basis"*: Karl Marx, *The Civil War in France*, in *M/ECW*, 22:34.

155 *"a new era in that long series of revolutions"*: Pyotr Kropotkin, "The Paris Commune," first published in *Le Révolté*, March 20, 1880.

155 *"The Chartist movement in Britain ended in defeat"*: Rosa Luxemburg, "Order Prevails in Germany," *Rote Fahne*, January 14, 1919.

155 *"totalitarian democracy"*: See J. L. Talmon, *The Origins of Totalitarian Democracy* (New York: Praeger, 1960). Though ignored in Talmon's account (which focuses on the French Revolution, not the Commune of 1871), Rigault perfectly embodies the political type Talmon describes.

156 *"one of real democracy's most important elements"*: Hans Kelsen, *The Essence and Value of Democracy*, trans. Brian Graf (Lanham, MD: Rowman & Littlefield, 2013), 38 (emphasis added).

157 *"The victories of the ballot box, no less than of the sword"*: James Bryce, *The American Commonwealth* (Indianapolis: Liberty Fund, 1995 [1910]), 2:749.

157 *recent research suggests*: Daniel Ziblatt, *Conservative Parties and the Birth of Democracy* (New York: Cambridge University Press, 2017).

158 *"nothing beyond the old democratic litany"*: Karl Marx, "Marginal Notes on the Program of the German Workers' Party" (1875), in *M/ECW*, 24:95; posthumously published by Engels in 1890 as *Critique of the Gotha Program*.

159 *"Gentlemen, do you want to know what this dictatorship"*: Friedrich Engels, Introduction, dated March 18, 1891, to the German republication of Marx's *Civil War in France*, in *M/ECW*, 27:191.

159 *"A neatly structured hierarchy of professional politicians"*: Carl E. Schorske, *German Social Democracy 1905–1917* (Cambridge, MA: Harvard University Press, 1955), 116.

159 *Eduard Bernstein's 1899* The Preconditions of Socialism: Eduard Bernstein, *Die Voraussetzungen des Sozialismus und die Aufgaben der Sozialdemokratie*, translated into English in 1909 as *Evolutionary Socialism*.

160 *Bernstein's heresy was swiftly reproved*: The classic account of this schism remains Schorske's *German Social Democracy*.

160 *"the old democratic litany"*: Rosa Luxemburg, *Reform or Revolution*, chap. 7, "Co-operatives, Unions, Democracy."

161 *"a classic example of a momentous historical event"*: Abraham Ascher, *The Revolution of 1905* (Palo Alto: Stanford University Press, 1988), 211.

161 *"Neither gas nor electric lights work"*: Ibid., 215. Cf. Orlando Figes, *A People's Tragedy: A History of the Russian Revolution* (New York: Viking, 1997), 189–192.

162 *"this people which produces everything"*: Quoted in Wilfrid Harris Crook, "The General Strike," in *Encyclopedia of the Social Sciences*, ed. Edwin R. A. Seligman and Alvin Johnson (New York: Macmillan, 1933), 6:608.

162 *some other advocates of the democratic control of industry*: See Georges Sorel, *Reflections on Violence*, trans. J. Roth and T. E. Hulme (Glencoe, IL: Free Press, 1950 [1915]; originally published in French in Paris in 1910), chap. 5,

"The Political General Strike," §1. (In Sorel's view, the Russian strike of 1905 was neither sufficiently violent nor authentically "proletarian" but merely a political simulacrum of a genuine myth-inspiring general strike—never underestimate the capacity of French philosophers to make a hash of historical reality.)

162 *On October 17, the new group met*: Oskar Anweiler, *The Soviets: The Russian Workers, Peasants, and Soldiers Councils, 1905–1921*, trans. Ruth Hein (New York: Pantheon, 1974; originally published in German in Leiden in 1958), 43–47; cf. Ascher, *The Revolution of 1905*, 219–222.

163 *"to grant the population the unshakable foundations"*: Figes, *A People's Tragedy*, 199.

163 *"We were certain in our hearts"*: Quoted ibid., 199.

164 *"the Russian Social Democratic Workers Party must be organized"*: Michael Waller, *Democratic Centralism: An Historical Commentary* (New York: St. Martin's Press, 1981), 20.

165 *"The principle of democratic centralism is beyond dispute"*: Ibid., 21.

165 *a party congress held in Jena*: Schorske, *German Social Democracy*, 43.

166 *"the living picture of a genuine movement"*: Rosa Luxemburg, *The Mass Strike, the Political Party, and the Trade Unions*, chap. 6, "Cooperation of Organized and Unorganized Workers Necessary for Victory." Cf. Schorske, *German Social Democracy*, 55–58 (I am using Schorske's translation of Luxemburg here).

166 *"The feeble embryo of the general strike"*: Robert Michels, "Le Socialisme allemande après Mannheim," *Mouvement socialiste: Revue de critique social, littéraire et artistique* 182 (January 1907): 6.

167 *"the iron law of oligarchy"*: The full title of the 1911 book (in part, a pastiche of the monographs) was *Zur Soziologie des Parteiwesens in der modernen Demokratie; Untersuchungen über die oligarchischen Tendenzen des Gruppenlebens* (The Sociology of Party Systems in Modern Democracy; Inquiry into the Oligarchic Tendency of Life in Groups), translated into English in 1915 as *Political Parties*.

167 *he joined the Partito Socialista Italiano*: See Arthur Mitzman, *Sociology and Estrangement* (New York: Knopf, 1973), 267–338, for a brief biography of Michels until World War I; and David Beetham, "From Socialism to Fascism: The Relation Between Theory and Practice in the Work of Robert Michels," *Political Studies* 25, no. 1 (March 1977): 3–24.

167 *In this highly speculative work*: Max Weber, "Die protestantische Ethik und der 'Geist' des Kapitalismus," first published in 1904–1905 in two parts in the *Archiv für Sozialwissenschaft und Sozialpolitik*, vols. 20 and 21, and then published as a book in 1920. In the final paragraphs, Weber alludes explicitly to Nietzsche's "Last Man" as an outcome of the developments he has traced (a reference expunged in the English translation), and refers to a civilization of *"mechanisierte Versteinerung."* See Max Weber, *Schriften 1894–1922*, ed. Dirk Kaesler (Stuttgart: Kröner Verlag, 2002), 225.

167–168 *He encouraged Michels to document the situation*: See Wolfgang J. Mommsen, *The Political and Social Theory of Max Weber* (Chicago: University of Chicago Press, 1989), 87–105; and Lawrence A. Scaff, "Max Weber and Robert Michels," *American Journal of Sociology* 86, no. 6 (May 1981): 1269–1286.

168 *Weber disagreed*: Max Weber to Robert Michels, August 4, 1908, Fondazione Luigi Einaudi, Turin. Max Weber, "Briefe 1906–1908," ed. M. Rainer Lepsius and Wolfgang J. Mommsen, in *Max Weber Gesamtausgabe*, 2:615–616.

169 *Weber himself would subsequently rethink his own views*: Max Weber, *Economy and Society*, ed. Guenther Roth and Claus Wittich (Berkeley: University of California Press, 1978), 268–269, 984–985, 1132–1133. Cf. Wolfgang J. Mommsen, *The Age of Bureaucracy: Perspectives on the Political Sociology of Max Weber* (Oxford: Blackwell, 1974), esp. 72–94.

170 *The radical democrats of the SPD*: Cf. Schorske, *German Social Democracy*, 50, summarizing why Karl Kautsky in 1906 thought that the members of the trade unions should be subordinated to the strategy propounded by the party leaders, who understood, and would promote, a "total struggle for the liberation of the proletariat," unlike the rank and file, who were compromised and corrupted by their short-term interest in winning material gains.

170 *like many other anarcho-syndicalists*: Roberto Michels, *First Lectures in Political Sociology*, trans. Alfred de Grazia (Minneapolis: University of Minnesota Press, 1949 [1927]), 121.

170 *In his lectures in the 1920s on political sociology*: Ibid., 123.

171 *"the Fascist State"*: Giovanni Gentile, "The Philosophic Basis of Fascism," *Foreign Affairs* 6, no. 2 (1928): 302 (emphasis added).

171 *"revolutionary dictatorship of the proletariat and peasantry"*: the title of a 1905 pamphlet by Lenin.

172 *"The democratic currents of history"*: Robert Michels, *Political Parties: A Sociological Study of the Oligarchical Tendencies of Modern Democracy*, trans. Eden and Cedar Paul (New York: Collier Books, 1962), 371.

5. A HALL OF MIRRORS

173 *"The world must be made safe for democracy"*: Woodrow Wilson, "Address to a Joint Session of Congress Requesting a Declaration of War Against Germany," April 2, 1917, the American Presidency Project, www.presidency.ucsb.edu/ws /?pid=65366; "Must Exert All Our Power; To Bring a 'Government That Is Running Amuck to Terms.' Wants Liberal Credits and Universal Service, for 'the World Must Be Made Safe for Democracy.' A Tumultuous Greeting Congress Adjourns After 'State of War' Resolution Is Introduced—Acts Today," *The New York Times* (April 3, 1917): 1.

174 *Wilson was astonishingly consistent*: On this key point, I agree with the interpretation of Ronald J. Pestritto, *Woodrow Wilson and the Roots of Modern Liberalism* (Lanham, MD: Rowman & Littlefield, 2005).

174 *Born into an extended family of Presbyterian ministers*: All biographical details are drawn from John Milton Cooper, Jr., *Woodrow Wilson: A Biography* (New York: Knopf, 2009), the first major work able to draw on all sixty-nine volumes of *The Papers of Woodrow Wilson*, ed. Arthur S. Link et al. (Princeton: Princeton University Press, 1966–1994).

174 *"Democracy . . . is, of course, wrongly conceived"*: Woodrow Wilson, "The Modern Democratic State," c. December 1–20, 1885, in *The Papers of Woodrow Wilson*, 5:63.

175 *"Starting, as from one terminus of history"*: Henry Sumner Maine, *Ancient Law* (London, 1861), 169.

175 *Karl Marx, for example, attacked Maine's account*: See, e.g., *The Ethnographical Notebooks of Karl Marx*, ed. Lawrence Krader (Assen, Netherlands: Van Gorcum, 1974).

175 *"to answer Sir Henry Maine's 'Popular Government'"*: Woodrow Wilson to Horace Elisha Scudder, May [12], 1886, in *The Papers of Woodrow Wilson*, 5:218.

176 *"Democracy in Europe," he explains*: Ibid., 5:69–70. In effect, Wilson puts America at the end of history, as Hegel put Prussia in his *Philosophy of Right*, and Marx put communism in his *Manifesto*.

176 *"It had not to overthrow other polities"*: Wilson, "The Modern Democratic State," Ibid., 5:67.

176 *Democracy "in its most modern sense"*: Wilson, "The Modern Democratic State," in *The Papers of Woodrow Wilson*, 5:70.

177 *"practical political education is everywhere spreading"*: Ibid., 5:74.

177 *this "sovereignty is of a peculiar sort"*: Ibid., 5:75 (emphasis added).

178 *"the many led by the few"*: Ibid., 5:83.

178 *Enlightened leaders in Congress*: Ibid., 5:70.

179 *This is the main reason an American conservative*: The subtitle of a blog post on Wilson by Tony Listi, May 29, 2008, on the website Conservative Colloquium, https://conservativecolloquium.wordpress.com/2008/05/29/woodrow-wilson-americas-worst-and-first-fascist-president/. A similar but more nuanced case is elegantly laid out against Wilson by the Straussian scholar Ronald Pestritto, in *Woodrow Wilson and the Roots of Modern Liberalism*.

179 *"should be used not to destroy representative government"*: Theodore Roosevelt, *A Charter of Democracy: Address by Hon. Theodore Roosevelt, ex-President of the United States, Before the Ohio Constitutional Convention on February 21, 1912* (Washington, D.C.: GPO, 1912), 9.

179 *"an industrial and social democracy"*: Eugene Debs, "Debs' Speech of Acceptance" (of Socialist Party presidential nomination), *International Socialist Review* 13, no. 4 (October 1912): 307.

180 *"born under other flags but welcomed"*: Woodrow Wilson, Third Annual Message to Congress, December 7, 1915, www.presidency.ucsb.edu/ws/?pid=29556.

180 *"And so the modern age began"*: Daniel Patrick Moynihan, *Secrecy* (New Haven: Yale University Press, 1998), 98–99.

180 *As a young scholar, Wilson had argued*: Woodrow Wilson, "Leaders of Men," *The Papers of Woodrow Wilson*, 6:646–671.

181 *"They are conscious of being represented by him"*: Woodrow Wilson, "The Democratic State," *The Papers of Woodrow Wilson*, 5:87.

181 *"every door is open"*: Woodrow Wilson, "Address Accepting the Lincoln Homestead at Hodgenville, Kentucky," September 4, 1916 (Washington, D.C.: GPO, 1916), 3.

182 *"a process that has no endpoint"*: Michael Walzer, *Spheres of Justice: A Defense of Pluralism and Equality* (New York: Basic Books, 1983), 310.

183 *For the first time, political banners appeared*: Figes, *A People's Tragedy*, 310.

183 *"warnings not to assemble were disregarded"*: *The Times* (Friday, March 16, 1917): 7.

183 *"the revolution found us, the party members"*: Figes, *A People's Tragedy*, 323.

183 *"We are sorry for you . . ."*: *The Times* (March 16, 1917): 7.

183 *"disorderly groups of grey greatcoats"*: N. N. Sukhanov, *The Russian Revolution 1917: A Personal Record*, ed. Joel Carmichael (Princeton: Princeton University Press, 1984), 34.

184 *The Executive Committee of the Petrograd soviet quickly emerged*: Ibid., 38–39. Anweiler, *The Soviets*, 104.

184 *"In order to conclude successfully the struggle for democracy"*: Anweiler, *The Soviets*, 105.

185 *"The worst of the fighting took place in the vestibule"*: Stinton Jones, *Russia in Revolution: Being the Experiences of an Englishman in Petrograd During the Upheaval* (London: H. Jenkins, 1917), 165.

185 *"To me it seemed, on the contrary, self-evident"*: Sukhanov, *The Russian Revolution*, 95–96.

186 *From the start, the Petrograd soviet's Executive Committee*: Anweiler, *The Soviets*, 105. Figes, *A People's Tragedy*, 359.

186 *the soviets themselves, like the Parisian sections*: Figes, *A People's Tragedy*, 326.

186 *The soviet's voting procedures*: Ibid., 325.

187 *The deputies debated in front of a standing-room-only crowd*: Richard Pipes, *The Russian Revolution* (New York: Knopf, 1990), 289–293.

187 *"A man of astounding strength of will"*: Maxim Gorky, *Days with Lenin*, trans.

Harry Gould (Bombay: People's Publishing House, 1944), "Lenin's Qualities," 34.

188 *"The party of the proletariat cannot rest content"*: V. I. Lenin, "Draft of Revised Program," *Collected Works*, 45 vols. (Moscow: Progress Publishers, 1960–1970; in English, translation approved by CPSU), 24:471 (emphasis added).

189 *"the Russian soviet movement"*: Anweiler, *The Soviets*, 112–113.

189 *In one of his first official acts*: V. I. Lenin, "Decree on Peace," in *Collected Works*, 26:249. On the Wilsonian flourishes, see Lloyd C. Gardner, *Safe for Democracy: The Anglo-American Response to Revolution, 1913–1923* (New York: Oxford University Press, 1984), 148–149.

189 *Wilson responded in kind*: Woodrow Wilson, "President Wilson's Fourteen Points," delivered to a joint session of Congress, January 8, 1918, World War I Document Archive, https://wwi.lib.byu.edu/index.php/President_Wilson's_Fourteen_Points.

191 *When the Japanese mustered majority support*: The language of the Japanese resolution shelved by Wilson: "The equality of nations being a basic principle of the League of Nations, the High Contracting Parties agree to accord, as soon as possible, to all alien nationals of States members of the League equal and just treatment in every respect, making no distinction, either in law or in fact, on account of their race or nationality." See Jay Winter, *Dreams of Peace and Freedom: Utopian Moments in the Twentieth Century* (New Haven: Yale University Press, 2006), 70.

191 *But for Woodrow Wilson, it was also*: Ibid., 64.

192 *the Dutch astronomer and labour activist*: Anton Pannekoek, "Massenaktion und Revolution," *Die Neue Zeit* 30, no. 2 (1912).

192 *Since everyone in such a society had an interest*: G.D.H. Cole, *Guild Socialism Restated* (London: Leonard Parsons, 1920), 33–34.

193 "The trouble with socialism" is generally attributed to Wilde, though I can find no written evidence he ever said any such thing.

193 *Cole took it for granted*: Cole, *Guild Socialism Restated*, 13.

193 *"For democracy in industry"*: Ibid., 115–116.

193 *"man is not interested enough to vote"*: G.D.H. Cole, *Social Theory* (New York: Frederick A. Stokes, 1920), 115–116.

194 *When news of the Petrograd uprising of February 1917*: Margaret Cole, *The Life of G.D.H. Cole* (New York: St. Martin's Press, 1971), 121.

195 *Wallas arguably had the best mind*: This is the judgement of Eric Hobsbawm, "The Lesser Fabians," pamphlet No. 28 of *Our History*, published quarterly by the Communist Party History Group (London, 1962), 8, http://banmarchive.org.uk/collections/shs/pdf/28%20less%20fabians.pdf.

196 *"I know of no better way than democracy"*: Wallas to Shaw, cited in M. J. Wiener, *Between Two Worlds: The Political Thought of Graham Wallas* (Oxford: Oxford University Press, 1971), 141.

196 *"the first time that democracy had been discussed"*: Harold J. Laski, "Graham Wallas: Address Given at the London School of Economics and Political Science, October 19th, 1932," *Economica* 38 (November 1932): 405.

196 *"The political opinions of most men"*: Graham Wallas, *Human Nature in Politics* (Boston: Houghton Mifflin, 1909), 103.

196 *But despite acknowledging that the democratic movement*: Ibid., 199, 240.

196 *"Socialism stands or falls by its fruits in practice"*: Ronald Steel, *Walter Lippmann and the American Century* (Boston: Little, Brown, 1980), 27–28.

197 *In an essay published in the* International: Walter Lippmann, "Political Notes," *International*, May 1912.

197 *"brighten the coinage"*: Herbert Croly, quoted in Steel, *Walter Lippmann*, 88.

198 *"the prelude to quarrels"*: Unsigned editorial, written by Lippmann, *The New Republic*, May 17, 1919.

198 *"the news about Russia"*: Walter Lippmann and Charles Merz, "A Test of the News," published as a stand-alone forty-two-page monograph in *The New Republic* (August 4, 1920): 3.

198 *"the reliability of the news is the premise"*: Ibid., 4.

198 *"all the testimony is uncertain"*: Walter Lippmann, *Liberty and the News* (New York: Harcourt, 1920), 55.

198 *"establishment of more or less semi-official institutes"*: Ibid., 91.

199 *Building on the work of Graham Wallas*: Research summarized in Daniel Kahneman, *Thinking, Fast and Slow* (New York: Farrar, Straus and Giroux, 2011).

199 *"government by popular opinion"*: Wilson, "The Modern Democratic State," in *The Papers of Woodrow Wilson*, 5:70.

199 *What follows suggests that the great majority*: See Lippmann, *Public Opinion*, 36.

200 *"approach a condition in which everyone"*: Condorcet, "The Sketch" (*Esquisse d'un tableau historique des progrès de l'esprit humain*, 1794), in *Political Writings*, ed. Steven Lukes and Nadia Urbinati (Cambridge: Cambridge University Press, 2012), 126.

200 *"looked at a complicated civilization"*: Lippmann, *Public Opinion*, 173.

200 *"a self-centered opinion into a social judgment"*: Ibid., 194.

200 *"presupposes an unceasing, untiring round"*: Walter Lippmann, *The Phantom Public* (New York: Macmillan, 1927), 28.

201 *"The individual man does not have opinions"*: Ibid., 195.

201 *"into clearer relief than any other writer"*: John Dewey, "Public Opinion," *The New Republic* (May 3, 1922): 288.

202 *"The next religious prophet"*: John Dewey, "The Relation of Philosophy to Theology," *Monthly Bulletin* (of the Students' Christian Association of the University of Michigan) 16 (January 1893): 66–68. The quote comes from a Q

and A with the audience; see John Dewey, *The Early Works*, ed. Jo Ann Boydston (Carbondale: Southern Illinois University Press, 1971), 4:367.

202 *"a form of moral and spiritual association"*: John Dewey, "The Ethics of Democracy" (1888), ibid., 1:248–249.

202 *In 1893, at a time when Woodrow Wilson*: John Dewey, "Renan's Loss of Faith in Science" (1893), ibid., 4:17.

203 *"We lie, as Emerson said"*: John Dewey, *The Public and Its Problems* (New York: Holt, 1927), 219.

203 *Born in Vienna in 1892, Bernays*: For biographical details, see Edward Bernays, *Biography of an Idea: Memoirs of Public Relations Counsel Edward L. Bernays* (New York: Simon & Schuster, 1965); cf. Larry Tye, *The Father of Spin: Edward L. Bernays and the Birth of Public Relations* (New York: Crown, 1998).

203 *Sensing an opportunity to promote public relations*: Edward Bernays, *Crystallizing Public Opinion* (New York: Boni & Liveright, 1923); cf. Lippmann, *Public Opinion*, 19, 140–141.

204 *Since Lippmann had in fact criticized*: See Lippmann, *Public Opinion*, 218: "The picture which the publicity man makes for the reporters is the one he wishes the public to see. He is censor and propagandist, responsible only to his employers, and to the whole truth responsible only as it accords with the employers' conception of his own interests." See also Sue Curry Jansen, "Semantic Tyranny: How Edward L. Bernays Stole Walter Lippmann's Mojo and Got Away with It and Why It Still Matters," *International Journal of Communication* 7 (2013): 1094–1111. Despite its cute title, it's a very fine piece of scholarship.

204 *To paraphrase Lippmann*: Cf. Lippmann and Merz, "A Test of the News," 3.

204 *Taking as his premise Lippmann's observations*: Cf. Bernays, *Propaganda* (New York: Liveright, 1928), where this argument is explicit.

204 *"The average citizen"*: Bernays, *Crystallizing Public Opinion*, 133.

204 *"there is a different set of facts"*: Ibid., 201–202, referring to the famous dissent of Oliver Wendell Holmes, Jr., in *Abrams v. United States* (1919).

205 *"the mirrors of the public mind"*: Ibid., 113.

205 *"under the impact of propaganda"*: Lippmann, *Public Opinion*, 158.

205 *Since the nineteenth century, American newspapers*: For the straw vote tradition, see Jean M. Converse, *Survey Research in the United States: Roots and Emergence, 1890–1960* (Berkeley: University of California Press, 1987), 116–120.

206 *By winning this bet, Gallup helped launch*: For Gallup, see ibid., 114–127.

206 *what "the common man is thinking"*: George Gallup and Saul Forbes Rae, *The Pulse of Democracy* (New York: Simon & Schuster, 1940), v.

206 *"if the will of the majority of citizens"*: James Bryce, *The American Commonwealth* (Indianapolis: Liberty Fund, 1995 [1888]), 2:919.

207 *"to the extent that polls also are accurate"*: American Association for Public

Opinion Research, "AAPOR's Statement on 2012 Presidential Election Polling," www.aapor.org/Communications/Press-Releases/AAPOR-s-Statement-on-2012 -Presidential-Election-Po.aspx.

207 *The more refined such data*: For a recent discussion of this problem, see Cass Sunstein, *The Ethics of Influence: Government in the Age of Behavioral Science* (New York: Cambridge University Press, 2016).

207 *"were increasingly listening to what people"*: James W. Beniger, "Comment on Charles Tilly," *Public Opinion Quarterly* 47, no. 4 (Winter 1983): 481–482.

208 *"What we are confronted with"*: Schumpeter, *Capitalism, Socialism, and Democracy*, p. 263 (quoting from the third edition; the first edition appeared in 1942, the second in 1947).

208 *"view that the role of the people is to produce a government"*: Ibid., 269.

209 *"democracy is the rule of the politician"*: Ibid., 285.

209 *In the United States, it entailed a dramatic increase*: Moynihan, *Secrecy*.

209 *"socialist democracy may eventually turn out to be"*: Schumpeter, *Capitalism, Socialism, and Democracy*, 302.

210 *After some hesitation, and with compromising caveats*: Mazower, *No Enchanted Palace*.

210 *One result was the active involvement*: See Mary Ann Glendon, *A World Made New: Eleanor Roosevelt and the Universal Declaration of Human Rights* (New York: Random House, 2001).

210 *Article 21 of the Declaration*: See ibid., 312-313. As Glendon points out (ibid., 155), section 3 of article 21 was a crucial (and controversial) passage, added to specify the actionable content of the right to participate in government.

211 *"a world in which faith, deference"*: Dunn, *Democracy*, 184.

211 *in the decades since the ratification*: See Condoleezza Rice, *Democracy: Stories from the Long Road to Freedom* (New York: Twelve, 2017).

212 *It has seen the election of demagogues*: See Müller, *What Is Populism?*

212 *Under these circumstances, it's perhaps not surprising*: See Jonathan Schell, *The Unconquerable World: Power, Nonviolence, and the Will of the People* (New York: Metropolitan Books, 2003), and Krastev, *Democracy Disrupted: The Politics of Global Protest*.

CODA: WHO ARE WE?

214 *"Grab 'em by the pussy"*: "Transcript: Donald Trump's Taped Comments About Women," *The New York Times*, October 8, 2016, www.nytimes.com/2016/10 /08/us/donald-trump-tape-transcript.html?mcubz=1.

214 *"Nobody knows the system better than me"*: Donald J. Trump, acceptance speech at the Republican National Convention, July 21, 2016, www.politico .com/story/2016/07/full-transcript-donald-trump-nomination-acceptance-speech -at-rnc-225974.

215 *"This is what democracy looks like!"*: Anemona Hartocollis and Yamiche Alcindor, "Women's March Highlights as Huge Crowds Protest Trump: 'We're Not Going Away,'" *The New York Times*, January 21, 2017, www.nytimes.com /2017/01/21/us/womens-march.html?mcubz=1.

215 *"Who was sovereign?"*: Steve Bannon, speaking at the victory party for Roy Moore, a white nationalist candidate in the Alabama Republican Senate Primary, on September 28, 2017. Alex Isenstadt, "Moore's win spells trouble for GOP establishment in 2018: The insurgent's victory in Alabama is likely to fuel other primary challenges in a year that was supposed to be kind to the GOP," *Politico*, September 27, 2017, www.politico.com/story/2017/09/27/alabama -republicans-moore-midterms-strange-243188.

216 *"Men fight and lose"*: William Morris, *A Dream of John Ball*, a novel first published in 1888.

217 *"ideological consensus"*: Huntington, *American Politics*, 11.

217 *"What the Marxists mistakenly attribute"*: Crozier, Huntington, and Watanuki, *The Crisis of Democracy*, 73.

217 *"a democratic distemper"*: Ibid., 102.

218 *"expertise, seniority, experience, and special talents"*: Ibid., 113.

218 *"there never was a democracy yet"*: John Adams to John Taylor, December 17, 1814, https://founders.archives.gov/documents/Adams/99-02-02-6371. Cf. Andrew Sullivan, "Democracies End When They Are Too Democratic," *New York*, May 2, 2016, http://nymag.com/daily/intelligencer/2016/04/america -tyranny-donald-trump.html.

218 *He descended from old Yankee stock*: Robert D. Putnam, "Samuel P. Huntington: An Appreciation," *PS* 19, no. 4 (Autumn 1986): 837.

219 *He was just the kind of learned expert*: My account of Huntington, whom I never met, is coloured by the years I spent working at the American Academy of Arts and Sciences in Cambridge, Massachusetts, from 2000 to 2008 as the editor of that august honorific society's flagship journal *Daedalus*. In the course of doing my job, I came to see from the inside—especially with the sympathetic mentorship of Daniel Bell, who was still intellectually active in the Academy in those days—how the country's self-selected intellectual ruling class understood itself and its political obligations and prerogatives.

219 *"hierarchy, coercion, secrecy and deception"*: Huntington, in Crozier, Huntington, and Watanuki, *The Crisis of Democracy*, 93.

219 *"nuclear brinksmanship"*: Alexandr Fursenko and Timothy Naftali, *One Hell of a Gamble: Khrushchev, Castro, and Kennedy, 1958–1964: The Secret History of the Cuban Missile Crisis* (New York: W. W. Norton, 1997). Cf. Jonathan Schell, *The Fate of the Earth* (New York: Knopf, 1982).

220 *A lifelong supporter of America's Democratic Party*: Robert D. Kaplan, "Looking the World in the Eye," *The Atlantic*, December 2001. This sensitive profile

of Huntington, along with the appreciation of Robert Putnam cited above, is my source for the biographical details that follow.

220 *It is worth noting that Niebuhr's 1944 maxim*: Reinhold Niebuhr, *The Children of Light and the Children of Darkness: A Vindication of Democracy and a Critique of Its Traditional Defense* (New York: Scribner, 1944), xxxvi.

221 *"average men succeeding"*: Samuel P. Huntington, *The Soldier and the State* (Cambridge, MA: Harvard University Press, 1957), 51, 464–465. Putnam, "Samuel P. Huntington: An Appreciation," 840.

221 *"hopeful air of unreality"*: Samuel P. Huntington, *Political Order in Changing Societies* (New Haven: Yale University Press, 1968), 35.

222 *as declassified documents subsequently revealed*: Andrew J. Gawthorpe, "'Mad Dog?' Samuel Huntington and the Vietnam War," *Journal of Strategic Studies*, December 20, 2016, www.tandfonline.com/doi/full/10.1080/01402390.2016 .1265510.

223 *"Men may have order without liberty"*: Huntington, *Political Order*, 7–8.

223 *"'Does anybody govern?'"*: Samuel P. Huntington, "The Democratic Distemper," *The Public Interest* 41 (Autumn 1975): 23.

223 *"A multicultural world is unavoidable"*: Huntington, *The Clash of Civilizations*, 318.

224 *"One very plausible reaction"*: Samuel P. Huntington, *Who Are We? The Challenges to America's National Identity* (New York: Simon & Schuster, 2004), 310.

225 *"which involved the enslavement"*: Samuel P. Huntington, Letter to the Editor, *Harvard Crimson*, March 19, 2004.

226 *"Can a people remain a people"*: Ibid.

226 *the Occupy Wall Street movement*: The account that follows is based on my own observations of Occupy Wall Street in the autumn of 2011, and is drawn in part from an essay published shortly after under the title "Is Democracy Still in the Streets?," in Janet Byrne, ed., *The Occupy Handbook* (Boston: Back Bay Books, 2012).

226 *Samuel Huntington had identified "three waves" of global democratization*: Samuel P. Huntington, *The Third Wave: Democratization in the Late Twentieth Century* (Norman: University of Oklahoma Press, 1991).

227 *other scholars have suggested a "fourth wave"*: Joshua Kurlantzick, *Democracy in Retreat: The Revolt of the Middle Class and the Worldwide Decline of Representative Government* (New Haven: Yale University Press, 2013), 51.

227 *"the power of organizing without organization"*: Clay Shirky, *Here Comes Everybody: The Power of Organizing Without Organizations* (New York: Penguin Press, 2008).

228 *one of the most radical forms of direct democracy conceivable*: For the instituting of participatory democracy within OWS, see David Graeber, "Enacting the Impossible: On Consensus Decision Making," *The Occupied Wall Street Jour-*

nal, October 22, 2011; Drake Bennett, "David Graeber, the Anti-Leader of Occupy Wall Street," *Bloomberg Businessweek*, October 26, 2011; and Jeff Sharlet, "Inside Occupy Wall Street," *Rolling Stone*, November 10, 2011. For an invaluable survey of some of the movement's participants (based, unfortunately, on a survey conducted on May 1, 2012, months after the movement's glory days in the autumn of 2011), see Ruth Milkman, Stephanie Luce, and Penny Lewis, *Changing the Subject: A Bottom-Up Account of Occupy Wall Street in New York City* (New York: Murphy Institute, 2013).

228 *"reignited hope in the possibility of a free society"*: Yotam Marom, "Occupy Wall Street Is Winning, So What's Next?" *MetroFocus*, October 6, 2011, www.thirteen.org/metrofocus/news/2011/10/were-winning-%E2%80%93-so-what-do-we-want.

228–29 *"the incompatibility of rule by consensus"*: Miller, *"Democracy Is in the Streets,"* 326, reiterating an argument made by others, notably Jane Mansbridge in *Beyond Adversary Democracy*.

229 *"for anyone who joined in the search for a democracy"*: Miller, *"Democracy Is in the Streets,"* 328.

229 *"every person is free to do as they wish"*: "Quick Guide on Group Dynamics in People's Assemblies," recommended on the New York City General Assembly website; available at http://takethesquare.net/wp-content/uploads/2011/07/Quickguidetodynamicsofpeoplesassemblies_13_6_2011.pdf.

230 *"When faced with a decision, the normal response"*: Commission for Group Dynamics in Assemblies of the Puerta del Sol Protest Camp (Madrid), "Quick Guide on Group Dynamics in People's Assemblies."

230 *"Prejudice and ideology must be left at home"*: Ibid.

230 *"new subjectivity"*: See Marina Sitrin, "Horizontalism," http://marinasitrin.com/?page_id=108.

230 *"If you want to see what real democracy"*: GE, "News from the Front," 16beaver website, www.16beavergroup.org/journalisms09.23.11.htm.

230 *"There is an energy and an amazing consensus"*: DG, "Some Impressions from Saturday and Monday," 16beaver website, www.16beavergroup.org/journalisms09.23.11.htm.

231 *"Consensus only works if working groups"*: David Graeber, "Some Remarks on Consensus," February 26, 2013, http://occupywallst.org, and http://occupywallstreet.net/story/some-remarks-consensus.

231 *the militancy of Occupy Oakland*: The infatuation with Oakland's Black Bloc anarchists and their tactics provoked a heated debate. See Chris Hedges, "The Cancer in Occupy," February 6, 2012, www.truthdig.com/report/item/the_cancer_of_occupy_20120206. David Graeber—the most prominent of those infatuated—responded to Hedges with an "open letter," "Concerning the Violent Peace Police," February 9, 2012, http://nplusonemag.com/concerning-the-violent-peace-police.

231 *"experiences of visionary inspiration"*: David Graeber, "Revolution in Reverse," in *Revolutions in Reverse: Essays in Politics, Violence, Art, and Imagination* (London: Minor Compositions, 2011), 64.

233 *"the law of group polarization"*: Cass R. Sunstein, "The Law of Group Polarization," John M. Olin Law & Economics Working Paper No. 91, www.law .uchicago.edu/Publications/Working/index.html.

233 *"the most important negative liberties"*: Arendt, *On Revolution*, 284.

234 *Instead of single-mindedly pursuing a new form of "collective thinking"*: Cf. John Gray, *The Two Faces of Liberalism* (New York: New Press, 2000), who has come to a similar conclusion. Analogous arguments appear in the work of William Galston, Bernard Williams, and Judith Shklar. My current views have been even more deeply shaped by the example of Montaigne, which I briefly describe in *Examined Lives* (London: Oneworld Publications, 2018).

235 *"democratic, federal, representative republic"*: Rice, *Democracy*, 297.

235–36 *"If democracy is broadly understood"*: Ibid., 6.

236 *"democratic recession"* . . . *"democratic disconnect"*: Larry Diamond, "Facing up to the Democratic Recession," *Journal of Democracy* 26, no. 1 (January 2015): 141–155. Roberto Stefan Foa and Yascha Mounk, "The Democratic Disconnect," *Journal of Democracy* 27, no. 3 (July 2016).

236 *In 1970, Robert Dahl*: See Robert A. Dahl, *Polyarchy: Participation and Opposition* (New Haven: Yale University Press, 1971).

236 *the political scientists Christopher Achen and Larry Bartels*: Achen and Bartels, *Democracy for Realists*, 8, 12.

237 *a convincing body of empirical research*: Martin Gilens and Benjamin I. Page, "Testing Theories of American Politics: Elites, Interest Groups, and Average Citizens," *Perspectives on Politics* 12, no. 3 (September 2015): 564–581. Cf. Bartels, *Unequal Democracy*.

237 *"This marked the 12th consecutive year"*: Freedom House, *Freedom in the World 2018*, "Democracy in Crisis," https://freedomhouse.org/report/freedom -world/freedom-world-2018.

237 The Economist *measures the functioning of government*: Democracy Index 2017: Free Speech Under Attack, http://pages.eiu.com/Jan-18-Democracy -Index_Thank-you-page.html?aliId=55895996.

239 *"the average levels of democracy in the world"*: Democracy at Dusk? V-Dem Annual Report 2017, compiled by the V-Dem Institute, housed at the University of Gothenburg, Sweden, and the Kellogg Institute at Notre Dame University, www.v-dem.net/en/news-publications/annual-report, 14.

239 *UN Human Development Index*: United Nations Development Programme, *Overview—Human Development Report 2016: Human Development for Everyone*, http://hdr.undp.org/en/2016-report.

239 *And the United States, which ranks "very high"*: The Economist Intelligence Unit, *Democracy Index 2016: Revenge of the "Deplorables,"* www.eiu.com/public

/thankyou_download.aspx?activity=download&campaignid
=DemocracyIndex2016.

240 *Both elections expressed a desire*: The Economist's *Democracy Index 2016* is especially nuanced in its treatment of Brexit and the Trump election, unlike the Freedom House report, which criticizes populist movements as an unambiguous threat to democracies.

241 *"We sometimes expect too little"*: Estlund, *Democratic Authority*, 259, 269.

241 *"men agree to share one another's fate"*: John Rawls, *A Theory of Justice* (Cambridge, MA: Harvard University Press, 1971), 102 (a passage dropped from the revised edition of 1999).

242 *"a modern democratic state is only possible"*: Lindsay, *The Modern Democratic State*, 261; he remarks on the rarity of common sense on 276–281.

242 *"is chiefly the manipulation of power and public opinion"*: Václav Havel, "Politics, Morals and Civility," in *Summer Meditations*, trans. Paul Wilson (New York: Knopf, 1992), 5–6.

242 *"the idea that the world might actually be changed"*: Ibid., 5.

242 *If we abandon a virtue like truthfulness*: In treating truthfulness as a virtue, I follow Bernard Williams, *Truth and Truthfulness* (Princeton: Princeton University Press, 2002).

243 *"I am convinced that we will never build a democratic state"*: Havel, "Politics, Morals and Civility," 18.

243 *"I feel that the dormant goodwill in people"*: Ibid., 8–9.

243 *In part, this failure has occurred because Condorcet's constitution*: Thomas Piketty, *Capital in the Twenty-First Century*, trans. Arthur Goldhammer (Cambridge, MA: Harvard University Press, 2014).

244 *"Censorship, the terror, and concentration camps"*: Havel, "What I Believe," in *Summer Meditations*, 62–63.

244 *Through online platforms like Facebook*: See Dipayan Ghosh and Ben Scott, *Digital Deceit: The Technologies Behind Precision Propaganda on the Internet*, January 23, 2018, https://www.newamerica.org/public-interest-technology/policy -papers/digitaldeceit; Tufekci, *Twitter and Tear Gas*; and Adrian Chen, "The Agency," *The New York Times Magazine*, June 2, 2015, www.nytimes.com/2015 /06/07/magazine/the-agency.html?_r=0. Cf. James R. Beniger, *The Control Revolution: Technological and Economic Origins of the Information Society* (Cambridge, MA: Harvard University Press, 1986), and Tim Wu, *The Attention Merchants: The Epic Struggle to Get Inside Our Heads* (New York: Knopf, 2016).

SELECTED BIBLIOGRAPHY
AND SUGGESTIONS FOR
FURTHER READING

There are innumerable ways to approach the topic of democracy—some historical, some empirical, some more philosophical. Readers interested in different points of view will want to consult a variety of works that take different approaches. Here is a selection of some (by no means all) of the important, relatively recent works available in English.

Achen, Christopher H., and Larry M. Bartels. *Democracy for Realists*. Princeton: Princeton University Press, 2016.

Anweiler, Oskar. *The Soviets: The Russian Workers, Peasants, and Soldiers Councils, 1905–1921*. Trans. Ruth Hein. New York: Pantheon, 1975.

Arendt, Hannah. *On Revolution*. New York: Viking, 1963.

Bachrach, Peter. *The Theory of Democratic Elitism: A Critique*. Boston: Little, Brown, 1967.

Badiou, Alain, and Marcel Gauchet. *What Is to Be Done? A Dialogue on Communism, Capitalism, and the Future of Democracy.* Malden, MA: Polity Press, 2015.

Barber, Benjamin. *Strong Democracy: Participatory Politics for a New Age.* Berkeley: University of California Press, 1984.

———, and Patrick Watson. *The Struggle for Democracy.* Boston: Little, Brown, 1988.

Bartels, Larry M. *Unequal Democracy: The Political Economy of the New Gilded Age.* Princeton: Princeton University Press, 2008.

Bobbio, Norberto. *The Future of Democracy.* Trans. Roger Griffin. Minneapolis: University of Minnesota Press, 1987.

———. *Liberalism and Democracy.* Trans. Martin Ryle and Kate Soper. New York: Verso, 1990.

Brennan, Jason. *Against Democracy.* Princeton: Princeton University Press, 2016.

Cartledge, Paul. *Democracy: A Life.* New York: Oxford University Press, 2016.

Crick, Bernard. *Democracy: A Very Short Introduction.* New York: Oxford University Press, 2002.

Crozier, Michel, Samuel P. Huntington, and Joji Watanuki. *The Crisis of Democracy: Report on the Governability of Democracies to the Trilateral Commission.* New York: New York University Press, 1975.

Dahl, Robert A. *After the Revolution? Authority in a Good Society.* New Haven: Yale University Press, 1970.

———. *Democracy and Its Critics.* New Haven: Yale University Press, 1989.

Dunn, John. *Democracy: A History.* New York: Atlantic Monthly Press, 2005.

———. *Breaking Democracy's Spell.* New Haven: Yale University Press, 2014.

Estlund, David. *Democratic Authority: A Philosophical Framework.* Princeton: Princeton University Press, 2008.

Finley, M. I. *Democracy Ancient and Modern*, rev. ed. New Brunswick, NJ: Rutgers University Press, 1996 [1973].

Fishkin, James S. *The Voice of the People: Public Opinion and Democracy.* New Haven: Yale University Press, 1995.

Hansen, Mogens Herman. *The Athenian Ecclesia: A Collection of Articles 1976–1983.* Copenhagen: Museum Tusculanum Press, 1983.

———. *The Athenian Ecclesia II: A Collection of Articles 1983–1989.* Copenhagen: Museum Tusculanum Press, 1989.

———. *Athenian Democracy in the Age of Demosthenes.* Trans. J. A. Crook. Norman: University of Oklahoma Press, 1991.

Huntington, Samuel P. *American Politics: The Promise of Disharmony.* Cambridge, MA: Harvard University Press, 1981.

———. *The Third Wave: Democratization in the Late Twentieth Century.* Norman: University of Oklahoma Press, 1991.

Keane, John. *The Life and Death of Democracy.* New York: W. W. Norton, 2009.

Kloppenberg, James T. *Toward Democracy: The Struggle for Self-Rule in European and American Thought*. New York: Oxford University Press, 2016.

Krastev, Ivan. *Democracy Disrupted*. Philadelphia: University of Pennsylvania Press, 2014.

Laclau, Ernesto. *On Populist Reason*. New York: Verso, 2005.

Lefort, Claude. *Democracy and Political Theory*. Trans. David Macey. Minneapolis: University of Minnesota Press, 1988.

Levitsky, Steven, and Daniel Ziblatt. *How Democracies Die*. New York: Crown, 2018.

Lijphart, Arend. *Patterns of Democracy: Government Forms and Performance in Thirty-Six Countries*, 2nd ed. New Haven: Yale University Press, 2012.

Lindsay, A. D. *The Modern Democratic State*. New York: Oxford University Press, 1943.

MacPherson, C. B. *The Life and Times of Liberal Democracy*. New York: Oxford University Press, 1977.

———. *The Real World of Democracy*. Oxford: Clarendon Press, 1966.

Manin, Bernard. *The Principles of Representative Government*. New York: Cambridge University Press, 1997.

Mansbridge, Jane J. *Beyond Adversary Democracy*. New York: Basic Books, 1980.

Miller, James. *"Democracy Is in the Streets": From Port Huron to the Siege of Chicago*. New York: Simon & Schuster, 1987.

———. *Rousseau: Dreamer of Democracy*. New Haven: Yale University Press, 1984.

Mouffe, Chantal. *The Return of the Political*. London, 1993.

Müller, Jan-Werner. *Contesting Democracy: Political Ideas in Twentieth-Century Europe*. New Haven: Yale University Press, 2011.

———. *What Is Populism?* Philadelphia: University of Pennsylvania Press, 2016.

Ober, Josiah. *Democracy and Knowledge: Innovation and Learning in Classical Athens*. Princeton: Princeton University Press, 2008.

———. *Mass and Elite in Democratic Athens: Rhetoric, Ideology, and the Power of the People*. Princeton: Princeton University Press, 1989.

Palmer, R. R. *The Age of Democratic Revolutions*. Princeton: Princeton University Press, 1959.

Pateman, Carole. *Participation and Democratic Theory*. Cambridge: Cambridge University Press, 1970.

Rancière, Jacques. *Hatred of Democracy*. Trans. Steve Corcoran. New York: Verso, 2006.

Roberts, Jennifer Tolbert. *Athens on Trial: The Antidemocratic Tradition in Western Thought*. Princeton: Princeton University Press, 1994.

Rosanvallon, Pierre. *Counter-Democracy: Politics in an Age of Distrust*. Trans. Arthur Goldhammer. New York: Cambridge University Press, 2008.

———. *Democracy Past and Future*. New York: Columbia University Press, 2006.

——. *Democratic Legitimacy.* Trans. Arthur Goldhammer. Princeton: Princeton University Press, 2011.

——. *The Society of Equals.* Trans. Arthur Goldhammer. Cambridge, MA: Harvard University Press, 2013.

Rose, R. B. *The Making of the Sans-Culottes: Democratic Ideas and Institutions in Paris, 1789–92.* Dover, NH: Manchester University Press, 1983.

Rosenblatt, Helena. *The Lost History of Liberalism.* Princeton: Princeton University Press, 2018.

——. *Rousseau and Geneva: From the First Discourse to the Social Contract, 1749–1762.* New York: Cambridge University Press, 1997.

Runciman, David. *The Confidence Trap: A History of Democracy in Crisis from World War I to the Present.* Princeton: Princeton University Press, 2013.

Sartori, Giovanni. *Democratic Theory.* Detroit: Wayne State University Press, 1962.

Soboul, Albert. *The Sans-Culottes.* Trans. Rémy Inglis Hall. Garden City, NY: Anchor Books, 1972.

Tilly, Charles. *Democracy.* New York: Cambridge University Press, 2007.

Tuck, Richard. *The Sleeping Sovereign: The Invention of Modern Democracy.* Cambridge: Cambridge University Press, 2016.

Tufekci, Zeynep. *Twitter and Tear Gas: The Power and Fragility of Networked Protest.* New Haven: Yale University Press, 2017.

Urbinati, Nadia. *Democracy Disfigured: Opinion, Truth, and the People.* Cambridge, MA: Harvard University Press, 2014.

——. *Representative Democracy: Principles and Genealogy.* Chicago: University of Chicago Press, 2006.

Wiebe, Robert H. *Self-Rule: A Cultural History of American Democracy.* Chicago: University of Chicago Press, 1995.

Wilentz, Sean. *The Rise of American Democracy: Jefferson to Lincoln.* New York: W. W. Norton, 2005.

Wood, Gordon S. *The Creation of the American Republic, 1776–1787.* Chapel Hill: University of North Carolina Press, 1969.

Woodruff, Paul. *First Democracy: The Challenge of an Ancient Idea.* New York: Oxford University Press, 2005.

ACKNOWLEDGEMENTS

Writing is a solitary enterprise—but it takes a village to make a book.

I thank my longtime literary agent and friend Rafe Sagalyn for persuading me that this was a book worth writing; and also the Renaissance woman, film-maker, and writer Astra Taylor, for urging me to stop making excuses and just do it.

I am grateful to my New School colleague and friend Elzbieta Matynia for inviting me to teach a course on people power and modern democratic revolts in Wrocław, Poland, in the summer of 2014, and to the students in this course who were veterans of Maidan in Ukraine and the anti-Putin demonstrations in Moscow and St. Petersburg in 2011—I learned a lot that summer, most of it disquieting.

The following summer, I had the opportunity to teach the same course in the politics department at the Technische Universität Dresden, thanks to an invitation from Professor Hans Vorländer. My students in Dresden were mainly left-wing activists trying to counter the growing influence of the city's far-right nationalist group Pegida; conflict was in the air, and some of it involved the very meaning of modern democracy.

Drafts of the present book were read in whole or in part by Stan Draenos, Jay Eisenberg, Greil Marcus, Ruth Miller, Bruce Miroff, Kresimir Petkovic, Helena Rosenblatt, Rafe Sagalyn, Astra Taylor, and Robin Wagner-Pacifici. I was also able to read parts of the book at the New York State Summer Writers Institute, where I am grateful for the encouragement I got from my colleagues and friends Robert and Peg Boyers, Henri Cole, William Kennedy, and Rick Moody.

Once again, I feel privileged to be able to publish a book with Farrar, Straus and Giroux—and to work, once again, with one of my favourite editors ever, the incomparable Alex Star. We first collaborated when Alex was editing the journal *Lingua Franca*, and he remains a paragon of intelligence, wide reading, and literary acumen.

The book was finished during a sabbatical from the New School for Social Research—what an honour to be able to teach at an institution that, historically, has stood tall for liberal and democratic ideals.

And through it all I had by my side my dear friends Michael Schober and Don Harrison; Tim Marshall and Janet Roitman; Robin Wagner-Pacifici and Maurizio Pacifici; Chivas Sandage and Vivian Felten; Gary Knoble and Robert Black; and, lucky me, my wife, Ruth Miller, a small-*d* democrat of the purest sort, and the kind of interlocutor who makes life worth living—even when the political horizon seems almost hopelessly dark.

Manhattan, February 2, 2018

INDEX

A NOTE ABOUT THE AUTHOR

James Miller is a professor of politics and liberal studies at the New School for Social Research in New York. He is the author of the critically acclaimed *Examined Lives: Twelve Great Thinkers and the Search for Wisdom, from Socrates to Nietzsche*; *The Passion of Michel Foucault*; *"Democracy Is in the Streets": From Port Huron to the Siege of Chicago*; and *Rousseau: Dreamer of Democracy*.

ALSO BY JAMES MILLER

EXAMINED LIVES

Twelve Great Thinkers and the Search for Wisdom, from Socrates to Nietzsche

JAMES MILLER

"Excellent."
Alain de Botton, *New Statesman*

"Fascinating...readers will be astounded to learn that philosophers make as much of a mess of their lives as anyone else."
Sarah Bakewell, *New York Times*

Plato risked his reputation to tutor a tyrant. Seneca, the philosopher of temperance, accumulated one of the greatest fortunes in Rome. Kant wrestled with hypochondria in private and advocated arch-rationality in public.

James Miller introduces twelve great philosophers who spent their lives examining who we are and how we should live.